THE
PERPETUAL
ORGY

Mario Vargas Llosa

THE
PERPETUAL
ORGY

FLAUBERT AND
MADAME BOVARY

Translated from the Spanish
by Helen Lane

Farrar Straus Giroux
New York

Translation copyright © 1986 by Farrar, Straus and Giroux, Inc.
Originally published in Spanish under the title La orgía perpetua,
copyright © 1975 by Mario Vargas Llosa
All rights reserved
First edition, 1986
Second printing, 1987
Printed in the United States of America
Published in Canada by Collins Publishers, Toronto
Library of Congress Cataloging-in-Publication Data
Vargas Llosa, Mario
The perpetual orgy.
Translation of: La orgía perpetua
Includes bibliographical references
1. Flaubert, Gustave, 1821–1880. Madame Bovary
I. Title.
PQ2246.M3V313   1986   843'.8   86-19515

TO CARLOS BARRAL,

the next-to-the-last *afrancesado*

The one way of tolerating existence

is to lose oneself in literature

as in a perpetual orgy.

Letter to Mademoiselle Leroyer de Chantepie,
September 4, 1858

Contents

THREE

The First Modern Novel 213

THE
PERPETUAL
ORGY

Introduction

There is, on the one hand, the impression that Emma Bovary leaves with the reader who for the first (second, tenth) time approaches her: affection, indifference, disgust. On another hand, there is what the novel itself is, without regard for the effect that the reading of it produces: the story it tells, the sources it uses, the way in which it transforms itself into time and language. And finally, there is what the novel means, not to those who read it, or as a sovereign object, but from the point of view of the novels written before or after it. To expand upon any one of these alternatives is to choose a form of criticism. The first, individual and subjective, prevailed in the past; its defenders call it the classic approach, its detractors the impressionist. The second, modern, claims to be scientific, to analyze the work objectively, following universal rules, although the nature of these rules varies, to be sure, depending on the critic (psychoanalysis, Marxism, stylistics, structuralism, and the combinations). The third has more to do with the history of literature than with criticism properly speaking.

In reality, the critics of every age have made use of all three perspectives at once. The difference lies in the fact that each era, person, and tendency emphasizes one of them, singles it out for particular attention. The critic of earlier days, who based his judgments on his sensibility, was persuaded that he personified a model of value and that his opinions were therefore universally valid. The contemporary critic knows that his reason and his knowledge are stimulated and oriented—if only as regards his choice of the theme of his study—by his subjectivity, by the impact that *this* particular work has had on him. Impressionists and scientists, moreover, have always endeavored to assign a work a place within a tradition, by showing what it means in relation to the past and to the future of its own genre.

In this book I propose to fulfill these aims separately, and have thus divided it into three parts. The first is a tête-à-tête with Emma Bovary, in which, naturally, I speak more of myself than I do of her. In the second, I do my best to concentrate exclusively on *Madame Bovary* and to sum up with some semblance of objectivity its gestation and its birth, what the novel is and how it comes to be what it is. And finally, in the third, I try to situate it, and therefore speak above all of other novels, insofar as their existence was made possible and enriched thanks to hers.

ONE

AN UNREQUITED
PASSION

Criticism would perhaps be simplified if, before setting
forth an opinion, one avowed one's tastes; for every work
of art contains within itself a particular quality stemming
from the person of the artist, which, quite apart from the
execution, charms us or irritates us. Hence only those works
which satisfy both our temperaments and our minds arouse
our unqualified admiration. The failure to make this fun-
damental distinction is a great cause of injustice.

—*Preface to* Dernières chansons *by Louis Bouilhet*

"The death of Lucien de Rubempré is the great drama of my
life," Oscar Wilde is said to have remarked about one of Balzac's
characters. I have always regarded this statement as being literally true. A handful of fictional characters have marked my
life more profoundly than a great number of the flesh-and-blood
beings I have known. Although there is no denying that when
literary characters and human beings are an immediate presence,
a direct contact, the reality of the latter prevails over that of the
former—nothing is as alive as the body that can be seen and
touched—the difference disappears when both become part of
the past, of memory, to the considerable advantage of the first
over the second, whose fading in our minds is irremediable,

whereas the fictional character can be brought to life indefinitely, merely by opening the pages of the book and stopping at the right lines. In that heterogeneous, cosmopolitan circle, a gang of friendly ghosts whose members come and go, depending on the period of my life and my mood (today I might mention, offhand: D'Artagnan, David Copperfield, Jean Valjean, Prince Pierre Bezukhov, Fabrice del Dongo, the terrorists Cheng and the Professor, Lena Grove and the tall convict); none of them has been present as persistently, and with none of them have I had as clearly passionate a relationship, as Emma Bovary. That story may perhaps serve as a small example that will help to shed light on the much-discussed, enigmatic relationships between literature and life.

My first memory of *Madame Bovary* is cinematographic. It was 1952, a stifling-hot summer night, a recently opened movie theater in Piura, on the Plaza de Armas with its waving palms; James Mason appeared as Flaubert; Louis Jourdan, tall and svelte, was Rodolphe Boulanger; and Emma Bovary took on visible form by way of the nervous movements and gestures of Jennifer Jones. I couldn't have been terribly impressed, because the film didn't cause me to rush out and hunt up a copy of the book, despite the fact that it was at precisely this period in my life that I'd begun to stay up nights devouring novels like a cannibal.

My second memory is academic. On the hundredth anniversary of the publication of *Madame Bovary*, the University of San Marcos, in Lima, organized a ceremony in honor of the occasion, in the main auditorium. The critic André Coyné was impassively considering Flaubert's reputation as a realist when his arguments suddenly became inaudible amid shouts of "Long live free Algeria!" and the war cries of a hundred or so San Marcos students, armed with sticks and stones, as they made their way through the hall toward the platform where their target, the French ambassador, awaited them, white as a sheet. Part of the celebration in honor of Flaubert was the publication, in a little booklet whose ink rubbed off on our fingers, of *Saint Julien l'Hospitalier*, in a translation by Manuel Beltroy. That was the first work of Flaubert's I ever read.

In the summer of 1959 I arrived in Paris with very little money and the promise of a scholarship. One of the first things I did was to buy a copy of *Madame Bovary* in the Classiques Garnier edition, in a bookstore in the Latin Quarter. I began reading it that very afternoon, in a tiny room in the Hôtel Wetter, near the Musée Cluny. It is at this point that my story really begins. From the very first lines, the book's power of persuasion was like an extremely potent magic spell. It had been years since any novel had vampirized my attention so quickly, blotted out my physical surroundings so completely, plunged me so deeply into the story it told. As the afternoon wore on, as night fell, as dawn began to break, the magical decantation, the substitution of the fictional world for the real one, held me spellbound. Morning had already come—Emma and Léon had just met in a box at the Rouen opera—when, dizzy with fatigue, I put the book down and went to bed: in my troubled sleep at that hour the Rouaults' farm, the muddy streets of Tostes, the figure of Charles, good-natured and stupid, the ponderous pedantry of Homais (who might well have been Argentine) continued to exist, as vividly as when I'd been reading about them—and above these persons and these places, like an image foreshadowed in a thousand childhood dreams, dimly glimpsed from the moment I'd begun devouring books so avidly in adolescence, there hovered the face of Emma Bovary. As I woke up so as to go on reading, two certainties flashed through my mind, like two bolts of lightning: I now knew what writer I would have liked to be; and I knew that from that moment on, till my dying day, I would be in love with Emma Bovary. In the future she would be for me, as for Léon Dupuis in the first days of their affair, "the beloved of every novel, the heroine of every play, the vague *she* of every volume of verse."

Since then I have read the novel from beginning to end half a dozen times and reread various chapters and episodes again and again. Unlike what has happened to me on going back to other cherished stories, I have never been disappointed; on the contrary, especially on rereading those scenes that are volcanic craters—the agricultural fair, the ride in the fiacre, Emma's death—I have always had the sensation that I was discovering secret facets, unpublished details, and, to varying degrees depending on the place and the circumstances, I have always felt precisely the same emotion. A book becomes part of a person's life for a number of reasons appertaining at once to the book and the person. I should like to explore what some of these reasons are in my case: why *Madame Bovary* stirred me to such profound depths of my being, what it gave me that other stories could not.

The first reason is, surely, my particular penchant, ever since childhood, for works that are rigorously and symmetrically constructed, with a definite beginning and a definite end, that form a closed circle and gave the impression of being perfect, finished works, in preference to those open-ended works deliberately aimed at suggesting something inconclusive, vague, in the process of becoming, only half over and done with. It is possible that these latter works are more faithful images of reality and of life—always unfinished, ever at some halfway point between this and that—but what I have doubtless sought instinctively and been pleased to find in books, films, paintings has not been the reflection of this infinite incompleteness, this boundless ongoing flow, but rather the exact opposite: definitive overviews, wholes which, thanks to their bold structure, arbitrary yet convincing, give the illusion of being a total picture of reality, of summing up all of life. That appetite was to be fully satisfied by *Madame Bovary*, the very exemplar of the closed work, of the book that is a perfect circle. On the other hand, an increasing preference, which up to that point in my reading had nonetheless remained quite vague, must have taken definite shape thanks to this novel. Between the description of objective life and subjective life, of action and reflection, I am more attracted by the former than by the latter, and I have always considered the description of the latter by way of the former a more impressive feat than the converse (I prefer Tolstoy to Dostoevsky, invention rooted in reality to that rooted in fantasy, and if I am left to choose between unrealities, the one closer to the concrete has my preference over the one that is abstract: I prefer pornography, for example, to science fiction, and sentimental stories to horror tales). In his letters to Louise Colet while in the throes of writing *Madame Bovary*, Flaubert was quite certain that he was composing a novel of "ideas," not a novel of "action" with a lively plot. This has led certain critics who have taken his words literally to maintain that *Madame Bovary* is a novel in which nothing happens except on the level of language. But this is not so; in *Madame Bovary* as many things happen as in an adventure novel—weddings, acts of adultery, balls, journeys, outings, financial skulduggery, sicknesses, theatrical spectacles, a suicide—even though for the most part these events turn out to be inconsequential or sordid ones. It is true that many of these happenings are narrated as seen through the emotions or the recollected memories of the character involved, but because of Flaubert's maniacally materialistic style, the subjective reality in *Madame Bovary* is possessed of a solidity, a physical weight, as palpable as that of objective reality. The impression that the thoughts and the feelings in the novel were *facts*, so concrete that they could be seen and almost touched, not only dazzled me: it revealed to me a profound predilection on my part.

These are formal reasons, stemming from the structure and conception of the book. Those concerning its subject matter are less invertebrate. The greater the role that rebellion, violence, melodrama, and sex, expertly combined in a compact plot, have played in a novel, the greater its appeal has been to me. In other words, the maximum satisfaction that a novel can bring me is to arouse, as I read, my admiration for this or that revolt against the established order, my anger at some stupidity or injustice, my fascination for melodramatic situations, for excessive displays of emotion that romanticism seemed to have invented, since it both used and abused them, though they have always existed in literature, as they have doubtless always existed in reality and in my secret desire. *Madame Bovary* is chock-full of these ingredients, they are the four great rivers that irrigate its vast geography, and the distribution of these contents in the novel reveals the same careful balance of its formal division into sections, chapters, scenes, dialogues, and descriptions.

Rebellion in Emma's case does not have the epic dimensions of that of the masculine heroes of the nineteenth-century novel, yet it is no less heroic. Hers is the rebellion of an individual, and to all appearances a self-centered one: she violates the codes of her milieu because she is driven to do so by problems that are hers alone, not in the name of all humanity, of a certain ethic or ideology. It is because she feels that society is fettering her imagination, her body, her dreams, her appetites that Emma suffers, commits adultery, lies, steals, and in the end kills herself. Her defeat does not prove that she is wrong and the bourgeois of Yonville-l'Abbaye right, that God punishes her for her sins, as was maintained by Maître Sénard, the attorney for the defense at the trial of *Madame Bovary* (his defense of the novel is as pharisaical as the accusation against it put before the court by Pinard, the public prosecutor, a composer in secret of pornographic verses), but simply proof that the battle was one-sided: Emma was alone, and because she was an impulsive and sentimental creature, continually inclined to go astray, to become more and more deeply enmeshed in situations that in the end gave her enemy the advantage (setting forth arguments doubtless suggested to him by Flaubert himself, Maître Sénard assured the judges at the trial that the moral of the novel is: Dangers lie ahead for a girl who receives an education superior to that of her class). This defeat, foredoomed due to the conditions governing the battle, takes on the overtones both of genuine tragedy and of a cheap newspaper serial, and that is one of the mixtures of genres to which—poisoned, like Emma, by certain books I read and movies I saw when I was an adolescent—I am most likely to succumb.

But it is not only the fact that Emma is capable of defying her milieu—family, class, society—but also the causes of her defiance that force me to admire that elusive little nobody. These causes are very simple and stem from something that she and I share intimately: our incurable materialism, our greater predilection for the pleasures of the body than for those of the soul, our respect for the senses and instinct, our preference for this earthly life over any other. The ambitions that lead Emma to sin and death are precisely those that Western religion and morality have most savagely combated throughout history. Emma wants sexual pleasure, she is not resigned to repressing this profound sensual need that Charles is unable to satisfy because he doesn't even know that it exists; she wants to surround her life with pleasing and superfluous things, elegance, refinement, to give concrete form by way of objects to that appetite for beauty that her imagination, her sensibility, and her reading have aroused in her. Emma wants to know other worlds, other people; she refuses to reconcile herself to the prospect of spending the rest of her days hemmed in by the narrow horizons of Yonville; and she also wants her existence to be different and exciting, to ensure that adventure and risk, the magnificent gestures of generosity and sacrifice, will play a role in it. Emma's rebellion is born of one conviction, the root of all her acts: I am not resigned to my lot, the dubious compensation of the beyond doesn't matter to me, I want my life to be wholly and completely fulfilled here and now. A chimera no doubt lies at the heart of the destiny to which Emma aspires, above all if it becomes a collective pattern, a common human goal. No society can offer all its members such an existence; it is evident, moreover, that in order for communal life to be possible man must resign himself to keeping a close rein on his desires, to limiting that will to transgress that Georges Bataille called Evil. But Emma represents and defends, in an exemplary way, a side of our humanity that has been cruelly disavowed by almost all religions, philosophies, and ideologies, and made out by them to be a cause for shame shared by our entire species. Its repression has given rise to as great and as widespread unhappiness as have economic exploitation, religious sectarianism, or the thirst for conquest. With the passage of time, ever broader and broader sectors of society—including even the Church today— have come to recognize that man has the right to satisfy his hunger, to think and to express his ideas freely, to enjoy good health and a secure old age. But the same taboos as in Emma Bovary's day still hold sway (and in this regard the right and the left are in total agreement and work hand in glove to enforce them)—taboos that universally deny men and women the right to pleasure, to the fulfillment of their desires. The story of Emma is that of a blind, stubborn, desperate rebellion against the social violence that stifles this right.

I remember having read, in the opening pages of a book by Maurice Merleau-Ponty, that violence is almost always beautiful as an image, that is to say, in art, and having felt more or less reassured thereby. I was seventeen years old at the time, and it frightened me to note that despite my peaceful nature, violence—whether implicit or explicit, refined or raw—was an indispensable requisite for a novel if it was to persuade me of its reality and arouse my enthusiasm. Those works that did not possess at least a little taste of violence seemed unreal to me (I have always preferred novels that pretend to be real, just as others prefer novels that pretend to be unreal), and as a general rule unreality bores me to death. *Madame Bovary* is steeped in violence, which manifests itself on many planes, ranging from the purely physical one of pain and blood (the operation, gangrene, and amputation of Hippolyte's leg; Emma's poisoning of herself) or the spiritual one of ruthless rapine down to the last sou (the merchant Lheureux), selfishness and cowardice (Rodolphe, Léon), to its social forms represented by the animalization of the human being through backbreaking labor and exploitation (covered with embarrassment and paralyzed with confusion amid the crowd at the agricultural fair, old Catherine Leroux, who has taken care of the animals on a farm for fifty-four years, receives a silver medal worth twenty-five francs; as she walks off, those standing near her hear her murmur that she is going to give it to the parish priest to pay him for saying Masses for her), and above all, in its most generalized form of stupidity and the insidious traps that men lay for themselves and one another: their prejudices, their envy, their intrigues. Against this background Emma's fantasy, her hunger for a world different from the one that shatters her dreams, stand out like snow against pitch-black darkness. It is precisely the scene, the most violent one in the book, in which Madame Bovary meets her final defeat, by her own hand, that moves me most. I know by heart this chapter which begins with Emma walking, in the fading light of day, to Rodolphe's château to try one last maneuver that may save her from ruin, from shame, from Charles's forgiveness, which would force her to change, and which ends the following day as Emma enters death as one enters a nightmare, overcome by the vision of the Blind Man covered with purulent sores, as he crosses Yonville humming a vulgar song. These are pages marked by an amazing mastery of the art of narrative and by a terrible cruelty—Maître Sénard couldn't have lost the case if he had shown what horrible punishment Emma's sin met with, thanks to the hideous effects of the arsenic—effects that have given me simultaneous pain and pleasure, that have totally satisfied my literary penchant for sentimentality and sadism a hundred times over. Moreover, I owe this episode a special debt of gratitude, for reasons that are a secret between Emma and me. Quite a few years ago now, for the space of several weeks, I suffered from the feeling of a definite incompatibility with the world, a stubborn despair, a profound distaste for life. At one moment the idea of suicide crossed my mind; on another night I remember having hung about outside the offices of the Foreign Legion (the fateful influence of *Beau Geste*) near the Place Denfort-Rochereau, with the idea of inflicting upon myself a romantic punishment, by way of that most odious of institutions: fleeing everything, changing my name, my life, disappearing by taking up a rough and despicable occupation. The help lent me in this difficult period by the story of Emma, or rather, the death of Emma, is a debt I cannot possibly repay. I remember having read, during those days, the episode of her suicide with anxious, avid anticipation, having hastened to my reading and rereading of this scene as others in similar circumstances take to religion and the parish priest, to drinking, or to morphine, and having each time found consolation and a sense of proportion, a revulsion against chaos, a taste for life in those heartrending pages. The fictional suffering neutralized the suffering I was experiencing in real life. To help me, Emma each night entered the deserted château of La Huchette and was humiliated by Rodolphe: she wandered out into the fields, where pain and helplessness brought her for a moment to the brink of madness; slipped like an elf into Homais's pharmacy, where Justin, innocence become death's henchman, watched her swallow the arsenic in the half-shadow of the *capharnaüm*; went back home and suffered her unspeakable calvary: the inky taste in her mouth, the nausea, the chill in her feet, the shivering, the fingers clutching the sheets, the cold sweat on her forehead, the chattering of her teeth, the wildly rolling eyes, the howls of pain, the convulsions, the vomiting of blood, the tongue lolling out of her mouth, the death rattle. Each time my sadness and melancholy were mingled with a curious sense of relief, and each time the agonizing ceremony left me with a feeling of admiration, of elation: Emma was killing herself in order that I might live. On other occasions when I have been deeply upset, depressed, or simply in a bad mood, I have had recourse to this remedy and almost always it has had the same cathartic effect on me. This experience and others like it have convinced me that the theories defending edifying literature *in terms of its results* are highly debatable. It is not necessarily happy stories with an optimistic moral that raise the spirits and gladden the hearts of readers (virtues attributed in Peru to Vargas Pisco★); in some cases, as in mine, the somber beauty of stories as unhappy and pessimistic as Emma Bovary's may achieve the same effect.

But Emma is not only a rebel plunged into a world of violence; she is also an overly sentimental, rather coarse young woman, and therefore a certain bad taste, a moderate touch of vulgarity appear in her story. I deeply appreciate these aberrations, I am irresistibly attracted by them, and despite the fact that I cannot bear literary melodrama in its pure state (though I am a devotee of melodramatic movies, and it may well be that this weakness of mine stems from the Mexican films to which I was addicted in the forties and fifties, and for which I still feel a keen nostalgia), when a novel is capable of using melodramatic materials within a broader context and with artistic talent, as is the case in *Madame Bovary*, my joy knows no bounds. To avoid a misunderstanding, I should perhaps explain my feelings in this regard. My fondness for melodrama has nothing to do with that disdainful, supercilious intellectual game that consists of aesthetically rehabilitating, by way of a lofty and intelligent *interpretation*, what is ignoble and stupid—as Hermann Broch did, for instance, with his concept of *kitsch* and Susan Sontag

---

★ A popular brand of Peruvian brandy. (H.L.)

with *camp*—but, rather, a primarily emotional identification with this material, by which I mean a total obedience to its laws and an orthodox reaction to its excitement and its effects. Melodrama may not be precisely the right word to express what I am trying to say, since it has a connotation closely linked to theater, films, and the novel, and I am referring to something broader that is present above all in real things and real people. I am speaking here of a certain distortion or exacerbation of feeling, of the perversion of the recognized "good taste" of each era, of that heresy, counterpoint, deterioration (at once popular, middle-class, and aristocratic) to which, in every society, the aesthetic, linguistic, moral, social, and erotic patterns established by the elite as models fall victim; I am speaking of the mechanization and vulgarization to which emotions, ideas, human relations are subject in everyday life; I am speaking of the intrusion of the comic on the serious, the grotesque on the tragic, the absurd on the logical, the impure on the pure, the ugly on the beautiful, as a product of naïveté, ignorance, laziness, and routine. Each country, each social class, each generation comes up with its own particular variants of, its own particular contributions to, vulgarity (in Peru it is known as *huachafería* and is one of the realms in which we Peruvians have been truly creative), one of the most persistent and most universal forms of human expression. This material does not interest me intellectually but emotionally. A movie such as *El último cuplé*,* with all its elephantine stupidity, does not attract me as a spider attracts an entomologist, as a phenomenon to be examined under a magnifying glass, but rather because during the hour and a half that it is shown on the screen, this spiderweb is capable of trapping me in its threads exactly as the black widow catches the imprudent fornicator of her species in hers,

---

* A Spanish film, starring Sara Montiel, celebrating the glories of Spanish popular songs at the turn of the century. (H.L.)

and provokes in me an identification, a recognition similar to that experienced by Emma on attending a performance of *Lucia di Lammermoor* in Rouen ("The soprano's voice seemed to her to be merely the echo of her own consciousness, and this illusion that charmed her part and parcel of her own life"). The thing is, however, that in the case of *El último cuplé* the effect vanishes the moment the cause disappears, reflection intervenes, and in the light of reason and a sense of proportion, stupidity blindingly reveals itself as sheer stupidity. But this happens—as in *El derecho de nacer* by Corín Tellado,* or in *Simplemente María*†— because in this movie reality is *only* melodramatic, there is *only* bad taste in life: the exclusion of everything else creates a sense of unreality. This strong propensity of mine, I grant, is no doubt symptomatic of my basic realist fixation: the melodramatic element moves me because melodrama is closer to the real than drama, as tragicomedy is closer to the real than either pure comedy or pure tragedy. When a work of art includes, in addition to other aspects (which are its opposites) and intermingled with them, this vulgar, pathetic, parodic, base, alienated, and stupid side, and does so without taking an ironic distance from it, without establishing a tone of intellectual or moral superiority, with respect and sincerity (the medieval hero who makes little buns out of the fingernails and hair of his beloved and eats them, another who kisses the princess three times on the mouth in homage to the Most Holy Trinity, the swaggering romantic swordsman whose eyes grow wet with tears at the smell of violets, the pair of pink panties bought by the maidservant with her carefully hoarded pennies so as to impress the chauffeur), I feel precisely the same emotion as that aroused in me by the literary representation of rebellion and violence.

In *Madame Bovary* this aspect is apparent above all in the

---

* The author of sentimental novels famous throughout the Spanish-speaking world. (H.L.)

† A very popular radio serial. (H.L.)

weaving together of episodes, situations, and characters drawn for the most part from the arsenal of the romantic novel—from the premonitory signs that all through the story announce the dire fate that awaits Emma, to figures such as the ragged Blind Man covered with sores, a symbol of tragic destiny, or Justin, another all-too-familiar nineteenth-century figure, the young lad secretly in love with the unattainable woman. It pleases me that *Madame Bovary* can also be read as a collection of clichés, that it is peopled with stock characters: that Lheureux the dry-goods merchant is greedy, anti-Semitic, and rapacious, that the notaries and functionaries are sordid and wicked, and the politicians garrulous, hypocritical, and ridiculous. But most of all I am charmed by the ambivalence shown by Emma, who coldly plans her acts of daring and excesses, is moved like a little ninny by the naïve books she reads, dreams of exotic countries dotted with picture-postcard scenes that are stereotypes of her day, gives the man she loves a signet ring that says *Amor nel cor*, asks him to "think of me at midnight," and sometimes utters grand-iloquent phrases ("There is no desert, abyss, ocean I wouldn't cross with you") that irritate the practical Rodolphe. I am de-lighted by the cheap-serial coincidences of the novel, such as the marvelous one during Emma's and Léon's outing on the river, just after they become lovers, when the boatman remem-bers having taken out, a few days before, a party of ladies and gentlemen who drank champagne, and Emma, with a shudder, discovers that one of them was Rodolphe; or that ineffable image of Charles Bovary tenderly smelling and admiring the bouquet of violets that Léon has given Emma after possessing her. I am haunted by the scene of Justin, alone, sobbing in the shadows alongside Madame Bovary's tomb, and I find it touching that Emma, when the world begins to cave in on her, tosses to a beggar the last five francs she has left to her name, and naturally I find it a perfect touch that the episode of the fiacre ride ends simply with a woman's ungloved hand scattering to the four winds the torn bits of the letter breaking with her lover that she had intended to give him.

On April 24, 1852, Flaubert, who had just read a novel by Lamartine (*Graziella*), writes to Louise: "And first of all, to put the matter bluntly, does he fuck her or doesn't he? The pair of them aren't human beings, they're mannequins. How beautiful these love stories are where the principal thing is so surrounded by mystery that one doesn't know what in the world is going on, sexual intercourse being systematically relegated to the shadow along with drinking, eating, pissing, etc! This partiality irritates me no end. Here's a strapping young fellow who is living with a woman who loves him and whom he loves, and never a desire! Not a single impure cloud ever appears to darken this pale blue lake! Had he told the real story, it would have been even more beautiful! But truth demands hairier males than Monsieur de Lamartine. It is easier in fact to draw an angel than a woman: the wings hide the hunched back."* I have very often had precisely the same reaction to a story: a novel that leaves out sexual experience annoys me as much as one that reduces life exclusively to sexual experience (although the latter irritates me less than the former; I have already said that among forms of unreality I prefer the most concrete one). I need to know whether the hero excites the heroine (and vice versa), and in order for these protagonists to seem lifelike to me, it is indispensable that I be caught up in their mutual excitement. The treatment of sex constitutes one of the most delicate problems in fiction; along with politics it is perhaps the most difficult subject of all to deal with. Since in both cases author and reader alike bring to the narrative such a heavy load of prejudices and stubborn convictions, it is hard to pretend to be natural and spontaneous, to "invent" themes dealing with these subjects, to make them autonomous: one inevitably tends to take sides for or against

* This and later translations from the French are mine. (H.L.)

something, to present arguments instead of showing. Just as, according to certain theologians, a majority of men go to hell by way of their trousers fly, a great number of novels are plunged into unreality by the same route. No other theme so patently demonstrates Flaubert's mastery as his dosage and distribution of the erotic in *Madame Bovary*. Sex lies at the base of what happens; along with money it is the key to the conflicts of the novel, and sexual and economic life are so intimately interwoven that one cannot understand the one unless one understands the other. Nonetheless, in order to get around the restrictions of the period (the sinister puritanism imposed by men of the cloth in the Second Empire brought before the bar of justice the two great books of that era: *Madame Bovary* and *Les Fleurs du mal*) and at the same time avoid the risk of giving the book an air of unreality by its total absence, sex is frequently present but hidden, cunningly bathing the episodes in sensuality from the shadows (Justin tremblingly contemplates Madame Bovary's intimate undergarments; Léon adores her gloves; after Emma's death, Charles relieves his tensions by acquiring the objects that she would have liked to possess), although at other times it parades in private triumph: the unforgettable scene of Emma letting her long hair down for Léon like a consummate courtesan, or preparing her person for lovemaking with all the refinements and foresightedness that the Egyptian houri Kuchuk Hanem must have possessed. Sex occupies a central place in the novel because that is the place it occupies in life, and Flaubert was out to imitate reality. Unlike Lamartine, therefore, he did not dissolve in a halo of spirituality and lyricism a phenomenon that is *also* biological; yet at the same time he did not reduce love to the *merely* biological. He made every possible effort to paint a love that, on the one hand, would be sentiment, poetry, gesture, and on the other (more discreetly), erection and orgasm. On September 19, 1852, he wrote to Louise: "The good old sex organ is the basis of human affection; it is not itself affection, but rather its *substratum*, as philosophers would say. No woman has ever loved a eunuch, and if mothers cherish their children more than fathers do, it is because they are the fruit of their womb and the umbilical cord of their love remains attached to their hearts without being severed." This philosophy, which with Freud will attain scientific respectability, pervades the entire story of Emma Bovary. The "good old sex organ" sheds light on the behavior and the psychology of the characters and frequently fuels the advancement of the plot. The discouragement, the restlessness that little by little turn Emma into an adulteress are a result of her frustration as a wife, and this frustration is largely sexual. The *officier de santé* is no match for Emma and her ardent temperament, and the infrequent nights of lovemaking that fails to satisfy her precipitate her fall. Precisely the opposite happens to Charles. This beautiful, refined young woman makes him so happy (he who has so few expectations in this regard, having come to her from the bony arms of Héloise, an old hag whose ice-cold feet made him shiver when he climbed into bed) that, ironically, she kills his ambition, puts an end to his striving to better himself: since he already has everything, why seek anything more? His sexual contentment explains in large part his blindness, his conformism, his stubborn mediocrity.

In the same letter to Louise in which he comments on Lamartine's novel, Flaubert sums up, in rather vulgar terms, his opinion of women: "They are not honest with themselves; they do not acknowledge their sensuality; they confuse their cunts with their hearts and think that the moon's reason for being is to light their bedrooms" (*Correspondance*, vol. II, p. 401). I fail to see why the same thing couldn't be said of men; they, too, are in the habit of being dishonest with themselves, of hiding their sensuality from themselves, and of mistaking their "cunts" (or the equivalent) for their hearts. Emma, however, tries to make what she can of herself within the "limitations" set upon her life, and by turning vice into virtue, the rule into the exception, breaks the bonds of the conditioning to which her person (her sex) has been subjected and sets in motion a process that is unquestionably an obscure, instinctive process of self-liberation. It is impossible not to admire Emma's capacity for sexual pleasure; once stimulated and educated by Rodolphe, she surpasses her teacher and her second lover, and from Part Two, Chapter IX on, envelops the novel in a passionate eroticism. As in the libertine literature of the eighteenth century (Flaubert was an enthusiastic reader of the Marquis de Sade), love is linked to religion or, rather, to the Church and the trappings of worship. Emma's sexual awakening takes place in a school run by nuns, at the foot of altars, amid the incense of religious ceremonies (a fact that made public prosecutor Pinard apoplectic), and her first rendezvous with Léon, which sets both of them on fire and precedes the great erotic scene in the fiacre, takes place, at Emma's suggestion, in the cathedral of Rouen. In accordance with a system of communicating vessels whereby the erotic is suffused with religiosity and religion with eroticism, the seduction is intertwined with the description of the beauties and treasures of the cathedral reeled off by the guide to this couple who are about to become lovers. One of the critical judgments that keep cropping up with regard to Emma (beginning with Maître Sénard and Flaubert himself) is that she is an unfortunate creature who deserves our pity. In reality, her fate is more human and desirable than that of those industrious procreating wombs, the women of Yonville—Madame Langlois, Madame Caron, Madame Dubreuil, Madame Tuvache, Madame Homais—who seem to be alive only to fulfill certain domestic functions and who are doubtless persuaded, like Emma's mother-in-law, that women ought not to read novels, for if they do they risk becoming flighty, irresponsible *évaporées*. Although she dies a terrible death at a young age because she has the courage to accept herself for what she is, Emma at least

has profound experiences that the virtuous bourgeois house-
wives of Yonville, in their existence as humdrum and circum-
scribed as that of their hens and their dogs, have no notion of.
I am pleased that, instead of stifling her senses, Emma did her
best to indulge them, that she had no qualms about mistaking
"cul" for *"coeur"* (the two of them are, in fact, close relatives),
and that she was capable of believing that the moon existed
only to light her bedroom.

It is not as a cold observer that the presence of sex in a
novel interests me; if I am going to study the subject I prefer a
manual. Every time a problem of censorship arises, those plead-
ing in defense of the banned book base their case on certain
fundamental arguments (such as those, for instance, put forward
by Maître Sénard in rebuttal of Maître Pinard's requisitory) that
are hypocritical: that the literary description of sexual acts and
organs, the invention of erotic situations have as their avowed
aim the furthering of science, the education of readers, or their
moral edification (depicting sin in order to combat it); or that
the beauty of the form has so sublimated the sexual content that
this latter can only provoke the loftiest of spiritual pleasures; or
that only commercial pornography seeks to excite readers, a
function incompatible with genuine literature. What humbug!
In my case, no novel arouses my fervent enthusiasm, holds me
spellbound, fulfills me, unless it acts, if only to a slight degree,
as an erotic stimulant. I have noted that my excitement is all
the more profound when the sexual element is neither exclusive
nor dominant, but instead complemented by other materials,
integrated in a complex and diverse vital context, as happens
in real life: a book by Sade, where the obsession with a single
theme devitalizes sex and turns it into something mental, excites
me less, for example, than the (very few) erotic episodes in
Balzac's *Splendeurs et misères des courtisanes* (I remember above
all the two pairs of knees rubbing against each other in a carriage), or those found here and there in the pages of *The Thou-*

sand and One Nights in Dr. Mardrus's version. In *Madame Bovary*
the erotic element is basic, but even though Flaubert wanted *to
tell all*, he was obliged to take precautions in order to avoid the
risk of censorship (and not only official censorship: his own
friend, the writer Maxime Du Camp, was in favor of the cuts
in the text made by the *Revue de Paris*). But the fact that the
sex in the book is more implicit than explicit does not mean
that the details that are *not* revealed, the events present in the
narrative precisely because they are *not* described, are any the
less effective thereby. The erotic climax of the novel is an inspired hiatus, a sleight-of-hand trick of genius that contrives to
give the material hidden from the reader the maximum possible
charge. I am referring to the interminable journey through the
streets of Rouen in the fiacre, inside which Emma is giving
herself to Léon for the first time. It is remarkable that the most
imaginative erotic episode in French literature does not contain
a single allusion to the female body or a single word of love,
that it is simply an enumeration of the names of streets and
places, the description of the aimless wandering back and forth
through the town of an old coach for hire. But it is not only
the erotic silences of *Madame Bovary* that I remember best. I am
also thinking of the Thursdays at the Hôtel de Boulogne, in the
port district of Rouen, where the trysts with Léon take place,
when all the elements of tragedy are closing in on Emma and
her feeling of imminent peril, her intuition that catastrophe is
not far off appear to heighten her sensuality. I have waited for
her countless times in that cozy room. I have seen her arrive,
each time *"plus enflammée, plus avide"*; I have heard the snake-
like hiss as her corset lace falls to the floor, I have spied on
her running to the door on tiptoe to make certain that it is
locked, and then, with indescribable joy, I have watched her
strip naked and come, pale and grave, into Léon Dupuis's
arms.

It is curious that, in all of the enormous Flaubertian bibliography that exists, no addict has as yet produced a research paper entitled "Flaubert and Shoe Fetishism," since there is more than enough material for such a study. I offer here a sample of the data I have chanced to come across. Albert Thibaudet tells us that, as a child, Flaubert often fell into rapt contemplation of a woman's button boots,* and hence the scene in *Madame Bovary* in which Justin begs her maid's permission to polish Emma's ankle boots, which the boy handles with reverent love, as though they were sacred objects, is more or less autobiographical. Sartre points out the passage in which, for the first time in Flaubert's works, the theme of footwear appears (one *"si important dans la vie et l'oeuvre de Flaubert,"* he adds, though he has no more to say on the subject: one of the many loose ends never tied up in his Cyclopean essay)†: the lines in Chapter IX of *Mémoires d'un fou* in which Flaubert delicately describes a beautiful woman's foot: ". . . her adorable tiny foot sheathed in a pretty high-heeled shoe trimmed with a black rose." It is a well-known fact, moreover, that Flaubert kept in a drawer of his desk, along with letters from his mistress and certain garments and objects belonging to her, the mules that Louise Colet had worn on their first night of love and that, as he frequently writes to her in his letters, he often took out to caress and kiss.

The theme of feet and footwear often crops up in his correspondence, at times in a most curious way. There is extant, for example, a letter of his to Louise, penned in Trouville on August 26, 1853, in which he tells her, jokingly, that if he were a professor at the Collège de France he would give ". . . a course on the important subject of Boots as compared with literature. *Yes, a Boot is a world, I would say*, etc." This whole long letter is a *divertimento* on the subject, consisting of several pages of

* Albert Thibaudet, *Gustave Flaubert* (Paris: Gallimard, 1968), p. 115.

† Jean-Paul Sartre, *L'Idiot de la famille: Gustave Flaubert de 1821 à 1857* (Paris: Gallimard, Vols. I and II, 1971, and Vol. III, 1972). The reference cited is in Vol. II, p. 1525.

surprising, ingenious, and vaguely perverted ramblings (the footgear in question here is masculine) on the shoe as a symbol of cultures, civilizations, and historical eras—China, Greece, the Middle Ages, Louis XV—and as emblems of books and authors—Corneille, La Bruyère, Boileau, Bossuet, Molière, and so on. All this is doubtless a game, but a disquieting one, symptomatic of an uncommon inclination: what allows him to fantasize with such great erudition on this particular theme reveals that in his reading and his observations he has always been very much aware of the appearance of this member, the foot, and its social envelope, footwear.

Another letter to Louise, written a few days before, is further proof of this. Having recently arrived at Trouville to spend a holiday, Gustave has gone down the beach to "watch the ladies bathing." His letter (dated August 14, 1853) tells of his astonishment at seeing how ugly these women look in the shapeless sacks they hide themselves in and the bathing caps they stuff their hair into to take a dip in the water; but what depresses him even more is what they leave visible, namely, their feet. "And their feet! red, skinny, with corns and bunions, deformed by their button boots, feet as long as shuttles or as broad as washerwomen's paddles." There is no doubting the fact: Flaubert was a connoisseur of feet. And it is significant that the name of the supreme father of foot fetishism—a phenomenon which in fact has been named after him—whose voluminous autobiographical oeuvre as a novelist revolves around this delicate feminine extremity and the footwear in which it is encased, appears as a scribbled notation in Flaubert's manuscripts of *Madame Bovary* preserved in the Municipal Library of Rouen: the picaresque melody that the Blind Man of the novel sings was taken from a book by Restif de la Bretonne.

In any event, this demon rears its head in *Madame Bovary*, where women's feet and women's shoes are very important in the erotic life of male characters.* I have already mentioned the spell cast over Justin by the sight of Emma's shoes; at another point the narrator tells us that Léon, who has wearied of Emma, tries to free himself of her hold on him, but that ". . . on hearing the creak of her button shoes, he felt his resolve weaken, like a drunkard at the sight of strong drink." During Emma's meeting with Maître Guillaumin, the notary to whom she has gone to ask for help in paying her debts, his senses are stirred and he apparently has in mind taking advantage of his beautiful visitor and having his way with her when his knee brushes against ". . . her shoes, the sole of which was curling and smoking as it rested against the stove." When Emma leaves, sickened by the notary's baseness, the latter stands there like an idiot, ". . . his eyes staring at his handsome carpet slippers," which were "a love-gift." The first time that Léon sees Emma, who has just come to Yonville, Madame Bovary is standing in front of the fireplace tucking up her skirts so as to warm "her foot sheathed in a black button shoe." And on the day of the horseback ride together, which will end with their making love, Rodolphe notes admiringly ". . . between the black cloth and the little black boot, her delicate white stocking, which seemed like a bit of her naked flesh." When Emma, at the height of her passionate affair with Rodolphe, is at her most radiantly beautiful, it is not surprising that the narrator, in describing her dazzling charms, states that ". . . a subtle, penetrating aura emanated even from the folds of her dress and the arch of her foot." In the early manuscript drafts of *Madame Bovary*, we

---

* Not only in *Madame Bovary*, of course, but here I want to limit myself to speaking only of this book. Traces of this same special interest can be glimpsed all through Flaubert's works. We need only call to mind the moving meeting, after so many years, of Madame Arnoux and Frédéric in *L'Education sentimentale*. After recalling his extraordinary and impossible love, Frédéric falls to his knees and endeavors to reawaken his desire of yesteryear. He is on the point of succeeding in doing so when he spies "the tip of her button shoe . . . peeking out from beneath her dress." On the point of fainting, Frédéric murmurs in a faltering voice: "The sight of your feet perturbs me."

discover that even Charles was a connoisseur. In one passage, which Flaubert later discarded, the *officier de santé* contemplates Emma's feet as she lies dying and is being given extreme unction, and suddenly he is overwhelmed by erotic memories; he sees himself once again in his mind's eye on his wedding day, undoing the laces of Emma's white shoes as ". . . he trembled at the dizzying thought that soon he would possess her." And indeed, the first symptoms of emotion that Charles displays on seeing Emma are of a fetishist nature: they are provoked by the wooden shoes that Père Rouault's daughter is wearing. The narrator is nothing if not explicit: he states that Charles used to be happy at the thought of visiting Les Bertaux because these powerful magnets drew him to the Rouault farm: ". . . he liked the sound of Mademoiselle Emma's little wooden clogs on the scrubbed stone flags of the kitchen; their thick heels made her just a bit taller, and when she walked in front of him, the wooden soles, clacking swiftly along, hit against the leather of her shoe inside with a sharp slapping noise." The theme is omnipresent, with different emotional overtones: sometimes sensual, sometimes overpowering, and in the end even worshipful, as the Abbé Bournisien anoints with the holy oil ". . . the soles of her feet, which once ran so quickly to quench her desires, and which now would never walk again." But in all this gallery of references, the one I cherish most, and the one that lingers longest in my mind, is the description of Emma's *"mignarde chaussure"*—a little embroidered pink satin slipper—which dangles from the instep of her tiny foot as she hops into her lover's lap in the cozy room in the Hôtel de Boulogne.

But on dissociating the indissociable, I know that I am falsifying: what is important is not that *Madame Bovary* contains these ingredients, but rather, that they are so intimately combined as to constitute a whole that is thereby more than the sum of its parts. Rebellion—vulgarity—violence—sex: it is form that makes this indivisible content what it is.

(30

While still under the sway of the enormous impression the novel had made on me, I immediately proceeded to read, one after the other like episodes in a serial, all the other books by Flaubert in the Garnier edition of his works, bound in yellow paper covers. All of them moved me, some more and some less, and made me a definite addict. I remember a number of Olympian discussions I had, in that summer of '59, with friends who laughed when I heatedly asserted that "*Salammbô* is a masterpiece, too." Everyone agrees today that this book is dated, and no one can help yawning or smiling on reading this story of the young woman who committed the sacrilege of touching the veil of Tanit, what with all its operatic décors and the Technicolor "antiquity" somewhat reminiscent of a Cecil B. De Mille production. There is no denying that a good part of the novel is dated, a product of the worst sort of romanticism: the hollow, cliché-ridden story of the love of Mathô and the daughter of Hamilcar, for instance. But there is another side of this work that has lost none of its power and vigor: its epic dimension, the crowd scenes, which no other novelist except Tolstoy has brought off as well as Flaubert. (In *Madame Bovary* there is a major example of this mastery in the chapter on the agricultural fair: the entire town of Yonville is present, almost all the characters who have appeared previously circulate about and speak, and the synthesis of the general and particular, the alternation of the collective and the individual, are impeccable.) The banquets, the fêtes, the ceremonies and rituals in *Salammbô*—the unforgettable, hallucinatory sacrifice of the children to Moloch—and, above all, the battle scenes are still possessed of a dynamism, a plasticity, an elegance that have not been seen since in literature. (We do find these qualities, on the other hand, in films, in the great Westerns of John Ford, for instance— another precocious vice to which I remain addicted.) But even though I liked all of Flaubert's other works, the only one that made as profound an impression on me as *Madame Bovary* was

L'Education sentimentale. For a long time I considered it the greatest of Flaubert's novels, because it was his most ambitious one, and to a certain degree this is a valid opinion: what in *Madame Bovary* is a woman and a town is a generation and a society in *L'Education sentimentale*. The whole is richer, we find in it a more complex variety of social types and a broader historical perspective, a more diversified representation of life, and, from the point of view of form, an equally striking originality, an equally spellbinding magic. And yet . . . the cast of characters in *L'Education sentimentale*, despite being so varied and so splendid, includes no figure comparable to Madame Bovary. The timid Frédéric Moreau and the elusive, maternal Madame Arnoux are admirable characters, but neither they nor the fauna surrounding them—the bankers, artists, industrialists, courtesans, journalists, workers, aristocrats—withstand comparison with Emma, for none of them in the end constitutes a human type in the Cervantine or Shakespearean sense that Flaubert himself defined so well: "What distinguishes great geniuses is generalization and creation. They sum up scattered personalities in a type and bring new characters to the awareness of mankind" (letter to Louise Colet, September 25, 1852). This is the case with Emma Bovary. Like Don Quixote or Hamlet, she sums up in her tormented personality and her less than glorious life story a certain permanent attitude toward life, capable of appearing in the most diverse guises in different places and different eras. And while it is a universal and enduring story, it is at the same time one of the most personal attempts to define the limits of the human, that quest from which all the heroic feats and all the cataclysms of mankind have derived: the capacity to fabricate illusions and the mad determination to make them real. Salammbô, Saint Antoine, Bouvard and Pécuchet, Saint Julien l'Hospitalier also harbor extraordinary illusions and formidable wills bent on realizing their chimerical fantasies, but their ambitions have to do with God or Science: Emma's utopia, by contrast, is strictly human. On the morning of May 22, 1853, Flaubert wrote to Louise: "The measure of a soul is the dimension of its desire, as one forms one's preconceptions of a cathedral by the height of its bell tower." His greatest glory may have been to have created, in the vulgar, fickle, fictional figure of Emma Bovary, the best demonstration of this truth, one of the bell towers that dominate the vast flat plain of human existence.

In 1962 I began to read Flaubert's *Correspondance*. I remember the exact date; I had just earned some money from a novel I had written, and my first investment was the purchase, in a bookstore in Tours, of the thirteen volumes published by Conard. Apart from the interest in following step by step such a difficult and harsh human life, and the excitement that the Flaubert addict* finds on retracing the Homeric gestation of his works day by day as described by the author himself, discovering at first hand what his readings, his hatreds, his frustrations were, experiencing the sensation of having broken through the barriers of time and space and entered his circle of intimates, the witnesses of his life—Du Camp, Bouilhet, Louise, George Sand, his niece Caroline—I believe that Flaubert's correspondence constitutes the best possible friend for a budding writer with a literary vocation, the most profitable example a young writer can have as he embarks upon the destiny he has chosen. Those who have read them will find it odd that I use the word "stimulating" to characterize letters in which the gloomiest pessimism reigns, in which curses against mankind in general and a great many men in particular sputter, in which humanity appears, with very few exceptions (almost all of them writers), to be a grotesque, vulgar lot. But while the great man gave vent

* And the sadness for one in love with Emma to discover that Flaubert sometimes spoke ill of her: "She is a somewhat perverse creature, a woman of false poetry and false sentiments," he assured Mademoiselle Leroyer de Chantepie (letter of March 3, 1857).

to the nervousness and fatigue accumulated during the ten or twelve preceding hours of work★ in these boiling fits of fury, the letters demonstrate better than anything else the humanity of his genius, how his talent was an inch-by-inch conquest, how, in the task of creation, the writer is left entirely to his own devices—to his misfortune (no one is going to come whisper the right adjective, the felicitous adverb in his ear), but also to his good fortune, because if he is capable of emulating the patience and persistence that these letters reveal, if he is capable of dissecting himself *in vivo*, as Flaubert was, in the end he too, like this vociferous old provincial bachelor, will succeed in creating something lasting. Pettiness and poverty that gradually become nobility and abundance, the process wherein perseverance and conviction play such an important role, can be a marvelous incentive for a writer, a powerful antidote against discouragement. It has been at times when I was having the most difficulties writing that I have most often turned to Flaubert's letters (skipping about, and continually cursing his niece Caroline for having insisted that cuts be made in the *Correspondance*), and invariably they have had a tonic effect on me.†

I am a literary fetishist: I delight in visiting the houses, graves, libraries of writers whom I admire, and if I could also collect their vertebrae to venerate, as believers collect those of saints, I would do so with the greatest of pleasure. (In Moscow,

---

★ These fits of rage at times move him to unexpected rash decisions, to setting himself time limits for proving his talents. After having worked for a number of weeks on the scene of the agricultural fair, he suddenly writes to Louise: "I give myself two more weeks to be done with it. At the end of this time, if nothing good has come of it, I'm abandoning the novel indefinitely" (*Correspondance*, Vol. III, p. 369). The twenty-nine-page episode was in fact to cost him four months of work.

† It is possible that this emphasis on willpower is false, that it plays only a very secondary role in literary success, that there are more decisive innate or causal factors involved. No matter: from the point of view of someone who wants to write, it will always be preferable to believe that all doors lie open before him and that everything will depend on his lucidity and his tenacity, rather than on processes that entirely escape his control. And in this regard there is no better model than Flaubert.

I remember, I was the only one, among a group of those invited on a well-nigh endless Tolstoy pilgrimage, to make the entire circuit without despairing, the only one to enjoy nosing about among all the memorabilia, from slippers and samovars to the last goose-quill pen.) I have not forgotten how disappointing my visit to Croisset was. We had first gone to Rouen, with Jorge Edwards, to have a look at the scene of Gustave's childhood, the Hôtel-Dieu, imagining the autopsy room, wanting to believe that over there was the very window through which he and his sister used to watch their father meticulously dissecting cadavers, and then we had strolled through the cemetery without finding the writer's grave, and we thought that Croisset would be exactly the right crowning touch for this Sunday visit to Flaubert country. What we found was a miserable image of the man: the house had been torn down and a factory erected on the site; the atmosphere was ugly and oppressive, with chimneys belching forth black smoke; the river had been dammed and no longer flowed past the house; piles of coal were visible everywhere, and the air was full of soot. The museum was simply the one remaining outbuilding, in which visitors could see a stuffed parrot that had served Flaubert as a model for *Un Coeur simple* and one of the carved stone slabs he had brought back from Tunis when he was writing *Salammbô*. There were also a few yellowed photographs. Everything was sordid and sad, and the only thing that moved us was our walk down the famous *"allée des gueulades,"* the little lane shaded by trees ("the same ones," the guide insisted) to which the Norman giant—hunting down assonances, consonances, maddening cacophonies—was in the habit of repairing each afternoon to bellow out the phrases he had composed the night before.

A lover enamored of truth does not limit himself to taking his pleasure with his beloved, but, as was required in the Middle Ages, he orders his entire life around this love and does battle for his lady whenever called upon. (Late 1960. A heated discussion with a Bolivian friend whose parting words were: "You won't give an inch when it comes to Cuba or Flaubert." Fourteen years later, I am more tolerant of criticism of the Cuban revolution; I am as intransigent as ever, on the other hand, when the subject under discussion is Flaubert.) My addiction led me to devour not only all Flaubert's works but all the critical or parasitical literature concerning him that came my way, and Flaubert has served in many instances as the thermometer by which I have measured other authors, the factor that has determined my eventual enthusiastic acceptance or my rejection of a given writer. I am certain, for instance, that my loathing for Barbey d'Aurevilly stems from his attacks on Flaubert, that the same reason underlies my scant sympathy for Valéry or Claudel (who called the consummately beautiful beginning of *Salammbô* the dullest prose in all of French literature), and that my sudden change of mind regarding Henry James, whose slow-moving novels had always sorely tried my patience, began when I read his intelligent essay on Flaubert. My lack of respect for journalistic literary criticism is due largely to my having become acquainted, thanks to the devoted labors of René Dumesnil, with what newspapers and reviews of the time had to say when Flaubert's books first appeared; and my conviction that, generally speaking, creative writers have had a greater flair than critics for detecting what is genuinely new is largely based on Baudelaire's review of *Madame Bovary*. I should also like to mention here Ezra Pound's bold statement, in his *ABC of Reading* (which made my heart leap for joy, as the saying goes, when I came across it) to the effect that, unlike the poet, who must read a great long list of authors beginning with Homer if he is to have an adequate background for the practice of his craft, the prose writer may simply begin with the author of *Bouvard et Pécuchet*.

The critics of Flaubert's day were unfair to him and short-sighted. Even *Madame Bovary*, which was a popular success—

due in large part to the trial, which gave it the reputation of a "scandalous" book—was mercilessly attacked by the penny-a-liner Paris literary columnists, but in the case of this novel at least, Sainte-Beuve and a handful of other critics realized its merits. Flaubert's other books were totally misunderstood, however, and provoked what amounted to mutiny among literary columnists (some sort of dubious record was achieved by Barbey d'Aurevilly, who declared *La Tentation de Saint Antoine* to be as indigestible as *Faust*, Part II), wherein envy and bad faith, along with ignorance and insensitivity, played a role. The following generation, on the other hand, claimed Flaubert as one of its own, and though he himself always declined to occupy the lofty place that Zola and the naturalists had set aside for him, it nonetheless considered him a master. But after this period French littérateurs scorned Flaubert—Claudel was no exception—and until the 1950s writers and critics more or less gave the impression that they remembered Flaubert only to denigrate him. The existentialists, convinced that literature is a form of action and that it is the writer's duty to participate in the battles of his time with every weapon at his command, beginning with his pen, could scarcely tolerate Flaubert's fanatic concern for form, his haughty isolation, his art-for-art's-sake aesthetic, his lofty disdain for politics. Forgetting that what is essential in Flaubert is the work and not his temperament and his personal opinions, the antipathy they felt toward this hermit of Croisset, who did battle with words as the world came tumbling down about his ears, was extended to his novels as well. This attitude finds its most exacerbated expression in Sartre's remarks about Flaubert in *Situations II*, an essay that I had read with fervor years before becoming addicted to the master of Croisset and that retroactively aroused in me a sort of anxiety attack, a clash of loyalties.

During the 1960s, the appraisal of Flaubert in France changed radically; scorn and neglect suddenly gave way to rescue, praise, worship of him as a cult figure. The French became addicts at the same time I did, and half pleased and half jealous, I saw the passion for Flaubert spread in those convulsive years of Gaullism, the Algerian war, the OAS, and for me, between writing and preparing radio broadcasts (I was earning my daily bread by working for the ORTF*), a work schedule that kept me on the go from morning to night. I remember clearly the satisfaction—as though a member of my family or a personal friend had been the one thus honored—with which I read François-Régis Bastide's preface to the new edition of *La Première éducation sentimentale*, published by Seuil, an early version of the novel that up to that time had been known only to university students and professors, and I would not have hesitated a second to post the last words of Bastide's preface on the door of my house: "We already realized it, but now we realize it once and for all: the real Boss is Flaubert."

In contemporary French literature, the *engagés* were succeeded by that heterogeneous group of novelists referred to by critics under the bushel-basket title of practitioners of the *"Nouveau Roman."* Although I found almost all of them extremely boring, with the exception of Samuel Beckett (he was included in the group because he was published by the same house), who also bored me but at the same time gave me the impression that in his case something lay behind all the tedium, I was always well disposed toward them because they proclaimed to the four winds how important an influence Flaubert had had on the modern novel. The first one to offer a theoretical analysis of this link was not a novelist, however, but a scholar, Geneviève Bollème, who in 1964 published an essay, *"La Leçon de Flaubert,"* pointing out those aspects of the work of the author of *Madame Bovary* on which the new narrators had based their own experiments: the concern for aesthetic values, the obsession with

* The French national radio-television network. (H.L.)

description, the autonomy of the text—in other words, Flaubertian "formalism." Her essay was a practical demonstration of a bold hypothesis: that in all of Flaubert, and in *Madame Bovary* in particular, what is most essential is the description, that it deliberately destroys the narrative line, that "describing" rather than "telling a story" was for him the only experience capable of expressing "the movements of life." It was an extremely clever way of erecting a bridge between Flaubert and the New Novelists, all of whom were merciless describers and rather apathetic storytellers. In interviews, articles, or lectures, Alain Robbe-Grillet, Michel Butor, Claude Simon had recognized Flaubert as a precursor of modernity. But it was Nathalie Sarraute, in a brilliant and tendentious article entitled *"Flaubert le précurseur,"* published in the review *Preuves* (February 1965), who took it upon herself to crown him officially as master of the New Novel. As I read it in a bistro in Saint-Germain, I was thunderstruck. I was pleased by certain statements ("At this moment, the master of all of us is Flaubert. As to this name the consensus is unanimous: it is that of the precursor of today's novel"), but when the article went on to explain the reasons for his status as the principal forerunner of the New Novel, I thought I was dreaming. Taking out of context a paragraph from a letter to Louise ("What seems beautiful to me, what I would like to write, is a book about nothing, a book with no attachments to the outside world, which would be self-sustaining thanks to the internal force of its style, as the earth holds itself in the void without being supported, a book that would have almost no subject, or one at any rate in which the subject would be almost invisible, if such a thing is possible"), Nathalie Sarraute confused this desire expressed by Flaubert with the reality of his work and arrived at the following extraordinary conclusion: "Books about nothing, almost without a subject, free of characters, plot, and all the old props, reduced to the sort of pure movement that makes them kin to abstract art."

It would have been difficult to distort Flaubert's meaning any more drastically; Borges's phrase according to which every author creates his precursors has never been truer. But in the last analysis a reader has a right to find in what he reads what he himself has put there. Nathalie Sarraute's quotation is taken from a letter written when Flaubert was laboring over *Madame Bovary*, and anyone who has followed the process of development of this novel or the others knows how scrupulous Flaubert was about every detail of the story—the situations, the background, the characters, the peripeteias—and how carefully he mapped out the plot. It would not be difficult to cite hundreds of passages from the *Correspondance* demonstrating how important he considered the subject matter (he called this "the ideas" of a novel), as is quite evident, for example, from his opinion of Lamartine's *Graziella*. It is more reasonable to take his desire to write "a book about nothing, a book with no attachments to the outside world," as being, on the one hand, a fit of enthusiasm for the style of a novel and, on another hand, as yet another defense of the autonomy of fiction—everything in a novel, its truth and its falsehood, its seriousness or its banality, is a product of the form shaping its content—yet another statement of the necessity for a novel to be persuasive in and of itself, that is to say, through its use of words and technique and not through its fidelity to the outside world (although he was well aware that once the book is in the hands of the reader, this comparison is inevitable, inasmuch as the latter can appreciate, understand, judge the book only in terms of that outside world of which he is a part). The quotation cited by Nathalie Sarraute is an argument in favor of narrative objectivity, not a negation of the narrative element in a novel. If she had gone on searching through the *Correspondance*, she would have found that a year and five months after the sentence she cites, Flaubert wrote—again to Louise—this other sentence that begins by taking up precisely the same idea (books about nothing) once again, only to correct it and complete it in the opposite sense: "I should like to compose books in such a way that the only thing necessary would be to write sentences (if I may put it that way), just as in order to live the only thing necessary is to breathe. I thoroughly dislike having to bother with the tricks of organizing, the combination of effects, all the calculations of the underpinnings, *and yet they are Art, for the stylistic effect depends on them, and on them alone*" (letter written June 26, 1853—my italics). All this is as plain as day: the exciting part for Flaubert was polishing the style, choosing the words, solving the problems presented by nouns and adjectives, euphony, rhythm. He was less fond of all the rest of it—the "tricks of organizing," the "combinations of effects," the "calculations of the under-pinnings" are, obviously, the problems having to do with facts, the order of the events that make up the story, the organization of the subject matter of the novel within a temporal system— but he did not deny that these concerns were artistic or im-portant. On the contrary, he states that the "stylistic effect" *depends* on all these things, and adds, categorically: *and on them alone*. An author may not have the slightest conscious awareness of the full import of his work, and it might very well be that Flaubert, by yearning to write novels that were simply words, books without a story, contributed to the modern novel by way of inventions that have as much to do with narrative technique— the "montage" of the story—as with the use of words, or per-haps even more. But it gives me great satisfaction to be able to prove that this is not in fact the case; besides being a great storyteller in practice, Flaubert had a crystal-clear idea of the importance of plot in fictional narration and was even persuaded that the effectiveness of prose (whereby he meant its beauty) depended exclusively on it. Having come across this quotation, which corroborates my own idea of the novel, is one of the pleasures the *Correspondance* has brought me, in these days when so many narrators savagely attack the "story" in fiction; another pleasure, more personal still, is the happiness with which I, like any admirer of *Amadis de Gaule* and *Tirant lo Blanc*, discovered that Flaubert had once written: "You know that it has long been one of my dreams to write a romance of chivalry. I think this could be done, even after Ariosto, by introducing an element of terror and of sweeping poetry that is missing in him. But is there anything I don't yearn to write? Is there any lust of the pen that does not excite me?" (*Correspondance*, Vol. II, p. 245).

But the important thing is that, even though critics were looking at him through more or less distorting lenses, Flaubert was rapidly becoming a key figure in modern literature. Not all the distortions came from the formalist contingent. Almost at the same time as the article by Nathalie Sarraute—rightist deviationism—I read, with equal astonishment, in *Recherches Soviétiques* (Cahier 6, 1956), the translation of an essay by a member of the Academy of Sciences of the U.S.S.R., A. F. Ivachtchenko, who offered a leftist-deviationist interpretation: Flaubert had turned out to be one of the fathers of critical realism!

And in these same years, Sartre began to devote himself to what may be considered a laborious, monumental autocriticism. Between his summary judgment of Flaubert in *Situations II* and his effort to situate him in his family, social, and historical milieu in a "totalizing" interpretation which, by recalling Marx, Freud, and existentialism, would constitute a complete analysis of the social and individual aspects of creation,★ Sartre's attitude toward Flaubert changed considerably: a shift from scorn to respect, to a determination to understand him that is radically different from his initial ukase. This process culminated in the three volumes of *L'Idiot de la famille* (Sartre announced a fourth one, dedicated to *Madame Bovary*, but it remains unfinished, as

★ As outlined in *"Question de méthode"* (in his *Critique de la raison dialectique*) and his two articles, *"La Conscience de classe chez Flaubert"* and *"Flaubert: du poète à l'artiste,"* in *Les Temps Modernes*, May–June 1966 and August 1966.

has happened with other series of works of his), which represent
the apotheosis of the interest in Flaubert that has characterized
French literature of the seventies. This most intransigent of
Flaubert's critics, the sworn enemy of what he stood for in
terms of his attitude toward history and art, devotes twenty
years of his life and three thousand pages to the study of his
"case" and acknowledges that the master of Croisset, along with
Baudelaire, was a founding father of the modern sensibility.
Happily for me, this reconciliation solved a personal problem.
Sartre is one of the authors to whom I feel most deeply indebted,
and at one time I admired his writings almost as much as Flaubert's. As the years have gone by, however, his creative works
have slowly faded in my memory, and his pronouncements
concerning literature and the role of the writer, which at one
time I regarded as articles of faith, seem to me today to be
unpersuasive—to my mind his most penetrating and most enduring works are the essays devoted to Baudelaire and Genet,
his polemical writings, and his articles. His moral stature, on
the other hand, has little by little assumed gigantic proportions
for me amid all the crises and dilemmas of these difficult years,
in view of the lucidity, the forthright sincerity, and the youthful
courage with which he has confronted not only Fascism, con-
servatism, and bourgeois snares and pitfalls but also the au-
thoritarianism and dogmatism of the left.

I am not an overly enthusiastic admirer of *L'Idiot de la
famille*; the book is of more interest to a Sartrean than to a
Flaubertian; after the two months' reading time that the essay
requires, one is left with the feeling of a gigantic task that will
never fulfill the aim announced in the preface—explaining the
roots and the nature of Flaubert's vocation, through an inter-
disciplinary investigation in which all the human sciences of our
time will be called upon to demonstrate what they can tell us,
today, about a man. It is of little moment if a literary essay—
and Sartre's work is that only in part—strays from the subject

at hand to speak of other matters, wherever and whenever the result will justify such divagations. But that is not what happens in *L'Idiot de la famille*: in the final analysis, one is left with an impression of atomization, of an archipelago of disconnected ideas, of a striking disproportion between the means employed and the end attained. An extraordinarily uneven book, there exist side by side in its pages the most penetrating analyses and the most luminous discoveries, on the one hand, and the most flagrant contradictions on the other. What is strange, in the case of such a fervent partisan of the concrete and the real as Sartre, is that a large part of the book is pure speculation, with a very tenuous anchor in reality. In the first volume, for example, the account of the relations between Gustave and his father, Dr. Flaubert, seems convincing and is supported by solid textual evidence; that of the relations between Flaubert and his sister Caroline, firstly, and between Gustave and Alfred Le Poittevin, secondly, are based, on the other hand, on mere suppositions, some of which are highly questionable. Another unexpected feature of the book is the fact that although Sartre announced in *"Question de méthode"* that the point of view he planned to adopt in his study of Flaubert would be at once existentialist, Marxist, and psychoanalytic, in *L'Idiot de la famille* itself, save for certain passages here and there (some of them strikingly brilliant, such as the description of the social and ideological origins of Flaubert's mother and father that he has tracked down, or the examination of social classes during the Second Empire), by far the greatest part of the interpretation is a rigorous (and, one might add, orthodox) Freudian one, though it is tricked out in an existentialist vocabulary. I do not point this out as a criticism, but merely as a curiosity. Furthermore, the best pages come off as brilliantly as they do precisely because Sartre has followed the Freudian method: the psychoanalytic explanation, for instance, of the "Pont-l'Evêque crisis," the endlessly debated question, that is, as to the precise nature of Flaubert's illness—

epilepsy, hysteria, and so on—a debate to which Sartre, with his theory of neurosis, contributes a solid, complex, and imaginative, albeit not an entirely persuasive, point of view. It is in the second volume, above all, that the essay leaves literature behind altogether and becomes pure psychology. Instead of "explaining" Flaubert and his oeuvre in terms of this neurosis that he has analyzed in such minute detail, Sartre appears to use Flaubert's person and his writings to illustrate the mechanisms of the neurotic personality. What the reader learns about mental pathology, the Oedipus complex, castration, symbolic displacements is instructive and fascinating; but at the same time all of this sheds very little light on Flaubert's works. The description of generic traumas, of typical situations reduces to an abstraction the *specificity* of Flaubert's case, despite the fact that the explicit aim of Sartre's essay, as he himself announced, was to account for the *specific nature* of the man and his genius. Moreover, in this second volume, even more than in the first, there are infuriating repetitions, and at times, as the reader follows this prose that reworks, reiterates, retraces, circles back, returns again and again to the same idea, he has the impression that Sartre has imprisoned himself in his own spiderweb, that he finds himself—to use one of his own favorite images—trapped in his own labyrinthine construction. The same thing could have been said in half the number of pages. This impression becomes a near-certainty in the last volume, the most unfocused of the three. Save for the section entitled *"Névrose et programmation chez Flaubert: le Second Empire,"* Flaubert has disappeared from these pages and the book endlessly describes, in what is often mere pompous, verbose rhetoric, psychic processes that have no connection with his particular case: the general has blotted out the uniquely personal, the abstract has effaced the concrete. The last section, by contrast, is the most interesting one, in particular the comparison between Flaubert and Leconte de Lisle—the summary of what Parnassianism represented and the links between its aesthetics and Flaubert's theory of art is admirable—and the same can be said of the intriguing analysis of the relations between Flaubert and the Second Empire, although Sartre advances very few convincing arguments in proof of his thesis that the writer most representative of this society was the author of *Madame Bovary*, who supposedly identified himself heart and soul with what the regime of Louis Bonaparte stood for. At the same time, this historico-social analysis is such a brusque departure from everything that has gone before—all of which moved exclusively on the psychological and psychic planes—that it gives the impression of being the beginning of another investigation, a radical departure rather than a complement. The book ends abruptly, as though exhaustion had overtaken its author before he was halfway through, on discovering that he had set himself a goal so distant that he did not have the strength to reach it, a goal too distant for any one man to reach by his own effort alone. In the end, it is disheartening to realize that the only texts of Flaubert's that Sartre has analyzed in detail are the writings of his childhood and adolescence, that the effort expended in scrutinizing these texts—almost all of them of scant literary value, mere prehistoric signs of a vocation—has consumed all the critic's time and energy, so that at the end of all these thousands of pages, through an error in planning, he has not yet gotten around to studying even the first novel of Flaubert's that reached print. Hence Sartre's work as it stands turns out to be what was doubtless intended in his original plan to be preliminary considerations before embarking upon his interpretation properly speaking. Unlike the character in Camus's *La Peste* who never manages to write a novel because he can never decide how to phrase the very first sentence of it, in this case the author has set about writing with such fury, has developed his prolegomena in such detail, and dealt with so many adventitious subjects that he has lost sight of the whole and soon discovers that the work has assumed such tremendous proportions that he will not have the time—or doubtless the desire—to finish what he has started. The result is a monstrous baby, a giant child, a monumental—and brilliant—failure. This is what is known, of course, as defeat with honor; falling short of the mark by aiming too high; *ailes de géant qui empêchent de marcher.*

One is naturally reminded of the striking similarity between what happened to Sartre in this book and what happened to Flaubert in the last book *he* wrote. Have there ever been two such equally admirable failures, for such identical reasons, as those of *L'Idiot de la famille* and *Bouvard et Pécuchet?* Both are impossible endeavors, undertakings doomed to miscarry, because both were aimed at an unattainable goal, both weighted down by an ambition that borders on the inhuman: embracing the whole of the human condition. The idea of representing in a novel the totality of what is human—or, if one prefers, the totality of stupidity, since for Flaubert the two terms were very nearly synonymous—was a utopia akin to that of capturing in an essay the totality of a life, of explaining a man by reconstructing *all* the sources—social, familial, historical, psychological, biological, linguistic—of his life story, all the tributaries that converged to form his visible and secret personality. In both cases the author tried to unravel a tangle that has a beginning but no end. But it is evident that in both cases the merit lies in the defeat itself, that defeat represents a sort of victory, that in both cases we recognize the work to be a failure only after we recognize the grandeur that explains that failure and renders it inevitable. For to have persisted in such an adventure—to have fallen into Lucifer's crime—is to have set the novel and criticism loftier heights to attain.

And so I have reached the end of my love story. It is a sad and glorious one, like that of any self-respecting romantic story, of the sort that pleased Emma and that pleases me. It is sad because this long and very faithful passion was doomed from the beginning, by the wretched law of life itself, to flow in one direction only, to be a plea without an answer, and because the last image of the story resembles the first: the lover, alone, his heart pounding with desire, his eyes fixed on the book clasped tenderly in his hands, and in his head, like a little mouse with cruel teeth crouching in a deep dark cavern, the terrible certainty that this most earthy of women will never leave her ethereal precincts to come to the rendezvous. But the lover does not give up, because this woman has filled his life with a pleasure doubtless less sublime but perhaps more enduring than if his love had been shared, since in the latter case, as Emma learns, he must continually confront the truth that everything is transitory, and since his lady, though she has never become incarnate or lain in his arms, will continue to be born for him on a farm lost in the hinterland of the *pays de Caux* and repeat her adventure as many times as he asks her to, with marvelous docility, with not the slightest sign of fatigue or boredom.

The ending of the story is glorious, because in recent years this little Norman peasant girl has attained a popularity that shows no sign of being a mere passing vogue and that in years to come will in all probability continue to grow. She has been admired by men and women of the most diverse classes and stations; austere professors have devoted their lives to studying her; young iconoclasts seek to do away with all the literature of the past and begin all over again, starting with her; wise philosophers who have offended her have tried to redeem themselves by writing thick volumes that will serve as a pedestal for her statue. And this is happening not only in her own country but in many others as well. In the Spanish-speaking world, too, after having long been forgotten, she is again becoming accessible to countless eyes, hands, hearts, in an estimable translation. I should be jealous, but I am not; like certain old perverts with their young spouses, I feel supremely flattered by these persistent attentions, this popular fervor, this seething excitement surrounding the young woman I love. I know that in the territory where her beauty shines forth, no one except the country doctor, Rodolphe, and Léon will possess her, and that in the territory where I find myself, she cannot give anyone more than she has given me.

TWO

THE PEN-MAN

*I am a pen-man. I feel by way of it, because of it, in
relation to it, and much more with it.*

—Letter to Louise Colet, February 1, 1852

What was the point of departure of Madame Bovary?

A frustration, it would appear. In mid-September of 1849, Flaubert
invites his friends Maxime Du Camp and Louis Bouilhet to his
house at Croisset, near Rouen, so as to read them a manuscript
he had begun on May 24, 1848, and finished a few days before,
on September 12, at 3:20 on a sunny, windy afternoon: the first
Tentation de Saint Antoine. The idea for this book was suggested
to him by Brueghel's painting, which he had seen in Geneva in
the spring of 1845, though in fact the idea of Hell and Satan
had preyed upon his mind ever since the days when, as a small
child, he had seen each autumn at the fair of Saint-Romain in
Rouen the mystery play of St. Anthony, in the booth of a
famous puppeteer of the region, Père Legrain. At the age of
fourteen he had written, in biblical verses, a *Voyage en enfer,*
the starting point of a Satan cycle not closed until almost forty
years later (the definitive version of the *Tentation* appeared in
1874); two years later, in 1838, a *Rêve d'enfer;* a *Danse des morts,*
in which the Devil is one of the characters; and in 1839, *Smarh,*
a vast Luciferian mystery, steeped in Byronic romanticism. The

anxiety with which Flaubert awaits the verdict of his friends is thus due in part to the importance that the subject matter of this book—a demon that had awakened his vocation fifteen years before—holds for him. He has, in fact, worked on this first *Tentation de Saint Antoine* with rigorous self-discipline (it has taken him sixteen months of writing, on top of nearly three years of documentation, during which he consulted all sorts of books: medieval incunabula, theologians such as Swedenborg and mystics such as St. Teresa of Avila, histories of the beginnings of Christianity, religious treatises); and what is more, with pleasure, suffering none of the apprehensions and depressions that will turn the writing of his later books into veritable calvaries. Years later, amid the sea of doubts and fevered agitation of *Madame Bovary*, he will confess to Louise: "*Saint Antoine* did not demand a quarter of the mental tension that *Bovary* is causing me. It was an outlet; I experienced only pleasure in writing, and the eighteen months I spent writing the 500 pages of it were the most profoundly voluptuous ones of my entire life" (letter of April 6, 1853).

There are other reasons why this reading that he is about to give his friends is very important for him. A few months before, Madame Flaubert has given her son Gustave permission to go on a long trip through the Orient* with Maxime Du Camp, but Flaubert has postponed his departure until the manuscript is finished. Hence the journey through the lands of antiquity, the supreme ambition for a young man brought up on romantic readings and athirst for exoticism and local color, has come to represent a sort of recompense for all the diligent labor of these sixteen months. Moreover, he has written this first *Tentation* in circumstances very different from those in which

---

* In both French and Spanish, the terms Orient and Oriental may refer to the East in general. They are also often used to refer to the Islamic countries of Africa and the Near and Middle East. Following both Flaubert and Vargas Llosa, I use Orient and Oriental in the latter sense throughout. (H.L.)

he composed earlier texts—the first *Education sentimentale, Novembre, Mémoires d'un fou, Smarh*—which he has not attempted to publish because he considers them failures.

His previous work dates from a period in which Gustave seemed destined to assume his place in society by practicing some liberal profession, like his father and his brother Achille, both physicians. These texts were written in time stolen from his studies in secondary school, as with *Mémoires d'un fou* or *Smarh*, or while attending university, as with the first *Education sentimentale* and *Novembre*. Gustave had already discovered that the only thing that interested him was literature, and the idea of a bourgeois future, of any activity except writing, had long tormented him, as his adolescent letters attest, but Dr. Flaubert had allowed him no way out: he was going to be forced to follow the path pointed out by this (God the) Father whose finger pointed straight at law school. In these earlier years Flaubert has been a part-time writer, a young man whose time and energy are divided between literature and occupations that he considers an obstacle. But by the time he writes the first *Tentation* his destiny has abruptly reversed poles: literature has now taken over as mistress and queen. On a dark night in January 1844, he has had the first attack of that illness which—whether he was suddenly overtaken by it or whether he chose to suffer from it—has come just in time to free him from his law studies, from the obligation to "carve out a future for himself" that was driving him mad. The chief surgeon of the municipal hospital of Rouen has had no other choice but to give in: Gustave will abandon his studies at the university and remain at home, living the life of an invalid. Two years later, his liberation becomes more definite still: Dr. Flaubert, the overpowering shadow that could still darken his prospects of freedom, dies (talk has it that the bitterness of seeing his son become a ne'er-do-well hastened his death). From this point on, Flaubert's future is the one that he has planned for himself: he will live with his mother, on the income his father has left him, devoting himself entirely and exclusively to reading and writing. The first work of creation, the product of this new existence dedicated to literature (the book on travels through Brittany, written in collaboration with Maxime Du Camp, is little more than a stylistic exercise), is this *Tentation* that the good-looking Norman giant with fair hair and blue eyes, soon to celebrate his twenty-eighth birthday, is about to read to his friends Bouilhet and Du Camp, the two of them writers as well. We may be quite certain that he is happy, nervous, fearful of their verdict as he begins reading.

Under what conditions did the reading take place and what was the reaction of the two friends?

The reading of the enormous manuscript—the first *Tentation* is double the number of pages of the definitive version—had as its setting Gustave's bedroom and study, and was staged in accordance with strict rules and a precise schedule. It was agreed from the beginning that Bouilhet and Du Camp would make no comment until the entire manuscript had been read. The ceremony lasted four days, each of them divided into two four-hour sessions: from noon to four in the afternoon, and from eight in the evening until midnight. The only reader was Gustave, who "modulated, sang, intoned" his text, as Bouilhet and Du Camp listened in silence, exchanging swift glances now and again. On the first day, before beginning his reading, waving the manuscript in the air, Gustave exclaimed in a burst of euphoria: "If you don't cry out with enthusiasm, nothing is capable of moving you!" Madame Flaubert did not attend the reading sessions, but she worriedly loitered about in the hallway, and every so often, unable to control herself, she would take Louis and Maxime aside: "Well then?" Their answers were evasive. But the two friends decided between themselves to be truthful with Flaubert. Up until the reading, they had had a mistaken idea of the book: they had thought it would be a monologue of the hermit saint recounting his experiences or a historical novel about Christianity in its first heroic days. These eight hours of daily reading remained engraved upon Maxime's memory as a "painful" experience.

At midnight on the fourth day, Gustave reads the last sentence, raps on the table, and says, in what is no doubt a hoarse voice: "Very well, it's your turn now. Tell me frankly what you think." The one who pronounces judgment is Louis Bouilhet, a shy sort who, according to Du Camp, could nonetheless be pitiless when it came to literary matters: "We think you should throw it in the fire and never mention it again." Flaubert's reaction is that of a wounded animal. The friends argue all the rest of the night, Gustave defending his book, Louis and Maxime criticizing it. Finally Flaubert gives in: "Perhaps you're right. I became so absorbed in my subject that I got carried away and could no longer see clearly. I admit the book has the faults you point out, but they're inherent in my nature; what can I do?" They answer: "Give up subjects so vague and diffuse that you're unable to get a grasp on them and bring them into focus; since you have an invincible tendency toward lyricism, you must choose a subject where lyricism would be so ridiculous that you'll be obliged to watch yourself and eliminate it. Pick some commonplace subject, one of those incidents that abound in bourgeois life, something like Balzac's *La Cousine Bette, Le Cousin Pons*, and force yourself to treat it in a natural, almost familiar tone, culling out those digressions, those ramblings, which may be beautiful in and of themselves but are mere frills, useless to the development of your conception and boring to the reader." Flaubert, *"plutôt vaincu que convaincu"*—more beaten and bowed than convinced—murmurs: "It won't be easy, but I'll try."

It was 8 a.m., daylight flooded the room, early-morning sounds could be heard all over the spacious house, and on leaving the bedroom Du Camp caught a glimpse of a woman's black dress disappearing down the stairs: Madame Flaubert had been eavesdropping at the door. She accepted the verdict even more grudgingly than her son, continued to harbor a resentment against Bouilhet and Du Camp, and was convinced that their opinion (Maxime's especially) stemmed from their jealousy of Gustave.

On the following day, after this tense, sleepless night, the three friends take a stroll in the garden of the Croisset house, contemplating the waters of the Seine, embarrassed about what has happened the night before. Bouilhet suddenly turns to Gustave: "Listen, why not write a novel based on the story of Delaunay?" Flaubert raises his head and exclaims enthusiastically: "What a great idea!"

His words might be taken as the birth announcement of *Madame Bovary*.

What degree of verisimilitude does this anecdote have? Was the opinion of Du Camp and Bouilhet just or unjust?

My impression is that the broad outlines of the anecdote are true and that the details have been colored or invented. The one source of the episode is Maxime Du Camp, who recounts it in his memoirs,★ published after all the others present—Madame Flaubert, Gustave, Bouilhet—are dead. Du Camp's testimony is regarded as questionable by critics and biographers, who are inclined to believe that, as Madame Flaubert intuited, Maxime was jealous of his friend. They adduce as evidence the fact that Maxime cut, or as editorial co-director approved of, the cuts made in the text of *Madame Bovary* as published in the *Revue de Paris*; declared *L'Education sentimentale* a failure and again rec-

---

★ Maxime Du Camp, *Souvenirs littéraires*, Vols. I and III (Paris: Hachette, 1882–83). The episode is related in Vol. I, Ch. XII.

ommended dozens of deletions; and, once Gustave was dead, perfidiously painted a portrait of him in which, on the one hand, he belittled his talent and, on the other, made himself out to be the one responsible, thanks to his suggestions and criticisms, for Flaubert's literary success. In all truth, I find this line of argument unconvincing. Maxime Du Camp, a mediocre pen-pusher whose every ambition was realized—social and literary success, decorations, the Academy—was scarcely capable of understanding Flaubert's sense of vocation, and less capable still of appreciating his genius. It is probable that, in the last analysis, his opinions were a sincere reflection of his sentiments toward Flaubert: an amicable scorn, a paternal deference toward the friend who, despite his efforts (and perhaps because of his epilepsy, to use Maxime's word), never managed, as he himself had done, to "triumph" in his pursuit of popularity, honors, and power. Maxime would undoubtedly be surprised to discover that the one reason why he has a place in literature today is that he was a friend of Gustave's, if we except those few specialists who mention him as a precursor of futurism because of a handful of poems of his hymning progress, the city, and the machine.

Be that as it may, we have no reason to doubt his testimony that the verdict that he and Bouilhet handed down against the first *Tentation* was an extremely harsh one. Critics, with their complacent inclination to hail already-hallowed talent, today accuse Du Camp and Bouilhet of not having been able to detect the work of genius in those four days. Many judge the first *Tentation* in the light of the radically pruned and polished version of 1874, whose merit is unquestionable. My opinion, however, of the 1849 version is not very different from that of the two friends. It is an amorphous and uneven book, prolix to the point of tedium, in which the few stylistic nuggets lie buried in a dross of long-winded eloquence, repetition, a mania for metaphor. The style gives evidence of a facility that the author misuses, an uncontrollable and verbose lyricism, and the structure betrays carelessness, a lack of proportion, thoughtless improvisation: faults which, from *Madame Bovary* on, Flaubert will avoid like the plague. It is surprising that those who admire "Flaubertian" literary virtues—the *mot juste*, impersonality, objectivity, rigorous composition, the rational control of intuition—do not reason as follows: If Bouilhet and Du Camp had not disabused Gustave so severely, he might well have continued to write the sort of literature full of exaggerated flights of lyricism and orotund rhetoric, rooted in blind faith in inspiration, toward which he was predisposed, and we would therefore never have had those books of his we love most. Flaubert begins to be a great creator when he reacts against this lyrical, sentimental, romantic bent that predominates in his early writings, and here the sentence passed by Maxime and Louis in the course of that long night at Croisset played a capital role. The judgment of the two friends was not only a quite fair one; even more importantly, it was a useful one: it helped Flaubert become a different writer.

In what way did Flaubert's literary transformation, which was to culminate in Madame Bovary, *take place?*

The disappointment was a severe one, and it took Flaubert some time to recover from it. On January 5, 1850, a letter to his mother from Cairo—a few days after the reading Maxime and Gustave set out for the Orient—shows him still a prey to doubt: "Is *Saint Antoine* good or bad? That's what I often ask myself, for example: who was mistaken: myself or the others?" He has difficulty accepting the verdict of his friends, but on the other hand, he is not sure of himself either: "I am full of doubts and indecisions." The wound does not close and is a constant source of reflection or, as we would say today, of self-criticism. Almost

a full year after the episode, Gustave reminds Bouilhet, from
Damascus, how awful what had happened had been for him:
"I have recovered, however (not without pain), from the terrible
blow dealt me by *Saint Antoine*. I can't boast that I'm not still
a little dizzy from it, but I'm no longer sick about it as I was
all through the first four months of my trip. I kept seeing
everything through the veil of despondency in which that disappointment had enveloped me, and kept repeating the same
helpless phrase you now send me: 'What's the use?' " (letter of
September 4, 1850). His traveling companion reproaches him
in his memoirs for having proved withdrawn and apathetic as
they toured Egypt, Lebanon, Palestine, Turkey, and Greece,
attitudes that Du Camp attributes to Flaubert's lack of curiosity
and to homesickness for his family and for Rouen, but the secret
reason for Gustave's indifference (which in any event is relative,
as can be seen from his own account in his *Notes de voyage*) was
the bitterness he was still nursing over the *"coup affreux."* Future
references in the *Correspondance* reveal that as the episode recedes
into the past he takes the verdict handed down by Bouilhet and
Du Camp more calmly. In October of 1851 (he has just begun
Madame Bovary) he takes out the *Tentation* and again reads a few
fragments to Bouilhet, who stands by his unfavorable opinion:
"Bouilhet's objection to publication is that I have put all of my
faults into it and only a few of my good points" (letter to Du
Camp, October 21, 1851). Four months later, Flaubert already
has a clear idea of the real worth of the first *Tentation*; half a
year of work on *Madame Bovary* has brought him round to
condemning improvisation and defending the "planning" of a
novel. He writes as much to Louise, who has read the manuscript of the *Tentation* and praised it: "It's a failure. You talk of
pearls. But it's not pearls that make the necklace; it's the thread.
I myself was the St. Antoine in *Saint Antoine* and I forgot that.
He is a character that remains to be created . . . *Everything depends*

on the plan. Saint Antoine lacks one . . ."* (letter of February 1, 1852). The final observation is of particular interest: this lack of *plan*, of structuring, is something that will not happen again in the novel he is writing; what is more, this time he will try not to "forget himself" in the character; he will endeavor to keep a distance between himself and this creature, the better to create it—describe it, make it move, think, and feel. In other words, Flaubert is in the process of deciding on a method for *Madame Bovary* as a negative function of the *Tentation*; out of the limitations of the one he is inventing the virtues of the other. This becomes crystal-clear eight days later, in another letter to Louise in which, his feelings still hurt, he continues to maintain that Bouilhet and Du Camp judged his *Saint Antoine* "lightly," but adds: "I am in a completely different world now, that of the closest observation of the dullest details. My gaze is focused on moldering mosses of the soul. It is a long way from the mythological and theological blazes of *Saint Antoine*. And just as the subject is different, so I am writing in a completely different way. I do not want my book to contain so much as *one* reaction, *one* reflection of the author" (letter of February 8, 1852). It might be said that the theory of impersonality—this is the first time he speaks of it—is born of a rejection, of a determination to do something different from that first *Tentation* in which the irrepressible intrusion of the subjectivity of the narrator has prevented his hero from taking on a life of his own and the work from existing in its own right. As he repeats to Louise on March 28 of this year, the novel that he is writing "will be the diametrical opposite of *Saint Antoine*, but I think the style of it will be a more profound art."

According to Du Camp, in the Orient Flaubert not only pursued his aim of writing a novel on a banal subject, inspired by the "story of Delamare" (through a slip of the pen Du Camp

---

* Flaubert's italics.

mistakenly wrote Delaunay), but also found the name of his heroine there. The discovery purportedly came about in lower Nubia, at the top of Mount Abu Sir, as the two travelers contemplated the second cataract of the Nile. All of a sudden Gustave shouted: "Eureka! I'll call her Emma Bovary!" And supposedly repeated the name several times, with intense pleasure.

This is the uncertain part of Du Camp's testimony: there is nothing to confirm that the idea of *Madame Bovary* was born on the day after the reading of the first *Tentation* or that Flaubert thought of writing a novel on the "story of Delamare" during the trip to the Orient. His letters of these two years and his *Notes de voyage* do not refer to the subject. They do mention other projects, however, that Flaubert tells Bouilhet he is considering. Thus, for example, on November 14, 1850, he writes to him from Constantinople that he is hesitating between three subjects which, in the last analysis, may perhaps all be the same: (1) *Une nuit de Don Juan*, the idea for which came to him while he was visiting the lazaretto at Rhodes; (2) the story of *Anubis*, the "woman who wanted to get laid by the God" (the germ of *Salammbô*); and (3) a novel situated in Flanders, about a virgin and mystic who lives and dies in a little provincial town, at the bottom of a cabbage garden. Five weeks before he had spoken enthusiastically to Bouilhet of carrying out on his return a long-cherished plan of compiling a *Dictionnaire des idées reçues** (letter from Damascus, September 4, 1850). And, according to Maxime, on listening to the thousand and one adventures recounted by the Europeans he met on the journey, in Turkey Gustave conceived the idea of a *roman comique* on the modern Orient. Of all these projects, the one that seems to be most firmly fixed in his mind at this point is the Don Juan one, since he continues to ponder it in Rome and tells Bouilhet that he has even "com-

---

* Best translated, perhaps, as "Dictionary of Universally Accepted Opinions." (H.L.)

mitted to writing" several rough outlines of it (letter of April 9, 1851).

Flaubert returns to France at the end of June or the beginning of July of this year, with a tremendous urge to write, but he still has not entirely made up his mind to recount the "Delamare story," since once back at Croisset almost the first thing he does after unpacking his suitcases is to correct his travel notes and put them in order. But already he is turning the idea of a novel on Madame Delamare over in his mind, as is proved in a letter which he receives in this month of July from Maxime Du Camp, asking him: "What are you writing? Have you decided? Is it still *Don Juan*? Is it the story of Madame Delamarre [*sic*] which is a really good one, and how is it that you know of it?"★ There are those who are of the opinion that this letter betrays the unreliability of Maxime's account of the origin of *Madame Bovary* in his memoirs. If on the day following the reading Bouilhet suggested the "Delamare story" to Flaubert, why does Maxime ask him how he learned of this same story? But this does not definitively call into question the truth of Du Camp's version of events. On his return to Croisset, Flaubert might well have learned new details about the story of the Delamares—they did exist: Eugène, the husband, had died during Gustave's trip—and perhaps Maxime's curiosity concerned the source of these new facts. He and Flaubert had separated in Rome in April, so that between that date and Du Camp's letter, Gustave has been hesitating between two subjects: Don Juan and the Delamare story. At the end of July Maxime came to spend a few days at Croisset, and doubtless the matter was discussed by the friends. By the time Maxime returns to Paris, Gustave has chosen the name of his heroine and she has ousted Don Juan, as is indicated by another letter from Du Camp, who in August writes to him from Paris about a personal drama and

★ Letter of July 23, 1851, published in the *Bulletin des Amis de Flaubert*, no. 14, 1959.

concludes as follows: "I could pass on to you, for your Bovary, everything that happens to me; I am certain that it will be of use to you."★ Although at this point his mind is wholly made up, Flaubert does not begin the novel until several weeks later. The date and the time are indicated, in his own hand, on the manuscript: September 19, 1851, in the night.

What may we conclude as regards the origin of Madame Bovary?

That the novel has, as its remote cause, the frustration Flaubert felt as a result of Bouilhet and Du Camp's verdict on the first *Tentation de Saint Antoine*—an opinion which, although it cost him great effort, he finally managed to accept in part, and one which led him to choose for his next novel a subject and a form different from those of the condemned book. It is not inconceivable that Bouilhet suggested to him on the morning after the judgment the "Delamare story," a local scandal that doubtless all Rouen and the surrounding countryside knew about. Perhaps this advice was accepted only vaguely by Gustave, too discouraged at the time to show the enthusiasm for the subject that Du Camp attributes to him. Then, as he traveled through the Orient and recovered from his failure, Flaubert considered various projects, old ones such as the *Dictionnaire*, or new ones, such as Don Juan, Anubis, the comic novel, and the Flemish story, without thinking too much about the adventures of Delphine Delamare, but at the same time not forgetting them. This subject must have been left slumbering, set aside until later yet for all that still alive, a little demon making its way to the forefront as the journey continued, in cadence with the homesickness Gustave was feeling for his home and family, for

★ Letter of August 3, 1851, conserved in the Spoehlberch de Lovenjoul collection and cited by Enid Starkie in *Flaubert: The Making of the Master*, p. 188. (Note: The above translation is mine. H.L.)

the landscape and the people of Normandy, which were the scene and the actors in the Delamare story. On his return to Rouen, Bouilhet or Madame Flaubert doubtless told him of Eugène's death, which brought the drama to its close at last, and perhaps it was this detail that finally determined his choice. He must have made inquiries, discovered new facts as he corrected the *Notes de voyage*, and communicated all this to Maxime; it is to this that his friend's question in the letter of July 23 might well refer. The decision to put Don Juan aside for Emma Bovary had surely been made by the end of July, perhaps when Du Camp was with him at Croisset.

My supposition that the idea of writing a novel by using the Delamare story took hold little by little in Gustave's mind stems not so much from Maxine Du Camp's testimony as from the fact that in his entire life as a writer Flaubert never chose a subject in a brusque or inopportune manner. All his other novels resulted from experiences and projects that he had long cherished, reflected upon, reconsidered; on occasion reaching the written stage, being abandoned thereupon for long periods, and then eventually being rewritten with major modifications. This is a creator in whom the gestation of the subject is always a slow process, a gradual infection, an ever-growing obsession. If this happens in the other books, in *Madame Bovary*, whose material represented such a great change from work produced previously, it is quite improbable that the choice was a matter of a few days or weeks. It is more likely that, like the others, this novel too began as a tiny seed which slowly germinated, watered by melancholy and by the painful acceptance of a defeat, in the course of these twenty-some months during which he got himself a "bellyful of colors" in the Orient—as he puts it in his letters—contracted syphilis, began to lose his hair, and approached his thirtieth birthday.

How much time did it take him to write Madame Bovary *and what are the characteristics of the manuscript?*

He began to write it on Friday night, September 19, 1851, and finished it on April 30, 1856, according to dates written in his own hand on the cardboard covers that protect the manuscript—a period that encompasses four years, seven months, and eleven days. I am not counting the time spent making corrections and cuts in each of the editions published in his lifetime, in certain cases a substantial number of very important ones: thus the first edition in one volume put out by Lévy in 1862 contains 208 changes made by Flaubert in the original edition, as discovered and counted by Madame Claudine Gothot-Mersch.*

The result of all this labor is preserved in the Municipal Library of Rouen: (1) 46 folio-size pages of *Scénarios*, the *plan* of the work: plot, characters, division into chapters, etc.; (2) 1,778 draft pages written on both sides, full of annotations in the margins, additions and deletions; and (3) 487 pages constituting the definitive manuscript.

What sources exist to enable one to follow Flaubert's labors in these years?

The main source is the correspondence with Louise Colet. They had met each other and begun their affair in 1846, but they broke with each other in 1848. Fortunately, they were reconciled a few days after Gustave's return from the Orient, and in his letters to Louise—a minimum of two per week, and sometimes three and even four—the reader is able to follow the composition of the novel almost day by day. Louise's letters to Gustave were burned by his niece Caroline because they contained "too many

---

* *Madame Bovary. Sommaire biographique, introduction, note bibliographique, relevé des variantes et notes* (Paris: Garnier, 1971), pp. 359–64.

horrors," an act that earned this nefarious relative the eternal enmity of all Flaubertians. The letters to Louise cease in April 1854, following the final quarrel between the lovers. From then on, the principal source is Flaubert's letters to Louis Bouilhet, who in this period was residing in Paris. In these five years Gustave also writes from time to time to Ernest Chevalier, his friend from childhood, to Du Camp (with whom his relations had cooled and concerning whom Flaubert expresses himself with greater and greater sarcasm in his letters to Louise as Maxime's literary opportunism becomes increasingly evident), and occasionally to Victor Hugo and to Maurice Schlésinger, though he does not write to them about his work. This part of the *Correspondance*—three of the thirteen volumes of the Conard edition—is of an interest comparable to that of Flaubert's best novels. They are, on the one hand, letters of an extraordinary literary and anecdotal richness: written with flying pen, they are a repository for Flaubert's social, artistic, and political opinions, his judgments and prejudices regarding people he met or remembered, the emotional ups and downs brought on by his labors. Moreover, and this is what is most important, they set forth his theory of the novel that is gradually taking shape, in these years during which the book is coming into being, as a result of his creative practice.* They constitute a much more creditable account than would a "Diary of Madame Bovary," had Flaubert kept such a journal, since there is not the slightest trace of literary premeditation in these letters but, rather, the most complete spontaneity and freedom. Flaubert not only did not know that these letters would be read by someone other

---

* Flaubert discovered, around the beginning of 1854, the interaction between the theory and the practice of literature, that is to say, the fact that every work of creation contains implicitly, whether the author perceives it or not, a general conception of textual writing and structure and of the relationships between fiction and reality. After two and a half years of work on *Madame Bovary*, he wrote to Louise: "Every oeuvre to be undertaken has its own inherent poetics, *which must be found*" (his italics) (undated letter, January 1854, *Correspondance*. Vol. IV, p. 23).

than the person to whom they were addressed but also did not know that in them he was writing the story of his novel and outlining the most revolutionary theory of his century.

Did Flaubert work continually during these four years, seven months, and eleven days, or with interruptions?

The interruptions were minimal and I calculate that the days on which he failed to work add up to less than a tenth of the total. Thus, in 1851, shortly after the book was begun, he journeyed to London for a few days, accompanied by his mother and his niece, to take in an international exhibition. That same year, between November and December, he spent three weeks in Paris, where he was a witness to, and very nearly the victim of, the *coup d'état* of December 2 whereby Louis Bonaparte enthroned himself as emperor. In the summer of 1853 he spent a month's vacation with his family in Trouville, during which he did not work, being a creature of habit who could write only in his own lair. The other interruptions are brief ones. His relations with Louise did not take up much of his time, since he imposed a *sui generis* régime: every three months, he journeyed to Mantes, where she came to meet him; they spent a few hours together in the inn, or at most a night. On occasion, these brief trimestrial encounters took place in Paris; Flaubert would remain there only two or three days. It is surprising that, despite her willing obedience to so strict a discipline, Flaubert's biographers accuse Louise Colet of being dominating and difficult; the truth is that, *if they were lovers*, Louise was an understanding enough woman to accept Gustave's amorous, almost exclusively epistolary, system of relations. The biographers also criticize her because she was unfaithful, but this is to be more of a papist than the Pope: in Flaubert's letters one sees how little this problem troubled him, since he sometimes went so far as to advise Louise to grant her favors more readily to her admirers.

Did Flaubert suffer attacks of his nervous illness during these years of Madame Bovary?

At certain times, the overwork, the tremendous excitement that an episode or a problem of style brings on send him into a state of emotional unbalance, a frenzy that borders on nervous collapse. On December 23, 1853, for example, he works twelve hours in a row—taking only a twenty-five-minute break to eat something—on Emma and Rodolphe's ride on horseback through the woods, and around six in the evening, reading his own sentences and feeling "so deeply what my little woman was feeling," he is so carried away that as he writes the words *"une attaque de nerfs"* he is on the point of suffering one himself. With his head spinning, he gets up from his table, staggers over to the window, and stands there breathing in the breeze from the river till he calms down. Afterward his whole body aches (letter to Louise, December 23, 1853). But these states of extreme elation are different from his old attacks; apparently he did not suffer from any of the latter in these years. The few times he refers to his "illness," he speaks as though it is something that belongs to the past, thereby supporting the thesis of those who maintain that his malady was neurotic in character and his attacks crises of his own election. In any event, literature was his best therapy. It is improbable that he would have hidden attacks of his old illness from Louise out of a sense of shame, since in his letters to her or to his friends he speaks freely of other ailments that at times make his work difficult. In addition to bouts of grippe and colds, in August of 1854 he suffered from mercury poisoning (he was taking a remedy based on this drug to treat his syphilis). For nearly three weeks his tongue was so badly swollen he was unable to talk and barely to eat. He was treated with applications of ice, enemas, and leeches.★ It was in these years also that—due, doubtless, to the progression of the syphilis—he broke out for the first time in the boils which were to be such a torment to him in the future.

What was Flaubert's method of work?

On December 26, 1858, Flaubert writes to Mademoiselle Leroyer de Chantepie: "A book for me has never been anything but *a way of living* in a given milieu. That is what explains my hesitations, my anxieties, and my slowness." The sentence miraculously sums up the Flaubertian method: that slow, scrupulous, systematic, obsessive, stubborn, documented, cold, and ardent construction of a story. Like his poetics, Gustave discovered (invented) his system of work as he was writing *Madame Bovary*; although his previous texts—above all the first *Tentation*—had required effort and discipline, it was only from this novel on that he hit upon the precise combination of routines, manias, preoccupations, and occupations that enabled him to produce the maximum output. *Une manière de vivre dans un milieu quelconque*: this profound identification with a "milieu," in order to re-create it verbally, is something that Flaubert achieves thanks to the total devotion of his time and energy, of his will and his intelligence, to the work of creation. A few months after this letter, he uses the same formula to explain his work to Madame Jules Sandeau: "A book for me has always been a special way of living, a means of situating myself in a certain milieu" (letter of August 7, 1859).

He gets up around noon, and after breakfasting with his mother, or alone with his dog, and reading his mail (Louise's letters arrived daily), he spends an hour giving lessons in gram-

★ Unpublished documents in the Spoehlberch de Lovenjoul collection, consulted by Benjamin F. Bart, *Flaubert* (Syracuse University Press, 1967), pp. 249 and 758.

mar, history, and geography to his niece Caroline, whose education he has taken in his own hands. At two o'clock in the afternoon he shuts himself up in the adjoining rooms, his bedroom and his study; the latter has a terrace overlooking what was for him in his day a beautiful and peaceful view: the waters of the Seine, the fertile land, the gentle hills with their poplars. He remains in his study with its great round oak table and bench. The table is covered with a length of fine green netting, to keep Julie and Narcisse, the servants, from making neat piles of the note cards, notebooks, and papers lying in meticulous disorder all over it. A bunch of goose quills spray out of a container next to the inkwell, a crystal frog. There are shelves of books, a divan with a white bearskin thrown over it, and here and there many of the souvenirs brought back from the Orient: a hookah, a great many pipes, a stuffed crocodile. In winter he keeps a fire going in the fireplace and in summer he works with the windows open, almost always dressed in a white silk dressing gown reaching to his feet. He writes until seven or eight at night, at which time he emerges to have dinner with his mother, lingering at table afterward to chat with her for a while. He then returns to his study, where he loses himself again in his novel until two or three in the morning. At that hour he still has the energy to pen lengthy letters to Louise that show him rejoicing at times because he has worked well, and at others, the majority, beside himself with rage because he has spent hours trying to improve a single sentence.

Up until October 1853, this rigid daily schedule varies slightly on the weekends, when Louis Bouilhet comes out to Croisset to be with him. The two friends shut themselves up together all day Sunday in the study, each reading and criticizing—implacably—the work that the other has done during the week. Gustave trusted Bouilhet's opinion completely and generally followed his advice; throughout the writing of *Madame Bovary*, he was a second critical conscience for Flaubert. But

Gustave and Louis also devote many Sundays to scrutinizing, verse by verse, the poems that Louise Colet sends them—and correcting them, rewriting entire stanzas of them. These visits by Bouilhet, whom Flaubert has always dearly loved, are one of the few distractions of his monastic life, hours of leisure he eagerly looks forward to throughout a solitary and exhausting week. When Bouilhet goes off to live in Paris, in October 1853, Sunday becomes a day like any other for his friend in Croisset.

There are times when he finds himself confronted with such seemingly hopeless difficulties that he fears he is about to lose his mind. The critical period is the four months of the agricultural fair, a chapter in which certain passages—such as the prefectoral councillor's speech—are rewritten seven times. During this monastic confinement, there are days when the characters seem to take on material form and affect him physically. This occurs in a most spectacular fashion as he is recounting the death of Emma. As he later confided to Taine: "My imaginary characters *affect me*, haunt me, or rather, it is I who inhabit them. When I was writing the poisoning of Emma Bovary, I had *such a strong taste of arsenic in my mouth*, I had poisoned myself so badly, that I suffered two attacks of indigestion in a row, two very real attacks, for I vomited up all my dinner."[*]

He is in the habit of smoking a large number of pipes a day, on occasion as many as fifteen. His lighted windows, which never go dark, are known to have been used as a beacon by the crab fishers in the region. He seldom goes to Rouen, save to hunt down answers to questions connected with his work. He goes, for instance, to the Hôtel-Dieu to secure information on clubfoot pathology from his brother Achille when he is describing the operation on Hippolyte, and makes another special trip to the hospital and the library to gather documentation on

---

[*] Undated letter, probably 1869, *Correspondance*, Vol. V, p. 350. Flaubert's italics.

arsenic poisoning before setting about committing Emma's suicide to writing.

Does Flaubert's mania for documentation reach the same extremes in this novel as in L'Education sentimentale *and* Bouvard et Pécuchet?

No. The travel, reading, consultation, and research that Flaubert undertook for *Madame Bovary* are not as important as those to which he devoted himself for his later works, if we remember, for example, the 1,500 books he is said to have read and taken notes on for *Bouvard et Pécuchet*. But another fundamental aspect of the Flaubertian method also became apparent during the writing of *Madame Bovary*: the deliberate sacking of real reality in order to construct the fictional reality. In order, for instance, to describe Emma's readings in her early years, he reread the old books of fairy tales and the histories that he and his brothers had read as children. Before beginning the sequence of the agricultural fair, he attended, paper and pencil in hand, an event of this sort in the village of Darnétal, and for the ailment of the Blind Man and the remedy that Homais prescribes for it, he questioned Louis Bouilhet, who had been a medical student, and asked him to consult specialists. In like fashion, in order to be "true to the facts" as to how Emma is financially squeezed by Lheureux, he went to Rouen to have a lawyer and a notary explain all the details concerning promissory notes, attachment of property, sales at auction, and amortization of debts.* On the other hand, of the hordes of exegetes who have been arguing for a century about the real models for Tostes and Yonville—fictitious place names—there is not one who has been able to prove that Flaubert ever made a special visit to copy the plan of any of the villages that claim the (dubious) privilege of having served as a background for the novel.

* Letters of August 31 and September 17, 1855.

The Pen-Man

Did he engage in any kind of sport in these five years?

As a boy, he had been an excellent swimmer, and this was his one form of exercise—occasionally, in warm weather. At dusk, when the heat of the day had died down, he would dive into the Seine for a swim in front of his house. At one time he had been fond of sailing, but gave it up at his mother's insistence. She doubtless pressed him to do so not out of fear of an accident, as he states in one letter, but on account of his nervous attacks. The doctors had prescribed complete rest.

And his sexual life from 1851 to 1856?

It consisted largely of sporadic trysts with Louise, of which there were in all likelihood no more than twenty or so in these five years. (During a number of them, the lovers spent the entire time bickering.) It is a proven fact that in the summer of 1853 he slept for a brief period of time with the ex-wife of the sculptor Pradier, Louise d'Arcet, who had been a friend of his for several years. His first attempt at lovemaking with Louise d'Arcet, as with Louise Colet, was a fiasco, but he soon made up for lost time and even allowed himself certain vulgar lapses of taste, such as suggesting to Bouilhet that he, too, should try to seduce the former Madame Pradier, assuring him that she was better in bed than the Muse (their nickname for Louise Colet).★ It is also said that in 1854, during a trip to Paris, he contrived to bed the actress Beatrix Person; there is, however, no very convincing proof of this.† Sartre is of the opinion that he masturbated frequently, but to judge from his letters this appears to be the case only in the first period of his affair with Louise Colet

★ Unpublished documents cited by Bart, pp. 258–59.
† Maurice Nadeau, *Gustave Flaubert, escritor* (Barcelona: Editorial Lumen, 1971); original edition, *Gustave Flaubert, écrivain* (Paris: *Lettres Nouvelles*, 1969), p. 331.

(1846–48), before the journey to the Orient. (He kept in one of his desk drawers a pair of slippers, a handkerchief, a lock of Louise's hair, along with a little green branch that had fallen onto the Muse's hat during their first rendezvous in Mantes, and as he was writing the first *Tentation*, on many nights he interrupted his work to stroke these objects in a state of burning excitement.) But in the second stage of the affair, the years of *Madame Bovary*, there are no signs of such practices, though there are definite indications that he had periods of total lack of sexual desire, such as this confession to Louise penned at dawn on April 13, 1854: "You tell me that you're not haunted by thoughts of sensual pleasure. I will avow the same to you, for I confess I no longer have a penis, thank God. I'll find it again if need be, and that is exactly as it should be." In later years, Flaubert arrived at the conviction that intense erotic activity was detrimental to literary creation, and that, contrariwise, a certain self-restraint was beneficial to the novelist. He repeated this again and again to his friend Ernest Feydeau, an incontinent man of the world, to whom Gustave offered wise counsel of this sort: "But take care not to ruin your intelligence in commerce with ladies. You will lose your genius at the bottom of the womb . . . Save your priapism for style, fuck your inkwell, appease your lust on meat, and be thoroughly persuaded, as Tissot (of Geneva) says (*Treatise on Onanism*, page 72, see the illustration), that: One ounce of sperm spent is more fatiguing than three liters of blood lost" (undated letter, beginning of February 1859).

It would be a mistake to take this advice to be puritan preaching. Flaubert did not regard sexual pleasure and literary creation as being incompatible. In his case, rather, both experiences were, at certain moments, one and the same; his inappetency does not mean that he renounced sex, but that he succeeded temporarily in substituting literature for women as his focus of desire and source of pleasure. Writing—in his case a surrender of self as passionate and as total as that of coitus—was for Flaubert an "orgy." "The one way of tolerating existence is to lose oneself in literature as in a perpetual orgy" (letter to Mademoiselle Leroyer de Chantepie, September 4, 1858). It is therefore not surprising that he should speak of his work in sexual metaphors. Here, for instance, is how he announces that his *Salammbô* is off to a good start: "An erection has finally been attained, my good sir, by dint of whipping and manustruprating myself. Let's hope that climax will ensue" (letter to Ernest Feydeau, December 19, 1858).

What authors did he read in those years?

The revolutionary of form, the pathfinder of avant-garde narrative of his time, was a reader contemptuous of the literature of his own day and a passionate devotee of the classics. His greatest idol, the writer to whom he returns again and again, the author who calls forth his joyous paeans of praise for the richness and "impersonality" of his world is Shakespeare: "The whole of his works leaves me as bedazzled and enraptured as the idea of the astral system. I can see in it only an immensity in which my gaze loses itself in dazed wonder" (letter to Louise Colet, on rereading *King Lear*, March 30, 1854). Among French writers, the author he loved most and reread most often was Montaigne: he calls him "my foster father," quotes him from memory, paraphrases him in his letters. Critics claim that Montaigne taught him skepticism, but I for my part think that Montaigne civilized in him a brute skepticism he already possessed. Coming immediately after the author of the *Essais* is Rabelais, his great passion, cherished for his wild imagination, his perception of the grotesque, and his world of unbridled appetites. He also reads, with ups and downs of enthusiasm, Racine, Rousseau (whom in these years he still tolerates but later comes to detest), Boileau (for whom he feels a "formal" attraction: a few years later he will deny him too), Buffon, Ronsard, Voltaire, whom he always appreciated (he studied, paper and pen at hand, all his works for the theater), Goethe, and Byron—passions of his adolescence—and among the moderns, Victor Hugo, whom he respected all his life; Balzac, of whom he generally spoke with no great esteem because his style (which he regarded as a lack of style) irritated him; and Leconte de Lisle, for whom he felt a certain quiet affection. During these five years he evinces a persistent desire to study classical Greek so as to be able to read Homer in the original (he never manages to do so) and from time to time immerses himself in a Latin author such as Plutarch (he has no difficulty reading Latin). His vast readings of the Greek and Roman classics do not date from this time in his life, however, but from the later period of the writing of *La Tentation de Saint Antoine, Salammbô,* and *Hérodias.* During these years he also rereads the *Quixote,* another classic for which he felt a particular fondness. He had read it before his travels in the Orient, and his memory of it remained a vivid one: he mentions it now and again in connection with a projected journey through Spain that never materialized. Among the writings of his own day he never fails to read the *Revue de Paris* (of which Maxime Du Camp is co-director), though most numbers leave him feeling out of sorts. And finally, in addition to those works read for friendship's sake (Louise Colet, Bouilhet, Maxime), there are those he reads because they serve a purpose: books on medicine, for certain episodes of the novel, and the manuals that he uses in tutoring Caroline.

How did Flaubert write Madame Bovary? *Into what stages can the writing of the novel be divided?*

Flaubert answered this question, in a metaphorical yet very precise way, in a letter to Ernest Feydeau: "Books are not made in the same way babies are, but rather as pyramids are, following a premeditated design, and by hoisting great blocks one atop the other by dint of sheer brute strength, time, and sweat."* The first step is the premeditated design, drawing up the *plan* of the work: a synopsis in which the overall lines of the story are laid down. The primary concern of this first step is the plot: the characters, the dramatic trajectory, the key incidents. In these early weeks there is no thought whatsoever as to form; Flaubert devotes himself entirely to outlining the subject of the book in *tableaux*, chapters, and sketches, while at the same time allowing himself to become thoroughly immersed in this material. As he explains to Louise: "It is altogether necessary to ponder one's objective before thinking of the form, for the right one comes only if the illusion of the subject becomes an obsession" (letter of November 29, 1853). The forty-six pages of the *Scénarios*† enable us to establish two things: (1) this initial plan is very detailed and precise; in it even the most insignificant facts are set down, thereby indicating that Flaubert wants to carry premeditation to its extreme limit, to eliminate all spontaneity; and (2) the plan will be modified as the actual writing proceeds, not in its overall lines, but with regard to the content of the *tableaux*, those "blocks" of which he speaks in his letter to Feydeau and which constitute the thematic units of the book.

Once the general outline of the work and the rigorous plan of the first chapter have been traced, the writing begins. And it is at this point that formal considerations take over and drive him to despair. "One arrives at style only by dint of frightful labor, of a fanatical and devoted determination" (letter to Louise, August 15, 1846). Since in his letters he speaks only of "style," most critics take it that Flaubert's obsession with form has to

---

* Undated letter, end of November or beginning of December 1857, *Correspondance*, Vol. IV, pp. 239–40.

† The *Scénarios* have been published by Gabrielle Leleu in *Madame Bovary, ébauches et fragments inédits*, 2 vols. (Paris: Conard, 1936), and in the critical edition of the novel by Gabrielle Leleu and Jean Pommier (Paris: Corti, 1949).

do exclusively with language. In reality, his preoccupation with details of structure—the ordering of the events of the story, the organization of time, the gradation of effects, the concealing or revealing of facts—is as acute as his concern for the writing itself. His great contribution to the novel is technical, having to do equally with the use of language and with the distribution of the narrative materials. I hope to demonstrate this by disassembling some of the parts that go to make up the "machine" of *Madame Bovary* and make it work (the words are his own).

It is almost certain that Flaubert works with two blank pages before him, one alongside the other. On the first one, in a small, regular hand, leaving wide margins, he sets down the first version of the episode, no doubt hurriedly, developing the ideas as they come to him, without bothering much about the form. He scribbles several pages in this way, and then goes back to the beginning and starts correcting, meticulously, slowly, sentence by sentence, word by word. The page gradually becomes covered with deletions, additions, repetitions, so many superimposed strata of words that finally it is no longer readable. Then he makes a fair copy of this page on the one thus far left blank. He proceeds very slowly, and this new version is put to the test of the *gueuloir* (that is to say, read aloud, though it might be better to call it a testing by ear). He has a firm conviction: a sentence is well written when it is musically perfect. "The more beautiful an idea is, the more sonorous the sentence; you may be certain of that. Precision of thought makes for (and is itself) precision of language" (letter to Mademoiselle Leroyer de Chantepie, December 12, 1857). Hence when a sentence seems to him to be more or less finished, he reads it aloud, acts it out, increasing the volume, striding about the room, gesticulating. If it does not *sound* good, if it is not melodious and irresistibly rhythmic, if its qualities as pure sound do not constitute a value in and of themselves, it is not correct, the words are not the right ones, the idea has not been perfectly expressed. And so the pages slowly accumulate, in pairs: the recto of one is the first version of the verso of the other. A good day's work may mean a definitive half page, but there are entire days devoted to composing—that is the proper verb—a single sentence. It is a real five years' war, in which little by little his enemies multiply, *bêtes noires* that become nightmares and the target of his most choleric fits of wrath: consonances and assonances, cacophonies, certain conjunctions that tend to repeat themselves, such as *que*. He uses eloquent images in his letters to describe the incidents in the long battle. "Words" take on material form in this belligerent declaration: "One must turn all the words over, on all their sides, and do like the fathers of Sparta, pitilessly cast those with crippled feet or narrow chests into the void" (letter to Louise, March 26, 1854).

And as for that superior instance of the word, the "sentence": "Sentences must stir in a book like leaves in a forest, all dissimilar in their similarity" (letter to Louise, April 7, 1854). Each *tableau* makes its appearance as at once a narrative and a musical unity. When he has finished one, he goes out of doors to read it, to the *"allée des gueulades,"* "the bawling walk," and usually this test turns up disharmonies in the whole that oblige him to rewrite the entire section. As a result of his obsessive concern for musicality, when the first chapters appear in the *Revue de Paris* and Frédéric Baudry asks him to change the name of *Le Journal de Rouen* so as to keep from wounding certain people's feelings (there existed a real newspaper of that name), suggesting that he call it *Le Progressif de Rouen* instead, Flaubert is deeply distressed because the proposed change is going to be aurally detrimental to the text: "That is going to break the rhythm of my poor sentences. This is a serious matter" (letter to Bouilhet, October 5, 1856). He manages to find a substitute with the same number of syllables and an identical *-al* ending: *Le Fanal de Rouen.*

He does not go on to write the following *tableau* (at times, as with Charles and Emma's wedding and the agricultural fair, a *tableau* takes up an entire chapter, but generally each chapter contains several) until he has a satisfactory version of the one he is working on. (I use the term *tableau*, the one he himself used, to call attention to another aspect of Flaubertian form, as important as the musical: the visual.) His progress on the novel is slow, but each part that has been worked over in this fashion is definitive.

On finishing each *tableau*, he devotes one or more days to making a detailed outline of the elements that are to constitute the following one. Usually this means adding details and incidents to the subject indicated in the general plan, but in some cases he drastically alters his original idea. He never begins a *tableau* without having first made a meticulous outline of its entire content, without knowing beforehand, with a wealth of detail, what he is going to recount. He calls this planning: *"faire du plan."* When he has finished one of the Parts of the novel, he reads it over from beginning to end, in order to make sure that the *tableaux* are properly linked together, and works on what he calls "proportions." In order for us to see how intensely preoccupied Flaubert is with subject matter and to what point his formal concern is focused not only on style but on structure, let us cite his impression after rereading the first nine chapters of *Madame Bovary*: "Yesterday I reread all the first part. It struck me as scanty. But it's coming along (?). The worst of it is that the preliminary psychological, picturesque, grotesque, etc., preparations, being very long, *demand*, I think, a development of the action that will be in proportion to them. The prologue must not outweigh the story (however disguised and well blended in with the rest the story may be), and I shall have a job on my hands establishing a more or less equal proportion between the adventures and the thoughts. By watering down everything dramatic, I think I can more or less manage to do so" (letter to Bouilhet, December 10, 1853). It is evident that he is in no way disregarding the effects of what he is narrating, and these effects, in his opinion, depend on the disposition of the elements that go to make up the story.

When the manuscript is finished, he reads the whole thing through, and before sending it to Du Camp for the *Revue de Paris*, he makes more changes still, the majority of them deletions: he drops some thirty pages in their entirety and eliminates many sentences here and there. There disappear in this pruning "three long-winded speeches by Homais, an entire landscape, the conversations of the bourgeois at the ball, an article by Homais, etc. etc. etc." (letter to Bouilhet, June 1, 1856). When the novel (with a dedication to Louis Bouilhet) comes out in the *Revue de Paris*, there are numerous cuts in it, some of which Flaubert has reluctantly agreed to and others imposed *manu militari* by the editors of the *Revue*. Gustave demands that the *Revue* print a note of his disclaiming responsibility for the text as published. The first edition in book form (April 1857) restores the passages deleted by the *Revue de Paris*, but there are new changes by the author, as will be the case with all the other editions that appear in Flaubert's lifetime. This means that in a certain sense Flaubertian perfectionism is an infinite process. This driving need for perfection ultimately finds expression in a system based on a simple principle: a book is published at a given moment, but it is never finished. The writing of it would never end were it not for that accident, the death of the author. What happened with *Bouvard et Pécuchet* is symbolic. Had Flaubert died ten years later, it is possible that the novel would still have been unfinished: by its nature and that of the Flaubertian method, it required, to be completed, nothing less than the immortality of the author.

Did Flaubert use real elements in Madame Bovary? *Did he do so consciously?*

In a letter to Madame Roger des Genettes, Flaubert explains to his friend something that seems obvious to those who write novels but is more difficult for others to understand: the decisive role played in the choice of a subject by the irrational factor, that domain in which will and the conscious mind do not rule but obey, and from which certain key experiences stored there (and, very often, forgotten) operate secretly on human actions, thoughts, and dreams as their distant source, as their profound explanation. It is to this that Flaubert is referring when he declares that the writer does not freely choose his subject. "One is not free at all to write this thing or that. One does not choose one's subject. That is what the public and the critics do not understand. The secret of masterpieces lies therein, in the accord of the subject and the temperament of the author."★ Eight years later, he says precisely the same thing to George Sand: "As for my mania for work, I'll compare it to a bad case of impetigo. I keep scratching myself and howling. It is at once a pleasure and a torture. And nothing I write is what I want to write. For one doesn't choose one's subjects, they impose themselves" (letter of January 1, 1869). This means that the novelist does not create *ex nihilo* but as a function of his experience, that the point of departure of the fictional reality is always real reality such as it is lived by the writer. Certain subjects are compelling, as are love and suffering, desires and nightmares. This does not mean, naturally, that "inspiration" descends on him like a celestial emanation, but simply that he has a past and a present, a sum of experiences, some of which serve him as work materials. Certain subjects touch deep fibers of his being, excite his sensibility, arouse in him the will to create, whereas others

★ Undated letter, probably end of 1861, *Correspondance*, Vol. IV, p. 464.

leave him indifferent. Why certain ones and not others? Because those subjects that stimulate him at a conscious level preexist in a vague, embryonic way in his subjectivity. They fascinate him because they provide a shape, an anecdotal envelope, a symbolic image for experiences that are the source of his vocation, radical disillusionments in life that have given rise in him to the necessity of re-creating life, experiences that, by setting him at odds with reality, have awakened in him the vocation of creating imaginary realities. It is symptomatic that the most rationalist and deliberate of writers, the one who made will the key factor in the entire creative process, should point to *the accord between subject and temperament* as the secret of the successful work. This also means that disaccord between the two—the author, for example, who for moral or political reasons takes it as a duty to deal with a subject that clashes with his temperament—suffices to explain, in many cases, the failure of a particular work.

If the choice of a subject is in reality an "acceptance," where did those subjects which are going to serve Flaubert as work materials and which he has "recognized" come from, where are they to be found? All around him, in the life of which he is part. His first procedure as a novelist consists of a systematic plundering of everything within reach of his sensibility. This is the meaning of the famous sentences he writes to Louise near the end of his second year of work on *Madame Bovary*: "Everything one invents is true, you may be sure of that. Poetry is as precise as geometry. Induction is as valid as deduction, and besides, after a certain point in one's calculations, one never is wrong about matters of the soul. My poor Bovary, without a doubt, is suffering and weeping in twenty villages of France at this very moment" (letter of August 14, 1853). And that is also what his other famous phrase about this book *("Madame Bovary, c'est moi")* means: that the novelist invents only stories based on his own personal story.

The novelist's degree of awareness of his thievery varies, of course, and the case of the author who is unconscious of the pillaging that underlies his work is not infrequent. On the other hand, it is no easy task for a novelist to arrive at a complete and conscious awareness of everything that has gone into his creation, for his ransacking is both extensive and complex. A novel is not the end result of a subject taken directly from life but, inevitably, the product of an aggregate of major, secondary, or seemingly insignificant experiences which, dating back to different periods and circumstances, some buried deep within the subconscious and others of fresh memory, some personally lived, others merely heard of at second hand, and still others garnered from reading, little by little converge in the writer's imagination, which, like a powerful blender, will break them down and transform them into a new substance to which words and a particular ordering give another existence. From the ruins and the dissolution of real reality something very different will emerge, not a copy but an answer: fictional reality.

Flaubert is one of the most lucid of writers on the subject of this process of conversion of the real into the fictional. From a very early age he maintained, with firm conviction and clear-sightedness, that his vocation not only permitted him to regard the world as a stone quarry but demanded it of him. He was twenty-one years old when he told his earliest school friend, Ernest Chevalier, that to him people were *nothing more* than pretexts for books and that this curiosity quarried "good" and "bad" alike, since there was truth to be found in everything. It is worth reading this quotation from his youth carefully, for it contains three precociously discovered elements of his theory of the novel: (1) the writer uses without scruple the whole of reality; (2) the ambition of the writer is to encompass that totality; (3) the novel must show, not judge: "We must get used to the idea of seeing nothing but books in the people round about us. The man of discernment studies them, compares them, and creates from all that a synthesis for his own use. The world is but a keyboard for the true artist; it is up to him to bring forth from it sounds that entrance or freeze the blood with horror. Both good and bad society merit study. There is truth in everything. Let us understand each thing and cast blame on none" (letter of February 23, 1842). The conviction that reality is merely a material with which to work manifests itelf, obviously, in Flaubert's mania for documentation, which he carries to titanic extremes. But the sources of his work lie not only in the books, the periodicals, the specialists he consults. He turns everything that happens to him into literature; his entire life is cannibalized for the sake of the novel. When he is hard at work on the definitive text of *L'Education sentimentale*, he explains to his niece how, *just as has always been his practice*, he uses for his story everything he sees and feels: "In the midst of all that I think constantly of my novel; this last Saturday I even found myself in one of the situations of my hero. I carry over into this work (as is my habit) everything I see and feel" (undated latter, January 1864).

We have evidence that he puts these ideas into practice as he is writing *Madame Bovary*. In June of 1853 the mother of a friend of his, a doctor by the name of Pouchet, dies, and Gustave, who is preparing to go the funeral, writes Louise a sad-hearted letter, which begins with somber reflections on his friend's grief. Then suddenly, without transition, simply and naturally, he adds that, *since it is necessary to put everything to good use*, he hopes that the funeral atmosphere and Pouchet's bereavement will provide him with elements for the novel: "Since, moreover, it is necessary to profit from everything, I am certain that tomorrow will provide a dark and gloomy scene, and that that poor scholar will be pitiable. I may come by things for my *Bovary*."* There is no cynicism in this. Flaubert will go to the

---

* Letter of June 6–7, 1853. Flaubert's italics.

funeral because he mourns this death and because he wishes to do so as a gesture of friendship. At the same time, he knows something that he does not allow himself to forget: it is possible that the ceremony will be useful to him. A novel is built of appropriations of this sort. If they are inevitable, there is no reason to feel ashamed; it is preferable to accept them as a necessary element in creation. This means that the writer is at all times a divided self, that in him two persons coexist: the one who lives and the one who watches the other live, the one who suffers and the one who observes this suffering in order to use it. This dual nature of the novelist, this living and sharing of human experience and at the same time being a cold and avaricious exploiter of one's own life and that of others, is something that was borne in upon Flaubert during his travels in the Orient. The condition of the creator—someone who participates without participating, who is in the midst of life yet stands apart from it—struck him as a "monstrosity." His reflections appear in a letter to his mother, written in Constantinople: "If a man, be he of high or low station, wishes to attain an intimate acquaintance with the works of the Good Lord, he must begin, if only as a hygienic precaution, by putting himself in such a position as not to be the dupe of them. You may depict wine, love, women, glory, provided, my good man, that you are not a drunkard, a lover, a husband, or a lowly private in the ranks. Involved in life, you don't see it clearly: you suffer from it or enjoy it too much. The artist, to my way of thinking, is a monstrosity, something outside nature. All the misfortunes providence visits upon him are a consequence of his stubborn denial of this axiom. He suffers thereby and makes others suffer" (December 15, 1850). The use of pat formulas dating from the romanticism of his adolescence—in less awesome terms "monstrosity" means "outsider"—does not make Flaubert's vision any the less telling. From this time in his life onward, he accepted his vocation on these terms: he made of life a literary warehouse, and when he corresponded with writers whom he respected, he did not hesitate to remind them that their trials and tribulations could be useful to them. (For Flaubert, who all his life repeatedly declared that he wrote to *take his vengeance* on reality, it was above all negative experiences that inspired literary creation.) In October 1859, he learns that Ernest Feydeau's wife is on her deathbed. He immediately pens a few lines of condolence before the fact to his friend, while at the same time alerting him to the profit to be garnered from this family tragedy: "Poor little woman! It's frightful! You have and will continue to have *fine tableaux* and will be able to make *fine* studies! It is a dear price to pay for them. The bourgeois have little notion that it is our hearts that we serve up to them. The race of gladiators is not dead; every artist is one. He amuses the public with his agonies."* The truth is that, by writing about them, "agonies" are mitigated: literature exorcises them or makes them endurable.

This "monstrous" vocation, in whose name a man comes to consider life as a mere pretext for literature, gives the writer an extraordinary freedom: he is able to use the whole of it for his work. But this is a double-edged sword: the dizzying abundance may also paralyze him. Not every experience is an incentive, however: only those that are the sources of the writer's vocation and sustain it. In Flaubert's case this is to say *la misère humaine*. No novelist has seen as clearly as he—and of none of them has it been more true—that this vocation, like a vulture, feeds by choice on carrion. So he wrote, unblushingly, to Louise Colet: "When one has a clear model before his eyes, one always writes well, and where, I ask you, is the true more plainly visible than in these splendid spectacles of human misery? They have something so raw about them that it gives one's mind the appetite of a cannibal. It flings itself upon them to devour them,

* Undated letter, mid-October 1859, *Correspondance*, Vol. IV, p. 340. Flaubert's italics.

to assimilate them. With what dreams I have often lingered in a whore's bed, contemplating the marks of her labor in her flesh! What pitiless dramas I have constructed in the morgue, which once upon a time it was my mania to visit, and so on! I believe, moreover, that on this head I have a particular acuteness of perception; when it's a question of the morbid, I know where-of I speak" (letter of July 7–8, 1853). The carrion of which he speaks so enthusiastically here is cut from the cloth of romantic melodrama: brothels, hospitals, corpses. The kind that served as raw material for *Madame Bovary* is less sensational.

In the list of elements taken from reality for Madame Bovary, *which of them have been able to be identified?*

A complete exegesis of the real materials used by Flaubert is not only impossible; tracking them down would be so vast an undertaking that it would occupy generations of sleuths: when one begins to trace the sources of a fiction, one discovers that each one leads to others, and these in their turn to more, so that sooner or later the ultimate source turns out to be the entire history of the human race. Moreover, it is of no interest to trace the real genealogy of the fiction back to its very beginning, since what is important is not what the writer uses but the way in which he uses it and what he transforms it into: it is only these last two steps that are of any literary concern. To see this al-chemical process at work we need take a closer look only at the principal models.

The most important one of all is the story of Eugène and Delphine Delamare, which, as Enid Starkie has put it, is the grain of sand buried in the center of the pearl, the handful of paper flowers that on being immersed in water—the mind of the genius—bloom as in the gardens of Babylon.* If certain doubts remain as to the precise moment at which Flaubert de-

* *Op. cit.,* p. 294.

cided to use this story—the day after his reading of the *Tentation* to his friends or on his return from the Orient—there are none whatsoever as to the fact that he did indeed use it: the general plot of the novel corresponds to a series of events that actually took place in a little backwater of Normandy. It is difficult, nonetheless, to pin down the precise details of the Delamare story, since there is no written record of it anywhere *before* the novel that made it famous, and afterward it was distorted so as to make it more like the fictitious story. I shall recount in brief the proven facts. Eugène Delamare studied medicine in Rouen, was one of the disciples of Flaubert's father at the Hôtel-Dieu, and having earned a diploma as an *officier de santé*—"health officer" being a lesser degree than that of surgeon but one that nonetheless conferred the right to practice medicine—he settled in Ry, a village some twenty kilometers from Rouen. There, in April 1836, he married a woman whose family name was Mutel, who was older than he and left him a widower the following year. Twenty months later he married a girl of seventeen, Delphine Couturier, the daughter of a well-off farmer. The couple had a child, a daughter. Delphine died on March 6, 1848 (the death certificate★ does not show the cause of death), and was given Christian burial in the village cemetery. Eugène died in 1849. In these facts we recognize the principal episodes of Charles Bovary's life: he, too, studies medicine in Rouen, and once he obtains his degree he settles in the provinces, where he weds a woman older than he, is left a widower, and then marries Emma, who also bears him a daughter and dies before him. But Flaubert did not choose this model because of Charles, but because of Emma, as is indicated by Du Camp's letter of July 23, 1853, in which he asks whether he is going to write "the story of Madame Delamarre [*sic*], which is a fine one." The one thing certain about this story is that there was some-

★ Published in *La Normandie Médicale*, April 15, 1910.

thing "scandalous" at the bottom of it. In the little world of Ry and its environs, Delphine's amorous escapades caused a great deal of talk and people swore that she had killed herself. In the early years of this century, Dr. Brunon, the head of the Rouen School of Medicine, tracked down a woman who had been a servant of the Delamares.* According to this woman, now far advanced in years, Delphine scandalized the villagers of Ry by her grand airs and the costly luxuries she indulged in; the black-and-yellow curtains of her parlor, in particular, aroused the envy of her neighbors. Like Emma, she was said to have been a voracious reader of novels from lending libraries in Rouen. As for her lovers, René Dumesnil identifies two of them: the first a powerful farmer, Louis Campion, who was brought to ruin by gambling and women and shot himself to death in a Paris street; the second a notary's clerk, who died around 1905 in the *département* of the Oise.† If these facts are true (and this is not certain), in addition to the models for Charles, Héloïse, Emma, and Berthe, Flaubert took those for Rodolphe Boulanger and Léon Dupuis from the Delamare story. In any event, it is evident that the story of Delphine as perpetuated in local gossip provided him with the skeleton plot of the novel, the nucleus of incidents that he summarizes in the first *Scénario*, to which it will conform in broad outline, although he alters all the rest: the story of a girl who marries a poor devil older than herself and who, in the town where she lives, dreams of love affairs, luxury, travel, has two lovers, falls into debt, and, with neither love nor money left, commits suicide. Her heartbroken husband dies shortly thereafter.

But if the Delamare story gives Gustave the bare bones of Emma's life, another feminine drama in which dissipation and

---

* *La Normandie Médicale*, December 1, 1907.
† *Madame Bovary de Flaubert. Etude et analyse par René Dumesnil* (Paris: Editions de la Pensée Moderne, 1968), p. 67.

money problems are commingled provides him with material to flesh out his novel. And in this case the source is certain, for it is a written one: the *Mémoires de Madame Ludovica*, discovered in 1947 by Gabrielle Leleu among the files and documents used by Flaubert for *Bouvard et Pécuchet*.* These *Mémoires* consist of forty manuscript pages, written on both sides, with the syntax and spelling of a child, whose author claims to be the wife of a carpenter and a person close to Madame Ludovica. The person concealed behind the name Ludovica is not difficult to identify, for the author of the manuscript, who in the beginning gives Ludovica's last name only as P., later forgets this precaution and writes it out in full: Pradier. She is Louise d'Arcet, the sister of a schoolmate of Flaubert's and the daughter of an eminent chemist, a friend of Dr. Flaubert's. After being widowed by a first marriage while still a young woman, she married the sculptor James Pradier. She was an extravagant creature, of easy virtue; she had countless lovers and ruined her husband, who obtained a legal separation from her in 1845. The *Mémoires de Madame Ludovica* recount—though that is too generous a word for this clumsy and rancorous prose; one might better say they cruelly expose—the story of Louise d'Arcet, from her first marriage to her divorce from Pradier, placing particular emphasis on her wild adulteries, her lies, and her money troubles. Several critics presume that the text was dictated by Louise d'Arcet to a maid, but this does not make sense; one need only read it to discover that its author is filled with bitter resentment and envy of Louise, who is portrayed from the most negative angle imaginable. To conjecture that Louise d'Arcet herself sent this text to Flaubert is absurd; in all likelihood she did not know it had ever been written.

* Gabrielle Leleu and Jean Pommier, "*Du nouveau sur* Madame Bovary," in *Revue d'Histoire Littéraire de la France*, July–September 1947, pp. 211–26.

Then why was it written, and how did it come into Flaubert's hands?

We may formulate a hypothesis if we set side by side what we know about Flaubert's method of working and the relations that existed between him and Ludovica (this, apparently, was the name she was known by among her intimate friends). All the references in Flaubert's correspondence to Louise d'Arcet are posterior to her separation (in 1845) from the sculptor James Pradier. The first of them dates from April 2 of that year. Flaubert, who is passing through Paris on his way to Italy with his family, writes Le Poittevin that he has visited Louise Pradier in her very humble quarters in the rue Laffitte. She is going through a critical period; her husband has obtained a legal separation, her children have been taken away from her, she is destitute, and she has just discovered that the parents of her lover—an adolescent—are having her followed by the police. Gustave tells Alfred that he assumed a worldly air, proclaimed himself a defender of adultery, and amazed this "lost woman" by his indulgence. Ludovica's situation arouses Flaubert's literary curiosity, to judge from the following phrase from the letter (the same one he uses elsewhere in his correspondence to refer to experiences that strike him as possibly being useful later): "Ah! What an interesting study it was!" (*Correspondance*, Vol. I, p. 162). Flaubert also tells Le Poittevin that Louise d'Arcet has invited him to lunch when he returns from Italy. In his reply, Alfred urges him to accept and, after asking if he has any literary project in mind, suggests that he subject her to a battery of questions.* There is no doubt that Le Poittevin has been able to read between the lines of Flaubert's letter: the story of the "lost woman" may be a good one. This incident occurred when Flaubert was twenty-four, six years before he began work on

---

* Alfred Le Poittevin, *Une promenade de Bélial et Oeuvres inédites, avec une introduction et des notes par René Descharmes* (Paris: Les Presses Françaises, 1924), p. 190.

Madame Bovary, and it is not known whether he lunched with her on his return from Italy or whether he subjected her to "interrogation" during this period. But it is known for certain that he continued to see Ludovica, for in February 1847, six months after he became Louise Colet's lover, Louise made a terrible scene at Du Camp's, in a fit of jealous rage because Gustave had seen Louise d'Arcet. The quarrel did not end there, and there is a letter from Flaubert, censored in the *Correspondance*, in which he denies having anything but a literary interest in Ludovica. The only thing between them is a vague friendship and all he wants to do is "analyze her," since she seems to him to be the prototype of the woman of instincts, an orchestra of feminine sentiments.* He unquestionably has a literary interest in her, but it becomes evident that he also has interests of another kind at about this time, for around the middle of 1847, on his return from a walking tour of Brittany with Maxime, Flaubert inquires as to the whereabouts of Madame Pradier, whom he hopes to visit in Paris. Du Camp informs him that since she is in the process of moving he will not be able to see her. In the interval between this trip to Brittany and the one to Egypt— August of 1847 to October of 1849—close ties of friendship are forged between Maxime Du Camp, Louise d'Arcet, and Gustave, who, on his brief visits to Paris, sees both Louise Colet and Ludovica. Maxime suspects that Ludovica feels a strong attraction for his friend. He tells him so on December 25, 1848, in a letter in which he recounts how Louise d'Arcet and he, Maxime, were about to make love but resisted the temptation because Ludovica was afraid it might hurt Gustave.† And Ludovica jokingly writes Gustave that she is going to come live in Rouen so as to be closer to him. In October of 1849, as he is about to take off for the Orient, Flaubert visits her to say

---

* Letter cited by Bart, p. 156.

† Letter published by Jean Pommier and Claude Digeon in *"Du nouveau sur Flaubert et son oeuvre," Mercure de France*, Paris, May 1952.

goodbye. Thus far there has only been a teasing, bantering friendship between them. Benjamin F. Bart has discovered the precise period in which Ludovica gave herself to Gustave: the summer of 1853.* The liaison was a relatively brief one, falling within the very period in Flaubert's life during which he was writing *Madame Bovary*. After that, the relationship between the two was one of distant cordiality; there exists a letter from Flaubert to Louise d'Arcet, dated February 17, 1857, announcing that the tribunal has absolved his novel, and toward the end of 1862 he sends her one of the first copies of *Salammbô*.

What can we deduce from these facts? That, beginning in 1845, when an open, uninhibited friendship begins between them, and above all after 1853, when they become lovers, Flaubert could well have heard the story of her life from Louise d'Arcet herself. He might nonetheless have intuited that Ludovica's life was more "literary" than it appeared to be in her confessions, and might then have asked a maid—the person who had won her confidence—for the facts that Ludovica had kept a secret. That he did so behind her back and no doubt paid for the information seems to me to be the most likely version of events: Flaubert had already said that he regarded people as mere pretexts for books, so why should we be surprised to find him acting accordingly? My only doubts concern the date of this underhanded business. What would appear to be most probable is that it was at the time of the letter to Le Poittevin (1845), since the *Mémoires* go no further than Ludovica's life in 1844, when Pradier abandoned her; Flaubert may well have thought of using them for a story and then forgotten all about them till he began writing *Madame Bovary*. But he might also have paid to have them written after he had already decided to write *Madame Bovary*.

Here is a brief summary of Madame Ludovica's life. She

* *Op. cit.*, pp. 258–59.

marries at a very early age so as to get out from under her father's authority, and her first marriage, a fiasco, ends with the death of her husband. The sculptor Pradier falls in love with the beautiful widow, and she, believing herself to be in love, too, agrees to marry him. Everything goes wrong from the start; the three children they have are not a solution to any of their problems. Ludovica tries to forget her troubles by taking countless lovers, either successively or simultaneously, and at the same time lives extravagantly, showers gifts upon her lovers, squanders money she does not have. She falls further and further into debt. Inventing lies, she contrives to secure a power of attorney over all of Pradier's worldly possessions, whereupon she signs promissory notes and liens and ends up with her back to the wall. She is threatened with court proceedings. Her belongings are seized and placed at public auction in order to pay off her creditors. In desperation, Ludovica appeals to her ex-lovers, sending them a trusted maidservant bearing heartrending letters. All of them turn down her pleas for help, not even bothering to give credible excuses. On returning home one day, the husband finds the notice of the sale at auction posted on the door. Only then does he discover the catastrophe of which he is the victim; the shock leaves him stunned and half out of his mind. Shortly thereafter, he obtains a legal separation from Ludovica.

Flaubert marked the manuscript with crosses and underlined the facts and situations that could be fitted into the story of Emma Bovary. The literal facts of Ludovica's slide downhill are used almost without change in depicting Emma's financial ruin; like her, Emma will always feel the need to couple adultery with luxury and extravagance, will get herself money by having recourse to moneylenders, will not hesitate to steal from her husband, and will reach the point of seeing her furniture seized by the law. Like the sculptor Pradier, Charles Bovary discovers on returning home one day that he is ruined and stripped of his good name by his wife's follies. Gustave made a mark in the Madame Ludovica manuscript alongside the passage that speaks of the meanspiritedness of ex-lovers ("Not one of these men who refused their help even bothered to make polite excuses"). The episode in the novel is basically the same, although it has been dramatically heightened; instead of having Emma send a maidservant, he has her go in person to beg Léon and Rodolphe to help her out, in order that the baseness of the two of them and Emma's humiliation will be even more starkly evident. There are other details that Flaubert borrowed: the manuscript describes the "weakness" of Ludovica, never able to resist male overtures, just as Emma makes little effort to resist the two men who court her favors. The men who obtained Ludovica's are taxed with being mediocre sorts, as are the two who win Emma's; among the gallery of Ludovica's lovers is one who is a notary's clerk, as is Léon Dupuis. Nadeau notes that Emma falls to dreaming of romance on hearing the tenor Lagardy at the theater in Rouen and gives herself to Léon the following day, just as Ludovica loses her heart to the tenor Mocker and yields next day to the amorous advances of a certain Charles Puis.★ Ludovica does not kill herself when she finds herself unable to pay her debts, but she thinks of throwing herself into the Seine, and has a dream about Italy that is not unlike Emma's exotic fantasies.

The stories of Delphine and Ludovica attracted each other and commingled because they had a common element: the downfall of a woman whose irresistible desire to live beyond her means and station leads first to adultery and then to catastrophe. This theme was an old demon that had pursued Flaubert since his adolescence. He had first encountered it in real life on October 4, 1837, by way of an article in *La Gazette des Tribun-*

★ *Op. cit.*, p. 160.

aux, entitled *"La moderne Brinvilliers"*★ (or perhaps read it the following day in *Le Journal de Rouen*), an account of an adulteress who had committed suicide that read like a popular serial. The heroine, a married woman, has fallen in love with a young man who takes her as his mistress. Later on, to extricate himself from a situation that is becoming uncomfortable for him, he takes off for Brazil. From there he writes to the woman, begging her to forgive him and trying to convince her that he could not have done otherwise, for his love would have brought her remorse and unhappiness. The woman decides to free herself so as to be able to marry her lover. Using the handiest means she can think of, she slips her husband a fatal dose of poison. No one is the wiser, but when her children die too, the authorities become suspicious and order her arrest. On arriving at her house, the police find her dead, her hand clutching a bottle of prussic acid. This happening so impressed Gustave that he wrote a *"Conte philosophique"* about it; he completed it on December 10, 1837, shortly before his sixteenth birthday, and gave it the title *"Passion et vertu."* This is his best adolescent piece of fiction and a sort of first draft of *Madame Bovary*. When he cloistered himself at Croisset for his long novelistic adventure, he may not have remembered this article that he had read fourteen years before or recalled the story that he had written. But the tragedy of the suicide—consciously or unconsciously—was to aid in the gradual process of elaboration that was taking place as from facts, names, situations gathered here and there he forged the material out of which Emma Bovary would emerge. Flaubert transfers key episodes from the life of the poisoner to the novel: like her, Emma is abandoned by a lover who is too craven to break with her in person and instead sends her a letter; both

★ The Marquise de Brinvilliers was a famous poisoner, the talk of Paris and the court at Versailles, found guilty and guillotined in the Place de Grève during the reign of Louis XIV. (H.L.)

women end their lives by taking poison. Emma has also usurped the ill-fated woman's strong personality, her boldness, her willingness to take risks. In *"Passion et vertu"* Flaubert made changes in the real story which he then carried over into the story of Emma. *La Gazette des Tribunaux* made the lover out to be a sensible man and the woman the guilty party; in the short story and the novel the roles are reversed, and while the lover is pictured as a contemptible man (Ernest Vaumont has Rodolphe Boulanger's self-conceit, his cold, calculating turn of mind), the woman's psychological motivations mitigate her faults and give her a certain moral stature. In reality there was one letter; in the short story there are two: Mazza receives the second one as she is about to elope with her lover, just as Emma does as she is preparing to take off with Rodolphe. In both cases the letter precipitates a crisis, on a clifftop in Mazza's case, in the attic of her house in Emma's; Mazza kills herself and Emma thinks for the first time of suicide. Like the latter, Mazza is a dreamer eager to experience passion, and in the short story there are moments—Mazza stretched out on her bed allowing herself to be carried away by her voluptuous daydreams; Mazza full of hatred each evening when her husband comes home, kisses her, and tells her what his day has been like—that read like early versions of moments in Emma's life.

Delphine Delamare, Ludovica, the poisoner (three real persons), and Mazza (one fictitious one): a sponge moving about and soaking up material from every plane of the real, Flaubert steals from others and steals from himself, does research on subjects that intrigue him, as at the same time his memory brings back buried images whose source is both life and the changes that his youthful imagination, obeying inner impulses, had imposed upon these early literary pillages the moment he made them. Thefts of thefts, changes of changes, mixtures of mixtures, wherein conscious intent and the subconscious work together, wherein observation and deformation of the real are simultaneous: from these complicated conjunctions and reductions, impossible to reconstruct in their entirety, wrought of fragments, copies, bits and snatches, readings, gossip, contrivances—a fabrication invented in obedience to a throbbing wound that begs to be closed, to a disgust for reality so boundless that it seeks to demolish that reality in order to reconstruct it, that gives the appearance of re-creating it, though in truth it is an attempt to annihilate it—from all of this there little by little emerges the plot of *Madame Bovary*.

But there is another poisoner—the crime was very much in vogue in the nineteenth century, one of the revival of things medieval for which romanticism was responsible—whom Flaubert might also have come across. In March of 1852, when he is up to his neck (his own metaphor) in Emma's *rêves de jeune fille*, he receives a letter from Louise advising him to read the memoirs of the widow Lafarge, a woman sent to prison for having fatally poisoned her husband, a brutal man who had kept her sequestered in a village in the middle of nowhere. "I'm almost sorry you advised me to read the memoirs of Madame Lafarge, because I'll no doubt follow your advice and I'm afraid I'll get more engrossed in them than I really want to be," Flaubert answers Louise on March 21. And a week later, on the twenty-seventh, he brings the subject up again: "You needn't send me the memoirs of Lafarge. I'll ask for them here." It seems certain that he read the thick volumes entitled *Les Mémoires de Marie Cappelle* (1842), despite the fact that he does not speak of them again in the *Correspondance*, for there are similarities between this poisoner and Emma, beginning with their personalities. The *Mémoires* reveal a creature who feels herself to be a total misfit and deserving of a better life; her dissatisfaction feeds on dreams, yet at the same time it has made her a woman who takes action to remedy her situation. This is Emma's case precisely. An attentive examination has led critics to conclude that certain scenes of the *Mémoires* served, at least in part, as a model for a number of episodes in the novel: there is a country wedding, a ball at the Palais-Royal, and a description of the death by poisoning of Marie Cappelle's husband that might well have influenced the sequences depicting the wedding of Emma and Charles, the ball at La Vaubyessard, and Madame Bovary's death throes. Moreover, a premonition the widow has of the future that awaits her daughter might be the germ of Charles's vague imaginings of how Berthe changes as she grows up, from a babe in arms to a little girl, from a little girl to an adolescent, and from an adolescent into a woman.

Yet another crime case and court trial might have supplied certain ingredients for the novel. When Gustave was twenty-four, Rouen had been the scene of a trial that created a great stir—the "Loursel affair"—which brought before the bar of justice a man accused of having murdered his wife and a maidservant so as to marry the woman he loved: a certain Esther de Bovery. The latter turned out to be the figure who attracted most attention in the course of the trial. A woman of passion who could well have been the heroine of a novel, she wrote Loursel daring love letters that were dramatically placed in evidence against him, but the defense attorney—none other than Maître Sénard, the future attorney for the defense in the *Madame Bovary* trial—pleaded that the ardor and the excesses of these letters was a reflection of the romantic literature that was the height of fashion at the time. Maître Sénard won a resounding victory: Loursel was acquitted for lack of evidence. There are those who are persuaded that Flaubert's memory retained the name of Bovery, Esther's impassioned temperament, and certain details of the drama that came to light during the trial. The death of the maidservant as testified to before the tribunal has, for example, a number of points of resemblance with Emma's: the young woman was treated by an *officier de santé* as incompetent as Charles and Dr. Canivet; like the pair in the novel, he did not call upon a capable medical colleague until it was too late.★

Esther de Bovery's surname is cited as a possible source of that of the Yonville *officier de santé*. There are any number of others, and it is amusing to ponder the proliferation of theories as to the real origin of the name that various exegetes have carpentered up. There is the linguistic theory, according to which Bovary is a name invented from the Latin words *bovarium*, *boarium*, referring to oxen: by giving him this patronymic, Flaubert wanted to suggest Charles's slow-witted, bovine, dull nature. There is the family theory: among Flaubert's remote maternal forebears, genealogists have tracked down a person named Anne de Boveri, from whom Gustave supposedly took Charles's surname. There is the regionalist theory: it has been noted that in 1843 the orchestra conductor of the Rouen theater—which Flaubert makes the scene of an important episode of the novel—was named Boveri. There is the sophisticated hybrid theory: as a child, Flaubert was acquainted with a certain Madame Bouvard who had a tobacco shop near the Rouen cathedral, and crossed her name with that of Delphine Delamare's village (Bouvard + Ry = Bovary) to baptize his hero, before using it yet again for the copyist of *Bouvard et Pécuchet*, his last novel. Flaubert himself proposed a theory. On March 20, 1870, he wrote to Madame Hortense Cornu that he had invented the name of Bovary "by denaturing that of Bouvaret," the owner of a hotel where he stayed in Cairo, a onetime actor who, according to Gustave's *Notes de voyage*, had decorated his place with copperplate engravings by Gavarni that had been published in *Charivari*, a magazine of the period (thus leading the Flaubert scholar René Dumesnil to assure us that in one of these 1833

★ Jean Pommier has carefully studied this possible source. Cf. *"L'Affaire Loursel,"* in *Les Lettres Françaises*, Paris, April 11, 1947.

copper prints a schoolboy is wearing the cap that served as a model for the famous description of the "strange headgear of composite order" worn by Charles Bovary in the first pages of the novel, a rash but not impossible hypothesis). Flaubert's theory is no more valid than any of the rest; as regards his sources, an author generally knows less then his critics and it would not be difficult to combine his exegesis with any one of the others: to explain, for example, that Flaubert thought he was disguising the name of Bouvaret when in reality he was merely using a conscious stimulus—Bouvaret—to fish up from the subconscious the name of an ancestor, of a tobacco vendor, of an orchestra leader, or a Latin class of his years as a school-boy . . . What is certain is the importance Flaubert attributed to names: he took a long time choosing them and did research so as not to hurt anyone's feelings, but once he had settled on one he never changed his mind. During the years of *L'Education sentimentale*, his friend Louis Bonenfant discovered a family in Nogent named Moreau and suggested that he change Frédéric's surname. Flaubert refused: "A proper name is a *capital* matter. One can no more change a character's name than one can change his skin. It would be like trying to turn a black into a white."[*] And in the *Carnets*, the notebooks in which we find his plans for his writings between the years 1862 and 1874 (published in an excellent book, marvel-ously pairing erudition and intelligence, by Marie-Jeanne Durry),[†] we see how often Flaubert writes the first and last name of the living model alongside the character he has in mind.

In what form did Flaubert project his personal and family life into Madame Bovary?

[*] Undated letter, end of 1868, *Correspondance*, Vol. V, p. 427. Flaubert's italics.
[†] *Flaubert et ses projets inédits* (Paris: Librairie Nizet, 1950).

Flaubert not only delved into other people's lives for his fiction; his own experience spreads like a blot over the fictional reality, manifesting itself in any number of different situations and characters, at times in a way one would never suspect. At least two of the women he loved contributed to the creation of Emma. Madame Bovary has something of the sensuality of Eulalie Foucault, the mysterious hotel owner in Marseilles who taught Flaubert the intoxication of sexual pleasure and the excitement of forbidden love when he was eighteen. Eulalie's lack of inhibition and her aptitudes as a voluptuary (or at any rate those attributed to her by Gustave in *Novembre*) form part of the personality of Madame Bovary. It is well known how much the creation of Emma owes to Louise Colet, the mistress of the years when the book was being written. Her tempestuous, somewhat masculine temperament, as well as her typical southern tendency toward truculent behavior and dramatic gestures are also outstanding traits of the heroine of Yonville. It is also possible that Flaubert made use of more transitory experiences. For Emma's adulteries and the figure of Charles, he might well have found material in the love affairs of Madame Roger des Genettes, who later became his friend. But during the period when he is writing *Madame Bovary*, he speaks very badly of her to Louise and pities her cuckolded husband: "I got a good look at old Roger as he passed by on the street with his frock coat and his dog. Poor simpleton! . . . How little he suspects. Have you ever thought of the countless women who have lovers, the countless men who have mistresses, the countless separate households kept? How many lies that presupposes! How many schemes and betrayals, tears and mortifications!" (letter of December 23, 1853). The picture he paints of "old Roger" makes one think of Charles. Thibaudet was of the opinion that Emma's terrible boredom at Tostes and Yonville was the transubstantiation of the ennui that Gustave himself had experienced during his trip to the Orient, for which his traveling companion Du

Camp reproached him so bitterly.* Just as he was completing fifteen months of work on *Madame Bovary*, Louise informed him that she might be pregnant as a consequence of their last rendezvous in Mantes. It was a false alarm, but Flaubert was plunged into despair for three weeks and penned her cruel phrases rejecting the very thought of fatherhood. ("The mere idea of bringing someone into this world *horrifies* me. I would curse myself if I were to become a father. A son of mine! Oh, no, no, no!").† Lying somewhere between indifference and frank disgust, Emma's feelings toward maternity are cast in almost the same mold.

Dr. Achille-Cléophas Flaubert, Gustave's father, also played a part in the creation of *Madame Bovary*. But this clue does not shed much light on the book. The truth of the matter is more or less the reverse: the novel tells us a great deal about Gustave's relations with Achille-Cléophas. Taking it for granted that sons adore their fathers, biographers have been persuaded that by using Dr. Achille-Cléophas, chief surgeon of the Hôtel-Dieu of Rouen, as a model for Dr. Larivière, Flaubert was paying his father nostalgic homage. Doesn't the novel tell us that the townspeople are more moved by the arrival of the celebrated physician and professor in Yonville than they would have been by the appearance of a god? These biographers have been the victims of their own good faith by so interpreting the Dr. Larivière of the novel, for Flaubert's portrait of him is so equivocal as to be Machiavellian (and a novel cannot be taken by the reader, in all good faith, to be a direct reflection of the reality that is its source without his being led badly astray). Precisely the opposite conclusions may be drawn from it. Like Dr. Achille-Cléophas, Larivière is an eminent scientist, a philosopher-practitioner revered by his disciples, who copy even his dress;

---

* *Op. cit.*, pp. 63–65.
† Letter to Louise Colet, December 11, 1852. Flaubert's italics.

a man in love with his profession, who disdains honors, whose manner is one of genial majesty, conscious as he is of his talent, his fortune, and his forty years of irreproachable conduct. That is the positive side of the portrait. And this is the other. The learned doctor confesses to a *fanatical* love for his profession, and those extraordinary plump hands, always ungloved, "as though to be the readier to plunge into suffering flesh," also have something sadistic about them. This liberal thinker is a man whose fits of rage terrify people, and it seems fair to conclude that the narrator's remark that he might have been taken for a saint "if he hadn't been feared as a devil because of the keenness of his mind" is a way of calling him a cruel man. Sartre is quite right when he points out that the following sentence describing Dr. Larivière sheds light on Gustave's true feelings toward his own father: "His glance, sharper than his scalpels, cut deep down into your soul, through all the excuses and reticences, and exposed every lie." This is Gustave's secret image of Achille-Cléophas: an authoritarian god who read his soul, a will he could choose only to obey. Moreover, what role do we see Dr. Larivière, that paragon of medical science, play in Emma's story? It is true that he is summoned too late and it is perhaps the case that when he arrives his professional acumen permits him to determine at a glance that there is no hope for the woman. It is odd nonetheless that he does not even examine the victim, that he does not make the slightest attempt to counteract the poison, that after this one swift glance he goes off to eat with such gusto and leaves the town with such an air of self-satisfaction. Even if the characters and the narrator make much of his great talent, his behavior is in no way proof of it; the reader is left, rather, with an impression of mere show, false prestige, coldness, a lack of professional conscientiousness. By using him as a model for Dr. Larivière, was Gustave paying his father tribute or taking his revenge on him? And doing so in the way that would hurt most: by mocking his "scientific knowledge." For there is another borrowing that confirms the hypothesis of a perhaps unconscious act of revenge on Flaubert's part against his father. Dr. Achille-Cléophas once tried to cure a little girl named Marlin of a clubfoot by keeping her in bed for several months with her foot encased in an iron boot. The experiment was a total failure. This is doubtless the source of the grotesque operation performed on Hippolyte's foot by Charles Bovary, who, after having severed the tendon of the foot, subjects his patient to an identical post-operative regime (the end result of which is gangrene and amputation). Thus the merits and faults of Achille-Cléophas provide material for at least two of the doctors of the fictional reality: Larivière and Charles. Flaubert's father was often called in as a consultant by former students of his practicing in Norman villages, and was in the habit of taking Gustave, when still a young child, along with him on these professional visits. The vivid memories of them that lingered in Gustave's mind are the basis of Charles's endless travels up and down the Normandy countryside caring for his patients.

Good memories transformed by nostalgia into aching wounds are not the only wellspring of a fiction. A richer source still are the wounds that continue to suppurate in a writer's spirit, the demons that spur his imagination on. Is a torturously prolonged Oedipus complex, as Sartre believes, the explanation for Flaubert's difficult relations with his father and the remote cause of his nervous illness? Up to the time of his crisis on the Pont-l'Evêque, Achille-Cléophas represents the most serious obstacle that stands in the way of Gustave's following the one calling that interests him, literature, the practice of which he regards as nothing less than a total gift of self. It is no doubt on the advice of his father (which for a docile son is tantamount to an order) that he instead begins his law studies. These two years at the Sorbonne (1842 and 1843) were a bitter experience for Gustave, and his letters of this period are the principal evi-

dence in support of the thesis that he "chose" his illness so as
to free himself from the fate that awaited him: a lifetime of
practicing law. His nightmarish studies of the statutes bring on
an irritated rash of letters to Ernest Chevalier: "God damn it
to sonofabitching bloody fucking hell . . . may the devil strangle
jurisprudence and those who invented it! Axiom as to the study
and profession of law: the study of it is a beastly bore and the
profession ignoble" (May 21, 1842); "The Law is killing me,
brutalizing me, tearing me limb from limb, it is impossible for
me to toil away at it. After three hours with my nose buried
in the Code, not understanding the first thing, I just can't go
on: I'd rather kill myself . . ." (June 25, 1842); "Law sends me
into a state of moral castration strange to conceive" (August 1,
1842). Dozens of similar passages could be cited. His future
writings will be full of practitioners of this "ignoble profession,"
their portraits serving as his revenge for those two years of
calvary: in his fictitious reality lawyers, notaries, judges will
inevitably represent what is earthbound, base, sordid. In *Madame Bovary* there are numerous characters connected with the
law in one way or another, and there is no doubt that he made
abundant use of his memories of the Sorbonne to portray Maître
Guillaumin and Léon Dupuis. Léon, a timid, romantic-souled
student who ends up as a prosperous, morally contemptible
notary in Yvetot, is modeled in part after Flaubert himself, and,
more closely still, after a friend of his early years, the recipient
of the foregoing imprecations against the study and practice of
law: Ernest Chevalier. Chevalier had been a fervent devotee of
literature, a schoolboy who wore a hidden dagger at his waist
like the heroes of romantic novels, but later in life he became
a typical well-heeled bourgeois, having carved out a brilliant
career for himself in the courtroom as a prosecuting attorney
and even managing to get himself elected a deputy to the leg-
islature. Léon Dupuis bears a resemblance to Flaubert, not only
because of the years in Paris as law students that both have in

common, but also because in his relations with Emma (which we intuitively sense are a repetition of an Oedipal situation) Léon gives proof of a sentimental attachment that is a constant with Flaubert: falling in love with a woman older than himself (Flaubert's three mistresses—Eulalie Foucault, Elise Schlésinger, Louise Colet—were all several years older).

Two years after having begun his novel (give or take a few weeks), Flaubert went to Trouville on holiday and took lodgings with a pharmacist. Thanks to a description of the atmosphere and the persons in this household, sent off to Bouilhet, we may deduce that much of what he saw and heard there inspired Flaubert's creation of Homais and his milieu. "Marvel yet again in this case at the courtesies of Providence, which are enough to make one believe in it. With whom am I staying? A pharmacist! And whose former student is he? Dupré's! Like him, he makes a great deal of seltzer water. 'I'm the one person in Trouville who makes seltzer water!' In fact once the clock has struck eight I am often awakened by the sound of corks unexpectedly popping. Bim! Bam! The kitchen is also the laboratory. A monstrous still curves in and out among the saucepans

L'effrayante longueur de son cuivre qui fume

and often the stew can't be put on to simmer because of the pharmaceutical products already bubbling away. In order to go out into the yard, one must step over baskets full of medicine bottles. A pump out there splashes water all over your legs. The two boys are busy rinsing apothecary jars. There's a parakeet that keeps repeating, 'Had a nice lunch, Jacko?' from morning to night. And finally, a youngster of about ten, the son of the family, the hope of the pharmacy, practices feats of strength, lifting weights with his teeth" (letter of August 23, 1853). In this description the reader of *Madame Bovary* recognizes Homais's pharmacy (which is also the Homais residence), the industrious hustle and bustle, to which the entire family contributes, and above all, the commingling of domestic and professional life. On reading that in this Trouville kitchen pharmaceutical remedies usurp the place of the pots and kettles, there inevitably comes to mind the picture of the Homais family making jam in the pharmacy, the image that greets Emma the day she receives the news of the death of her father-in-law. The inevitable cheerful confusion, the children washing jars who might be the Athalie and Napoléon of the novel, the bourgeois pridefulness of the real pharmacist ("I'm the one person in Trouville who makes seltzer water" is something that Homais might have said, in precisely those words), along with the expression "hope of the pharmacy," which is an anticipation of Justin, show that this vacation was one that Flaubert put to extremely good use. During a previous season also spent at Trouville, he had had as his table companion at a banquet a little country priest who all of a sudden began to hold forth very excitedly about the life of "champagne and actresses" that students lived in Paris. This was the source, as the *Correspondance* confirms, of the mythical idea of *"la vie parisienne"* as lived by university students to which Homais gives voice when Léon leaves Yonville, a passage in which Flaubert strings together "all the stupid things people in the provinces say about Paris" (letter to Louise Colet, June 14–15, 1853).

But at the time that Gustave took lodgings at the pharmacy of Trouville, Homais already existed, his features clearly outlined, in Flaubert's mind (the letter to Bouilhet speaks of a surprising coincidence). The character had been around for some time—perhaps since his childhood, when Gustave and his schoolmates at the lycée in Rouen took turns impersonating the outrageous character they had invented and baptized the Garçon. The Goncourts believed that the Garçon was the prototype of Homais, and though there are any number of scholars who refuse to believe them (no character of Flaubert's has stirred up as much excitement among his exegetes as the pharmacist of

Yonville: they have scoured all of France for his model), I believe that they are right.* The Garçon was a jointed doll whose strident peals of wild laughter shattered moderation, reason, and good manners to bits and created bloody farce, sheer absurdity, breakdown, anarchy. It is evident that this aspect of the Garçon is not reflected in any way in the person of the pharmacist in the smoking cap, who never strays from the world of the serious-minded or from the intellectual, moral, and social conventions of his milieu. But the Garçon was also a perambulating ventriloquist, mouthing commonplaces and bromides of the moment. As he passed by the cathedral of Rouen, for instance, he marveled at the beauties *that one cannot but marvel at* and said of the Gothic *what must be said.* As well as being a fierce Mephistopheles who materialized to prove that life is a grotesque fraud, the Garçon gave voice to the *rhetorical level* of the day: he was a walking encyclopedia of the current sayings, the clichés, the pat formulas that express the inert, institutionalized thought of a society. This is no doubt the foremost trait of Homais's formidable personality: storing up and giving a pompous, self-satisfied stamp of approval to the hackneyed phrase; existing as an epiphenomenon of the established fact. Moreover, during his school years—the period of the Garçon—Flaubert wrote a *physiologie*, in the manner of Balzac, of a social type, the *"commis,"* the shop or office clerk, and this satire penned when he was fifteen is to Homais what the Mazza of *"Passion et vertu"* is to Emma: a preliminary sketch.†

---

* It will be noted that with regard to Flaubert's models, I follow a liberal, maximalist policy: everything convinces me, except exclusivism. My basic premise is that there is never one real model, but several, and that hybridization is so complex a process that it can never be completely resurrected.

† *"Une leçon d'histoire naturelle. Genre commis"* appeared in a Rouen student publication, *Le Colibri*, March 30, 1837. Parenthetically, Flaubert's school years undoubtedly furnished him with the material for the opening episode of the novel: Charles arriving at the lycée after the school year has begun and made a victim of their bullying. Gustave, too, had enrolled late at his school and was made a butt of his schoolmates' merciless ragging.

The supposed models for Homais are legion. For a time, it was taken as certain fact that he was a caricatural version of the apothecary of Ry in the time of Delphine Delamare, an individual named Jouanne whose pharmacy, according to Raoul Brunon, resembled the one described by Flaubert. This thesis was challenged by the argument that Jouanne, unlike Homais, had been a stubborn defender of the Church (as though Flaubert could not have stolen the pharmacy from him without swiping a single one of his ideas). Following this trail, René Dumesnil found at Forges-les-Eaux, where Flaubert had spent several months in 1848, a rabid anticlerical who, during the revolution of 1848, "sacrificed his silver on the altar of the motherland"; attracted by the reputation this colorful local character had made for himself, Flaubert had gone to have a look at him. Following another trail, that of stupid pomposity, Gérard Gailly came up with another model, producing evidence that, in the little village of Veules, Flaubert had met a pharmacist whose name, Esprit Bellemère, suited him perfectly; as mayor of the hamlet, he had once received Victor Hugo with a phrase that would not have sounded at all out of place coming from Homais: "You, Monsieur Victor Hugo, so worthy of that name!" It has also been maintained that the model for Homais was a literary one. Enid Starkie is of the opinion that Joseph Prudhomme, the famous character created by Henri Monnier, who for half a century symbolized laughable pedantry and the empty cliché, was Homais's immediate ancestor.* Flaubert often speaks of Joseph Prudhomme, particularly when he thunders against the bourgeoisie, and there are unquestionable resemblances between the garrulous pharmacist of Yonville and Monnier's self-important Parisian. But though Monnier's play *Grandeur et décadence de Joseph Prudhomme* was first performed in 1853 (Flaubert

---

* Raoul Brunon, *"A propos de* Madame Bovary,*"* in *La Normandie Médicale*, December 1, 1907; Dumesnil, p. 68; Gérard Gailly, *A la recherche du pharmacien Homais*, 1939; Starkie, p. 330.

makes no mention of it in these years), his *Mémoires de Joseph Prudhomme* did not appear until after the publication of *Madame Bovary* (1857). Homais, like other Flaubert characters, is the fruit of many grafts; the novelist might very well have come upon his type in any number of country villages, or yet again, in the streets of Rouen, excellent sources of material for his book. In a letter to Bouilhet, Flaubert, who has just returned from a trip to Rouen to do on-the-spot research, writes that since the novel will be a portrait of that city, it is absolutely necessary that *cheminots*, little rolls in the shape of a turban that are typical of it, be accorded a place in the fictional reality, and that it is Homais who will be responsible for their appearance: they are to be his "sole" human weakness (letter of May 24, 1855). As it turned out, they are made out to be that of Madame Homais, whose husband buys her *cheminots* every so often in the city.

The models proposed, by contrast, for Homais's diametrical opposite and complement, the Abbé Bournisien, are rare. It has been said that he was copied after a certain Abbé Lafortune of Ry, the Delamares' village, but this hypothesis was demolished when it was proved that there had never been a priest by that name anywhere in the diocese. What is certain is that the name Bournisien, like those of other characters in the novel— the tax collector, Binet, and the undertaker, Lestiboudois, for instance—were chosen out of Flaubert's concern for realistic effect: they are typically Norman, popular names. Like Homais and Emma, Bournisien long haunts Flaubert's mind before he sets about writing his novel. Inspired perhaps by his anticlericalism—which becomes a fixed attitude at an early age, never wavers, and explains his unfailing admiration for Voltaire—the uneducated, down-to-earth village priest, his mind closed to any and every form of spirituality, already appears as a type in the juvenilia of Gustave's adolescence. In a story written when he was sixteen, *"Agonies, pensées sceptiques,"* the narrator, a nihilist who has fallen prey to despair, seeks out a priest to ask for his counsel, but the man of the cloth is more occupied by the thought of the potatoes cooking in the kitchen nearby than by what the young man is confiding. This earthbound priest and this scene are an evident prefiguration of Father Bournisien and the episode in which Emma has a religious crisis and the priest is unable to understand what she is trying to tell him because he translates everything he hears into something altogether ordinary and prosaic and because he is paying more attention to the youngsters in his catechism class than to his visitor.

When he was fifteen, Gustave attended a ball given by a great landowner, the Marquis de Pomereu, in his château at Héron, and used this experience in one of his early stories: *"Quidquid voleris."* A romantic memory of the party lingered on and he remembered it during his trip to the Orient: "I had stayed up all night and early the next morning I had gone boating on the pond, all by myself, in my school uniform. The swans watched me row past and leaves of the shrubbery drifted down into the water" (letter to Louis Bouilhet, March 13, 1850). Twenty-six months later, he is hard at work on *Madame Bovary* and has arrived at the ball at La Vaubyessard: "I have to have my heroine attend a ball. It's been so long since I've been to one that it's taking a great effort of imagination. And then, too, it's such a trite subject, so hackneyed. It would take a miracle to avoid the vulgar touch, and yet I am determined to do so" (letter to Louise, May 2, 1852). There is no question that the principal source for the ball that changes Emma's life—her first encounter with luxury that leaves her *dissatisfied* forever after— was this party that Gustave attended as an adolescent, which left him with the memory of a languid boat ride amid swans and falling leaves. On the morning after the ball, Emma too wanders off by herself, pondering her life as she walks through the grounds of La Vaubyessard.

As in this case, it is possible to discover in Flaubert's own life the seed of other episodes in the novel. We are assured that the picaresque song that the Blind Man sings as Emma is dying is one that Madame Flaubert crooned to Gustave in his cradle, and at the same time it is said to be proven fact that Flaubert took this song from Restif de la Bretonne. One investigator has discovered that Emma's little lap dog, Djali, has the same name as the goat belonging to Esmeralda, the young gypsy girl in Hugo's *Notre-Dame de Paris*, a novel that enthralled Flaubert and his schoolmates.* The episode of the fiacre, in which Emma gives herself to Léon, may be traced back to Flaubert's affair with Louise Colet. Gustave recounted to the Goncourt brothers, in 1862, how the Muse had *begun* to give herself to him one night as he was taking her home in a hackney coach, a confidence that the memoirists recorded in Flaubert's own vulgar words: "The fuck began as I was taking her home in a fiacre" (letter of December 6, 1862). But we also know that during the time that Flaubert was writing *Madame Bovary*, Louise was very nearly raped in a carriage by Alfred de Musset, by then a lustful old roué: Gustave and Louise discussed the incident between themselves, and Flaubert may have used it when recounting the fiacre episode in the novel. He might also have used for the same purpose a cheap semi-erotic novel by the Chevalier Andrea de Nerciat, an eighteenth-century army officer and pornographer, who devotes an entire chapter of his *Félicia ou mes fredaines* [*Felicia, or My Amorous Escapades*] (1775) to a description of a couple making love in a carriage as it crosses Paris.

Flaubert was born and lived as a child and an adolescent in a hospital; his father and his brother were doctors. His memory teemed with images of sick people, physical suffering, blood, death. In a famous letter he tells Louise Colet how he and his

---

* See René Descharmes and René Dumesnil, *Autour de Flaubert*, 1912, Vol. I, p. 306, and Dumesnil, pp. 63–80.

sister Caroline used to stand in the garden of the Hôtel-Dieu looking down through a window at the morgue with its cadavers crawling with flies; Dr. Flaubert would sometimes catch the two looking on as he was dissecting and chase them away. When *Madame Bovary* appeared, Sainte-Beuve was the first to point to the connection between Flaubert's family background and the "scientific" style and minute descriptions—autopsies— in the book: "The son and brother of distinguished doctors, Monsieur Gustave Flaubert wields the pen as others the scalpel. Anatomists and physiologists, I find you everywhere!"★ This is an astute observation—in a mediocre article—and it has become a commonplace of Flaubert criticism. Admittedly the atmosphere of the Hôtel-Dieu and precocious familiarity with the ruin of the human body left their imprint on the fictional reality. Illness and medicine occupy a prominent place in the novel: there is Hippolyte's clubfoot, the operation, the treatment, the gangrene, the amputation; there are other less daring and more successful medical interventions by Charles: his setting of the fractured leg of Père Rouault, his future father-in-law, and the bleeding of Rodolphe's farmhand; there is the Blind Man covered with purulent sores and the remedies recommended to him by Homais, who, besides being a pharmacist, practices medicine without a license and spends his days amid prescriptions and organic illnesses; Emma's poisoning of herself brings on a flurry of Hippocratic activity—the arrival in Yonville of Dr. Canivet and Dr. Larivière—and leads to a meticulously detailed description of her death throes and demise. Sicknesses, treatments, cures, operations are all described with perfect accuracy: we have already seen how Flaubert consulted physicians on at least two occasions in order to make certain his facts were absolutely correct. But the influence of

★ Article published in *Le Moniteur*, Paris, May 4, 1857, and reprinted in *Lundis*, XIII, pp. 346–63.

Flaubert's family milieu is felt not only at the level of plot incident in *Madame Bovary*; as Sainte-Beuve suggests, it also has a primordial influence on the author's vision of the cosmos and on his style. The objectivity—that is to say, the impersonality acquired through the use of a certain technique—to which Flaubert aspired is tantamount to viewing the novel as a scientific product, as the result of a combinatory process whereby ingredients chosen and measured out in exact proportions according to precise laws by virtue of the intelligence of the creator will take on the life of a positive truth. The so-called coldness with which Flaubert recounts the adventures and misadventures of his characters was no different from the attitude with which Achille-Cléophas auscultated, prescribed, amputated, treated his patients, or pronounced their case hopeless. But along with the ideas and suggestions that came his way from within the family circle, we also find reflections of developments occurring within a wider circle, of the revolution in philosophy and science that was taking place in France. Flaubert writes *Madame Bovary* in the same era in which Auguste Comte proclaims that the "scientific" attitude is the only valid approach to an understanding of man and thought, in books that argue that society explains the individual and not vice versa, as the "metaphysicians" believe, the same era in which Claude Bernard begins his lectures and his research, which are to culminate in the dogma of scientific experiment as the sole method of discovering truth. Objectivity, social determinism, the rejection of metaphysics and intuition, faith in intelligence and logical reasoning—elements, all of them, that contribute to the shaping of *Madame Bovary*—are concepts that were imbibed by Flaubert and his entire generation, for it was during their youth and early adulthood that these ideas began to take root in France.

If the doctors and patients of his early years served him for his novel, is it not logical to suppose that his own illness would also be reflected in *Madame Bovary*? Sartre is of the opinion that

the physical ailments that befall Emma when her romantic illusions are shattered by Rodolphe are a literal reproduction of
the illness that overtook Flaubert. Sartre maintains that Flaubert's "nervous disease" was a response or a psychosomatic
solution to the terrible crises that marked his childhood and his
early youth. After having cited Flaubert's own description of
his attacks: "The pain does not remain confined to the cranium:
it extends to the limbs and then, once it has been communicated
to the body, becomes convulsive," Sartre makes this suggestive
comparison: "Flaubert always regarded his neurosis as the most
meaningful occurrence in his life: far from taking this 'death
and transfiguration' to be an accident, he does not distinguish
it from his very person: it is *himself*, in that he thereby became
what he was; he never thought, as Dumesnil believes, that he
was adapting to or would adapt to his illness but, quite to the
contrary, thought that his illness was, in and of itself, an ad-
aptation: in a word, he regarded it as a *response*, as a *solution*.
The proof of this is that later his Bovary will produce an explicit
somatization response: abandoned by Rodolphe, she falls sick,
her life apparently endangered by a terrible bout of fever; and
then, after several weeks, she finds herself cured at once of the
fever and of love. Or, to put it another way, love *transformed
itself* into a fever in order to put an end to itself by way of her
physical disorders."* In this way, Sartre finds arguments in
Madame Bovary for his hypothesis that Flaubert *chose* his neurosis
as a solution to his problems. There are others who argue along
somewhat similar lines. Two physicians, Drs. Galeran and Alen,
supporters of the theory that Flaubert suffered from epilepsy,
assure us that hallucinations of the sort produced by this malady
left their mark on the style of *Madame Bovary*. According to
these two doctors, one of the symptoms of epilepsy, which
stems from a disturbance in the temporal-occipital lobe, is mul-

* *Op. cit.*, Vol. II, pp. 1809–10.

ticolored visions: this, in their view, explains Flaubert's obsessive use in the novel of adjectives describing color, and of visual imagery.* There is no denying that in *Madame Bovary* the pictorial element is as important as the musical, but what weakens this argument is the fact that many other authors of the romantic and post-romantic era—Gautier, Leconte de Lisle, Baudelaire—shared this inclination for plastic effects, and in their cases epilepsy is ruled out as the cause. But there is no reason to doubt that in Flaubert's case his nervous attacks were "cannibalized" for the sake of the fictive reality. It is quite obvious, for instance, that certain hallucinations he suffered from during his crises bear a marked resemblance to the one that Emma has. On June 7, 1844, Gustave describes the attacks of those days in a letter to Ernest Chevalier: "Not a day goes by but that I do not see, from time to time, what looks like tufts of hair or of Bengal lights float past my eyes." As she is leaving the château of La Huchette after being humiliated by Rodolphe, Emma, alone in the dark, has a hallucination in which she sees the same balls of fire: "It suddenly seemed to her that fiery particles were bursting in the air amid the branches of the trees like exploding bullets, flattening out and whirling down and finally melting on the snow."

What are the principal literary sources of Madame Bovary?

If the real-life models (authentic or not) are innumerable, this is also more or less true of the literary models. In this domain too, trying to track down all the proved or probable connections would be like chasing shadows. I shall do no more than point to a few examples. A parallel which all commentators, from Thibaudet to Lukacs, have particularly stressed is that between

---

* Dr. Galeran, *"Flaubert vu par les médecins d'aujourd'hui,"* in the issue of *Europe* devoted to Flaubert, Paris, September–October–November 1969, pp. 108–9.

Emma Bovary and Don Quixote. The man of La Mancha was a misfit in life because of his imagination and certain books he had read, and like that of the young woman of Normandy, his tragedy lay in wanting to make his dreams a reality. The frequent references to Cervantes in the *Correspondance* indicate that the story of Don Quixote held young Gustave spellbound when his Uncle Mignon first recounted it to him, and that it continued to have the same effect on him every time he reread it as an adult. The affinities between the two novels are not limited to the character of the protagonists (whose drama does not lie, as has been so often said, in their being unable to perceive reality as it is, in their confusing their desires and objective life, but in their trying to *realize* those desires: therein lies their madness and their grandeur). Both works achieve the admirable symbiosis that Flaubert saw in the *Quixote*: "What is prodigious in *Don Quixote* is the absence of art and the perpetual fusion of illusion and reality that makes it so comic and so poetic a book" (letter to Louise, November 22, 1852). In *Madame Bovary* there is the same interweaving of illusion and reality: what occurs objectively is as important as what takes place only in Emma's imagination, as in Cervantes's story of Alonso Quijano.

Another of the parallels a critic feels obliged to point to is that between Balzac and Flaubert. Gustave had mixed feelings regarding the creator of *La Comédie humaine*. He learned of his death during the trip to the Orient, and on November 14, 1850, he penned these deeply felt words to Louis Bouilhet: "One is always saddened by the death of a man one admires. I had hoped to know him later and win his affection. Yes, he was a man of great powers with a staggering understanding of his era." At other times he was less sympathetic to him and called him a second-rate genius. What is certain is that on the one hand he admired the extraordinary scope of Balzac's world, the seething imagination capable of breathing life into multitudes and of effortlessly creating characters who evolve from one story to another; on the other hand, his own perfectionism, his mania for accurate detail, his "artist's" conception of language made it impossible for him to forgive Balzac for the offhandedness with which he wrote, and the latter's repetitions, his faulty grammatical constructions, his cacophonies, made Flaubert think that he lacked style (the truth was that the author of *La Comédie humaine* had a style different from his own). Balzac is one of the writers he reads in these five years. He mentions him frequently. One of these references sums up Gustave's ambivalent attitude toward him: "What a man Balzac would have been, if only he had known how to write! But that is the one ability he lacked. An artist, when all is said and done, would not have produced as much, would not have had his breadth" (letter to Louise, December 17, 1852). There is a certain truth in this. If Balzac had had Flaubert's conception of style, he would never have written all that he did. But the contrary is also true: had Flaubert shared Balzac's conceptions of novelistic style and structure, *Madame Bovary* would never have come into being. Hence the parallels that it is possible to establish between the two have to do primarily with the subjects they dealt with. Jean Pommier, for example, has proved that one of the novels of Balzac's "provincial" series, *La Muse du département*, develops the theme of the unhappily married woman in a way that reminds us of *Madame Bovary*: like Emma, Balzac's heroine is bored to death in a remote little town and dreams of a better life, but unlike Madame Bovary, she manages to escape provincial life by going to Paris to live with her lover.* A more interesting discovery is one made by Claudine Gothot-Mersch, who points out that the various phases of Emma and Charles's conjugal life faithfully follow Balzac's description in his *Phys-*

---

* Jean Pommier, "La Muse du département *et le thème de la femme mal mariée chez Balzac, Mérimée et Flaubert,*" in *L'Année Balzacienne* (Paris: Garnier, 1961), pp. 191–221.

iologie du mariage (a book that won Flaubert's praise in 1839) of the successive stages of a marriage that fails.* But there are more differences, by far, than similarities between the two narrators. Ernst Robert Curtius saw very clearly what separates them:† Balzac's optimism and Flaubert's pessimism, fundamentally opposed attitudes which permeate their respective novelistic worlds. In the first, the imagination of humanity is still capable of making its dreams come true and of renewing life. In the second, imagination is a crime that reality punishes by breaking those who try to live their dreams. Curtius says: "In Flaubert the wish to live enters into conflict with the actual living of life, and the conflict ends with an irremediable divorce between the two. In Balzac we find precisely the contrary: an unlimited imagination that contrives to penetrate all of reality and assimilate it." It is also true that Balzac finds life logical while Flaubert finds it absurd, but unlike Curtius—an optimistic liberal who cannot manage to hide the antipathy he feels for Flaubert the eternal killjoy—I for my part do not think that this makes Balzac more our contemporary than Flaubert. Curtius concludes his comparison with these words: "Balzac feels a passionate interest in life and passes his fire on to us; Flaubert, his nausea." This is so, and it is precisely for this reason that Flaubert is the first modern novelist.

Critics soon discovered that *Madame Bovary* was the novel of "disillusioned romanticism" and hastened to track down its romantic sources. Almost all of them have pointed to Chateaubriand. Dumesnil hears a distinct echo of *Atala* in the description of the natural setting of *Madame Bovary*,‡ but what he sees as an analogy I see as a diametrical opposite. The landscapes

---

* *Op. cit.*, pp. xii–xiii.
† In a 1950 essay, *"Reencuentro con Balzac,"* included in *Ensayos críticos sobre la literatura europea* (Barcelona: Seix Barral, 1972), pp. 209–32.
‡ *La Vocation de Gustave Flaubert* (Paris: Gallimard, 1961), p. 209.

of the romantics—and Chateaubriand's in particular—are a pro-
jection of the character's feeling and emotion, a totally subjec-
tified reality. Quite the contrary is true of Flaubert's, and this
is one of the great originalities of *Madame Bovary*: in it the natural
order infects the human, and thoughts and feelings are described
objectively. In Chateaubriand trees and lakes are humanized; in
Flaubert happiness and nostalgia become things. This representation of man and nature in such a way that the one stands for
the other is what links both writers; their respective originality
lies in the difference between them.

What further proof is needed that Flaubert built *Madame Bovary*
out of his own life, that of his family, that of his society—that
in a word his stone quarry was the reality of his time? And yet
we may set over against one another passages in which, on
the one hand, Flaubert acknowledges having mined his own
experience for material, and a host of others in which, with
the same sincere conviction, he denies that there is any personal element in *Madame Bovary* and insists that it is a totally
invented story. On December 18, 1853, he writes to Louise:
". . . by imagining, one reproduces what is general, whereas
by sticking to a *true* fact all that emerges from your work
is something contingent, relative, restricted." The novel he
is writing will be a work of pure imagination; it will not
be contaminated in any way by his experience, there will be
not one thing in it that is *true*. He emphatically assures Mademoiselle Leroyer de Chantepie of this: "*Madame Bovary* has
nothing true in it. It is a totally *invented* story; I have put none
of my own sentiments into it and nothing of my own life.
The illusion of reality (if such there be) comes on the contrary
from the *impersonality* of the work. It is a principle of mine
that a writer must not make himself a subject of his work.
The artist must be in his work like God in his creation, invisi-

ble and all-powerful; he must be everywhere felt, but never seen."★

The statement that *Madame Bovary* has nothing of himself in it is as true as his claim that he wrote only true things. Personal experience is a point of departure (the process of gestation); the point of arrival (the finished work) is reached through the *transmutation* of this material. The sum of experiences that constitute the basis of a fiction are not the fiction itself; the latter always differs from its materials because it is first and foremost a piece of writing and an order, and by being set down in words and arranged in accordance with a technique, these ingredients inevitably become something else.

This is what we must now see, what is really important: how the novel freed itself from its sources, how the fictional reality contradicted the real reality that inspired it.

★ Letter of March 18, 1857. (The italics are Flaubert's.) It may be noted that in this quotation there is a confusion of two ideas. Flaubert appears to be saying, on the one hand, that a writer's experience can be set aside when writing a novel, but this is impossible. On the other hand, it is not impossible for the narrator to be an unseen presence. Objectivity and impassibility are not moral precepts; they are a narrative technique, and nothing else.

THE ADDED
ELEMENT

Conjunctions and Substitutions

On August 26, 1853, Flaubert writes to Louise: "I am devoured now by a need for metamorphoses. I would like to write everything I see, not just as it is, but transfigured. An exact account of the most magnificent real fact would be impossible for me. I would still need to *embroider* it." The quotation sums up the two movements of novelistic creation, the relations between fiction and reality: (1) the point of departure is real reality ("everything I see"), life in the broadest sense (what I see may well be what I hear, read, dream); (2) but this material is never narrated "exactly"; it is always "transfigured," "embroidered." The novelist adds something to the reality that he has turned into work material, and this *added element*★ constitutes the originality of his work, that which gives autonomy to the fictional reality, that which distinguishes it from the real.

One of the key characteristics of the world of *Madame Bovary* is its materiality, the extraordinary importance that phys-

★ The *added element*, or manipulation of the real, is not gratuitous: it is always an expression of the conflict that is the source of the writer's vocation, a conflict of which he may be scarcely conscious, or indeed totally unaware. The *added element*, naturally, is detected by the reader in terms of his own experience of reality, and since this latter is continually changing, the *added element* also changes, as a function of different readers, places, periods.

ical reality, the inert, has in it. This fact, according to certain critics, can undoubtedly be traced back to the influence on Flaubert of his father, a scientist and an unbeliever won over to the new ideas of scientific experiment and the positivist philosophy of the day; and to Gustave's childhood and adolescence spent in the Hôtel-Dieu amid sick people and cadavers. In any event, despite his scorn for materialist philosophers, Flaubert often maintained that to him the physical was more important than "the moral." "I for my part hold that the physical outweighs the moral. No disillusionment causes one as much suffering as a decayed tooth, and no idiotic remark grates on my nerves as much as a squeaky door, and that is why a phrase set down with the best intention fails to come off once it turns out to have an assonance or a grammatical quirk in it" (letter to Louise, February 19, 1854). Every novelist re-creates the world in his image and likeness, corrects reality at the prompting of his demons; in the fictional reality, Flaubert's subjective materialism is an objective fact.

The instrument whereby the *transfiguration* is wrought is style. In *Madame Bovary* there is admittedly a sort of descriptive frenzy; in its greed language wallows all around, roots about everywhere, and fastens on anything and everything so as to bare reality in all its complexity, relief, detail. Universal, cannibalistic, it knocks down barriers and tirelessly describes objects, persons, landscapes, feelings, actions, thoughts, even other words, as in the chapter at the opera in Rouen in which the narrator describes (something that is not the same as reproducing) the words of the arias of *Lucia di Lammermoor* as they are sung onstage. This descriptive frenzy is not an end in itself but a procedure the narrator uses to destroy reality and re-create it as a different reality. The verbal substance that swallows up innumerable real facts does something more insidious than enumerating the properties of men and things; the intent behind it is to render all these heterogeneous ingredients that have been wrested from life homogeneous by endowing them with properties that are its own—those of language itself, formal properties. The materiality of the fictional world is the result of an adulteration, perpetrated by language, of objects, persons, sentiments, actions, thoughts, and even words. In the fictional reality the boundaries separating them fall; applied with a particular bias to men and things, the descriptive system of the novel produces that marvelous inversion whereby in Emma Bovary's world, contrary to what is the case in the reader's world, emotions and ideas appear to have corporeality, color, taste; and objects seem to possess a mysterious intimacy, a mind. Though no great novel can be called realistic without more or less misconstruing the term (for either all novels may be so termed, since they are all nurtured by real facts, or else no novel is realistic, since even the most mediocre of them transfigure their material to at least a minimum degree in order to turn it into fiction), it is nonetheless surprising that for more than a century *Madame Bovary*, a novel in which mind becomes matter and matter mind, has been taken as an example of realism, in the sense of a pure literary duplication of the real.

Things Humanized

Why is it that certain objects of the fictional reality linger in one's memory as clearly, as suggestively, as real persons in the flesh? Because they have been uprooted from the dead world of the inert and raised to a higher dignity, endowed with unsuspected qualities, such as, for example, a hidden psychology, an ability to communicate messages and awaken emotions, which, despite their immobile, rocklike, blind, mute bodies, make them beings possessed of profound animation, a secret life. From the opening pages of the novel, one of these humanized objects, Charles Bovary's cap, establishes, thanks to a memorable description, a distinctive characteristic of the fictional reality: the ability of certain things to compel recognition of themselves, through their color, their richness of shading, their power to convey information and to symbolize, as beings that are as complex, mysterious, enduring, and palpable as their owners: "It was a headgear of composite order, with recognizable elements of a busby, a cavalry schapska, a bowler, a sealskin cap, and a nightcap, one of those wretched things, in short, whose mute ugliness hints at unplumbed depths of expression, like the face of an idiot. Ovoid and stiffened with whalebone, it started at the bottom with three circular pads; there then followed alternating lozenges of velvet and of rabbit fur, separated by a red band; next came a kind of sac terminating in a cardboard-lined polygon covered with intricate braid embroidery; hanging from it, at the end of a long, excessively thin cord, was a little crosslet of gold wire, by way of a tassel. The cap was new; its peak was shiny." This, then, is what is meant by the famous Flaubertian "coldness" for which the book was condemned by the critics when it appeared. The novel ran completely counter to traditional narrative practices, which called for the narrator to assume one attitude when describing things and a quite different one when describing human beings. In *Madame Bovary* the narrator pays things the same close, respectful attention usually reserved for persons, and assigns them functions that had always been prerogatives of characters and were unthinkable on the part of objects whose sole duty, before Flaubert, was to constitute a decor, a background, a setting within which man, that absolute monarch, master of the domain of action, intelligence, and sentiment, monopolized all the adventures of the soul and the body. Thanks to the description of them, certain things in *Madame Bovary*, Charles's *casquette* for instance, are more eloquent and of more transcendent importance than their owners, and are more revealing of the person who possesses them than are that person's own words and acts: his/her social and economic status, manners and morals, aspirations, imagination, artistic sensibilities, beliefs. The *casquette* is humanized not only because it is capable of conveying a considerable amount of information, because it speaks, but also because, owing to certain adjectives ("*wretched* thing," "*mute* ugliness") and comparisons ("depths of expression like the face of an idiot"), it has taken on an idiosyncratic particularity, is capable of suffering human misfortunes, and hence merits, to the same degree as any hominid, our commiseration, our affection, our solidarity. The description of the *casquette* is minutely detailed, scientific, objective, but it is not cold: there is a secret tenderness in this desire to specify its hybrid nature, a discreet love in the perfection with which it is re-created through the medium of words. This object, so banal in real reality, so prodigiously transfigured by the power of language, is the demonstration of a truth that Flaubert discovered at the age of twenty-four and hastened to pass on to his friend Le Poittevin: "In order for a thing to be interesting, one has only to look at it for a long time."★

But in *Madame Bovary* the object not only displays individual human characteristics; at certain moments it stands in the stead of the human person as a social being whose nature cannot be determined apart from its situation, that is to say, in terms of the place it occupies and the functions it fulfills within a community of its fellows. Objects thus constitute a parallel society: they reflect classes and interests, levels of wealth, the degree of refinement of groups and families. In one of the "craters" of the book, Emma's wedding, the narrator, who is describing the odd lot that the guests represent, suddenly abandons the men and women arriving at Les Bertaux to concentrate instead on their dress, a rich and diverse assortment, yet structured along solid hierarchical lines reproducing those of the human social order: "Depending on their position in society, they were wearing tailcoats, frock coats, long jackets, short

★ Undated letter, September 1845, *Correspondance*, Vol. I, p. 192.

ones—good clothes, prized family possessions, taken out of the wardrobe chest only for solemn occasions: frock coats with flaring skirts billowing in the wind, round collars, pockets as big as sacks; heavy wool jackets, most often worn with a cap of some sort, its bill edged with brass; the short jackets very short indeed, with two buttons at the back set close together like a pair of eyes, and lopped-off tails that gave them the appearance of having been hacked out of a single block, by a stroke of some carpenter's ax. Others still (but these, naturally, would be dining at the very end of the table) were wearing dress smocks, that is to say, ones with collars turned down over the shoulders, fine pleats in back, and gathered in below the waist by a low stitched belt." The human suffuses things and things the human, the boundaries between inanimate and animate disappear, and within the fraternity between objects and their owners, the narrator uses them interchangeably to describe each other. In this way, he not only alters real reality, in which this confusion is impossible, but at the same time realizes in the part—situation, episode, chapter—the aim of the novelistic whole: totalization, the will to construct a reality as vast as the real one. By describing human beings as objects and objects as human beings, the narrator turns two independent, and in a certain sense antagonistic, orders of reality into a single one. As with the apparel of the wedding guests, there is a shift from owners to things in the description of the letters that Rodolphe has received in the course of his career as a seducer: "As he rummaged about among his souvenirs, his attention lingered on the differences in handwriting and style in the letters, as varied as their spelling. Some were affectionate, others lighthearted, facetious, melancholy; some begged for love and others for money."

The narrator's egalitarian attitude toward human beings and things becomes most pronounced in the episode of the fiacre, when Emma gives herself for the first time to Léon in a hackney cab that plies endlessly back and forth with lowered window blinds through the streets of Rouen. Here the confusion of orders becomes extraordinarily useful. This substitution of the fiacre for the couple as the focus of the attention of the narrator, who obstinately, obsessively, limits himself to describing the aimless wanderings of the fiacre through the streets and squares and crossways of the town, never casting so much as a glance at what is happening inside, has the virtue of transforming that absence—action replaced in the description by its setting—into an ardent presence: what is happening inside the fiacre is enhanced by the draperies in which the reader's inflamed imagination cloaks the invisible interior. The replacement of the couple by the object is believable; it does not give the impression of being merely a clever sleight-of-hand trick, because it occurs within a context in which we have gradually become accustomed to such situations. The exchange of properties is quite evident in this episode. From the beginning the fiacre is described as an entity possessed of a will and a movement of its own: "And the ponderous machine started up." For three pages the reader has the impression that it is the cab, not the cabman, who is taking the initiative: "The cab started off again . . . came out the gates . . . proceeded at a gentle trot . . . went along the river . . . leapt forward . . . wandered aimlessly about . . ." The cabman, perspiring, looks longingly toward the bars, grows desperately bored, and seems to be at a loss as to what is going on, not so much driving as driven, as the coach, despite its *"lourdeur,"* its ponderousness, proves both willing and bold. In its massive armature we glimpse a spark of intelligence such as is never kindled in the poor cabman, who has not the least idea what is behind his passengers' strange caprice; it is as though the fiacre, on the other hand, understands, and obligingly, cleverly, connives with the lovers.

Charles's telltale *casquette*, the attire of the wedding guests, the erotic coach: a mere sample of the vast collection of dissimilar objects that as a function of the way in which they are described take on unsuspected new potentialities, interact with men on an equal footing, or relegate them to the background as the protagonists of a given episode. Letters, seals, garments, items of furniture, personal adornments, books, coaches, vials, dwellings, statues, stones, towns, cities: at times merely hastily mentioned in passing, at other times described at length in minute detail, their presence in the fictional reality is never negligible or fortuitous, invariably demanding of the reader a minimum of consideration, if not of appreciation, since along with an aesthetic value, language has invested these objects with a sort of human dignity.

Human Beings Turned into Things

This raising of the object to the realm of the human has been made possible only because of a simultaneous operation that lowers the human to the status of the object: in order for them to fraternize, both have been obliged to journey the same distance. As things in *Madame Bovary* are spiritualized and take on life, the materiality of human beings is accentuated, and often the description, by being restricted to their outward aspect, transforms these latter into no more than a physical form, a silent and motionless presence, things. But mere carnal presence and the veiling of any sign of inward life do not suffice; the reduction of human beings to things is above all the result of a complementary procedure, which consists of dismembering the character and describing only one or several parts of him while omitting others; these detached parts—mostly faces or heads, but also hands or trunks—severed from human anatomy by the narrator's descriptive surgery and exposed as units of predominant or exclusive physical value, cease to live, turn into inanimate, almost inert, beings. The guests at Emma's wedding, for instance, are a gallery of ears and skin: "Every man was newly shorn, ears stood out from heads, faces were closely scraped; some of the ones who had had to get up before dawn and shave in the dark even had slanting gashes under their noses or, along their jawlines, patches of raw skin, big as three-franc pieces, inflamed by the wind during the journey, so that many a big, beaming, white face was marbled with red blotches." Severed from trunks and limbs, these faces have also lost another attribute: their individuality; they are as identical and inter-changeable as mass-produced consumer items. This is another of the means employed by the narrator to give the inhabitants of the fictional reality the appearance of things: describing them as wholes in which what is particular and individual disappears, leaving only the general and the common, with the result that they take on a uniform, identical character, a nature that makes each of them indistinguishable from any other—as is typical of the products of industry, the mechanical reproduction of an archetypical matrix. That is the reason why the reification of the human is particularly evident in the episodes describing group gatherings: the wedding, the ball at La Vaubyessard, the agricultural fair, the performance at the Rouen opera, Emma's funeral. On these occasions, by virtue of the astute egalitarian language employed by the narrator, the inanimate and the an-imate approximate each other so closely as to be nearly indis-tinguishable. In the ball scene, objects and the amputated mem-bers of their owners are caught up in a round dance in which fans and faces, hands and gloves, flowers and coiffures whirl past one by one like so many different forms of a single, in-divisible substance: "Along the line of seated women the painted fans fluttered, bouquets half hid the smiles on faces, and the gold-stopped scent bottles turned in cupped hands whose tight white silk gloves marked the shape of the nails and bound the flesh at the wrist. A froth of lace, diamond brooches, gold medallion bracelets trembled at décolleté necklines, flashed at throats, whispered on bare arms. Hair, in smooth sweeps at the forehead and knotted at the nape of the neck, had garlands, clusters, sprigs of forget-me-not, jasmine, pomegranate blossoms, wheat sprays, or cornflowers tucked in it. Matrons with scowling faces, wearing red turbans, sat imperturbably in their places." The two orders interchange properties: whereas the fans *flutter*, the bouquets of flowers *hide* smiles, the scent bottles *turn* in hands, the gloves *mark* the shape of nails, the adornments *tremble*, *flash*, *whisper*—dynamic, active verbs—the hands, bosoms, wrists, nails, hair of the women remain immobile and passive, allowing this to be done to them by restless, nervous things, under the vigilance of those granite statues, the mothers, the entire truth about whom would appear to be summed up in the fact that they are wearing red turbans. We see here in a few lines that inversion of the terms of reality which is one of the principal keys to the added element in *Madame Bovary*.★

As the outer setting comes to life, the inner aspect of feelings becomes visible, takes on substance. Once Léon leaves Yonville, Emma becomes deeply depressed; she immerses herself in the memory of the young man, associating it with everything that happens and trying to revive it by means of the new experiences she has. But this love declines as time passes and finally dies altogether. All this is expressed in the novel by way of a metaphor, the longest in the book and doubtless one of the lengthiest in literature. The memory of Léon in Emma's mind is compared to a campfire left burning on a Russian steppe, and the permanence of this memory, the avidity with which Emma hoards it and brings it back to life, despite which it languishes and dies, is the description of this fire whose flames are fed with new materials until finally it goes out—"either because the sup-

★ According to Sartre, the theme of man's "becoming a thing" fascinated Flaubert all his life, as is evident from the autopsied corpses (bodies turned into things by death and the scalpel) that appear in his writings. Marguerite, a character in a story written in his adolescence, ends up on the dissection table, and in this novel Charles Bovary is autopsied (*op. cit.*, Vol. II, p. 1867).

ply of herself gave out or because so much was piled on it that it was smothered." The image (twenty-three lines in the Garnier edition) is so complex and meticulous that to a certain extent it constitutes a series of metaphors, an allegory. This material reality—the campfire that flares, burns steadily, revives, dies down, and goes out—the function of which should be to explain the spiritual reality of which it is the symbol, ends up instead by absorbing it. Initially a reference, the campfire comes to be what is referred to; the explanation becomes what is explained. A change typical of the fictional reality occurs, in which, just as people's garments take on life, love literally catches fire, crackles, dances in red and yellow and blue flames, devours tree trunks and dry leaves, and then, little by little, turns into gray ashes. Another example of the crystallization of feeling into a visible landscape is the description of Emma's inward emotions after she has given herself to Rodolphe as a vista of majestic peaks and gorges spread out beneath the azure sky. "She was entering a marvelous realm where all would be passion, ecstasy, rapture: an immense blue expanse surrounded her, the heights of feeling gleamed as her thought soared above them, everyday life was so distant it could scarcely be seen, lying far below, in the dark valleys between those peaks." This is something more than a comparison intended to make an idea more precise: Emma's feelings *are* these magnificent mountain crests that challenge heaven; ordinary life *is* this earthbound orography humbled by those heights.

Money and Love

At a certain moment in the story the narrator, describing Léon's feelings for Emma, tells us that the notary's clerk "admired the loftiness of her soul and the lace trimmings of her skirt." This is not intended as a criticism of the young man; it does not mean that he is a callous bounder unable to appreciate the difference between a woman's soul and her skirts: in the fictitious reality there is no essential difference between the two. The spirit and objects belong to one and the same category—that which exists—and there is no reason why they should not awaken similar feelings. In much the same way, we are told that Charles's first wife, Héloïse, was in the habit of asking him for "another tonic for her health and a little more love." Placed on an equal footing, men and things complement each other; the latter are inseparable, for example, from states of mind such as enthusiasm or boredom. As for love, objects not only serve to decorate the scene of a romantic affair but, in the case of the heroine, erotic passion is inextricably bound up with a passion to possess, with a drive to own more and more things. In the novel there is thus an intimate relationship between love and money (the symbol of things), and during Emma and Léon's romance in particular, the two never speak of the one subject without speaking of the other.

In her early days in Yonville, Emma falls in love with the young man but takes pains to conceal the fact; this repressed love is as great a torment as her unsatisfied longing to be rich, and the narrator makes it clear that both frustrations converge to form a single source of suffering: "Then the appetites of the flesh, the cravings for money, and the melancholies of passion all merged into a single torment." Later, love and money will be so commingled as to bring her one and the same pleasure. Emma's first journey to Rouen to spend three days with her new lover (Part Three, Chapter III) also has as its object a visit to a notary to have him draw up the power of attorney that will give her the right to manage all of Charles's assets. The reader might think that this money matter is a mere pretext, something secondary that Emma forgets during those three days of passion; but at the end of the chapter we learn—a fact veiled in hyperbaton—that between embraces Emma has repeatedly mentioned the power of attorney to her lover, for after she has left, as Léon walks through the streets of Rouen he ponders the question: "Why the devil is she so set on getting that power of attorney?" This collusion of the erotic and the monetary spans the period of their affair; the one thing infiltrates the other until the two form one irreducible entity. Shortly thereafter Léon, head over heels in love and impatient, comes to Yonville and the lovers are able to spend a few moments alone in the little lane behind the Bovarys' house. They bid each other a tender farewell and Emma promises to try to find a way to steal off regularly to Rouen. The narrator adds: "She had, moreover, every hope for what the future would bring." And in fact, Emma begins to buy things, redecorates the house, spends money recklessly: "She bought for her bedroom a pair of yellow curtains with bold stripes that Monsieur Lheureux had assured her were a great bargain; she dreamed of a rug . . ." Love and money sustain each other, excite each other. When Emma is in love, she needs to surround herself with beautiful objects, to embellish the physical world, to create a setting for herself as lavish as her sentiments. She is a woman whose enjoyment is not complete unless it takes on material form: she projects her body's pleasure into things, and things in their turn augment and prolong her body's pleasure. In the following chapter, in which the passion of the two lovers reaches its climax, Emma's satisfied sexual appetites awaken in her parallel appetites for extravagant luxuries; for her journeys from Yonville to Rouen, she would like nothing better than to have "a blue tilbury, drawn by an English horse and driven by a groom in boots with turned-down cuffs." It is this greed for material possessions that will hasten her fall; as her love affair with Léon grows both more daring and more refined, the debts she owes Lheureux, the dry-goods merchant, mount, and he tempts her covetous fancies and satisfies them with so masterful a hand that in the end he ruins her.

Emma's passionate desire to possess objects is closely related not only to her love affairs but to her disillusionments and her boredom as well. This latter is a more subtle, less prominent relationship, yet in certain periods of her life it is quite evident. A hundred years before her flesh-and-blood sisters and brothers, Emma Bovary, in a little Norman town, tries to compensate for a fundamental emptiness in her life by acquiring objects, by looking to commercial products for the help that her fellow humans fail to give her. In *Madame Bovary* we see the first signs of the alienation that a century later will take hold of men and women in industrial societies (the women above all, owing to the life they are obliged to live): consumption as an outlet for anxiety, the attempt to people with objects the emptiness that modern life has made a permanent feature of the existence of the individual. Emma's drama is the gap between illusion and reality, the distance between desire and its fulfillment. On two occasions she is persuaded that adultery can give her the splendid life that her imagination strains toward, and both times she is left feeling bitterly disappointed. Her idea of love is shattered by both "the defilements of marriage and the disillusionment of adultery." Even during the days when her romance with Léon is in full flower and no shadow threatens, Emma discovers on each of her visits to Rouen that reality falls forever short of dreams: "She continually promised herself profound happiness, on her next visit; and then admitted to herself that she had felt nothing extraordinary. This disappointment was soon effaced by a new hope, and Emma returned to him more ardent, more avid than ever." Emma is cast into despair by this sabotage whereby her mind continually destroys her happiness. She asks herself: Where, then, did this lack of satisfaction in life, this instantaneous decay of things she was counting on, come from? The answer is: from her imagination, which continually impels her to desire things that are beyond things. This abyss between desire and reality perhaps explains Emma's vocation to possess, her appetite for objects. If in the beginning it seems to be a means—of beautifying her surroundings, of dispelling in some small measure the tedium of her days—it later becomes an end, a buying for the sake of buying, spending for the sake of spending. Fulfilling the same function as modern advertising, Lheureux is the orchestrator of this process, cleverly orienting Emma's vague longings in the direction of his shop. The case of Emma Bovary is a presage of that extraordinary phenomenon of the modern world whereby things, once the servants and instruments of mankind, become its masters and destroyers.

Madame Bovary, a Man

But in the fictitious reality it is not only things that become human and humans things. There is another, equally subtle inversion of substances: certain men and women change sex. Emma is a basically ambiguous character, in whom contrary sentiments and appetites coexist—at one point the narrator says that in her "one could no longer distinguish selfishness from charity, or corruption from virtue"—and this fundamental trait, which at the time of the book's appearance seemed absurd to critics accustomed to the Manichaean distribution of vices and virtues among separate and distinct characters, seems to us today to be the best proof of her humanity. But her lack of precise definition is not only moral and psychological; it also applies to her sex, for beneath the exquisite femininity of this young woman a strong-willed, determined male lies hidden.

Emma's tragedy is that she is not free. She sees her slavery as not only a product of her social class—the petty bourgeoisie as mediatized by certain modes of life and prejudices—and of her provincial milieu—a tiny world where the possibilities of accomplishing anything of note are few—but also, and perhaps most importantly, as a consequence of her being a woman. In the fictional reality, to be a woman is to be tied down, to find doors closed, to be condemned to more mediocre choices than those open to a man. During the amorous exchange with Rodolphe that has the agricultural fair as its background, when the seducer speaks of the class of beings to which he belongs, to whom dreams and action, pure passions and furious pleasures, are indispensable, Emma stares at him as though he were someone who had traveled through "exotic lands," and answers bitterly, in the name of her sex: "We poor women don't even have that distraction!" This is true: in the fictional reality not only are amorous escapades forbidden the woman; dreaming as well appears to be a masculine privilege, since those who seek to escape by way of the imagination, by reading novels, for example, as Madame Bovary does, are looked down upon, are considered to be *"évaporées,"* females who are featherbrained and flighty. Emma is well aware of the inferior status in which women find themselves in the fictional society—a typical "male-chauvinist phallocracy," as it would be called in today's feminist vocabulary—as becomes even more evident when she finds herself pregnant. She ardently hopes the baby will be a boy, "and this idea of having a male child was like the potential revenge of all her past frustrations." Immediately thereafter, using the *style indirect libre* with its elusive transitions, the narrator sets down the following reflection, undoubtedly Emma's, describing the sexual discrimination of the day: "A man is free, at least; free to range passions and the world, surmount obstacles, taste the most exotic fruits of pleasure. Whereas a woman is constantly thwarted. At once inert and compliant, she has both the weaknesses of the flesh and legal subjection to contend with. Her will, like the veil tied to her hat, quivers with every breath of wind; there is always a desire that leads her on, a rule of decorum that holds her back." Being a woman—above all, if one has imagination and a restless temperament—is a real curse in the fictitious reality: it is not surprising that on learning that she has given birth to a daughter, Emma, her hope deceived, faints dead away.

But Emma is too rebellious and active to content herself with dreaming of a vicarious "revenge," by way of a possible male child, for the powerlessness to which her sex condemns her. Instinctively, gropingly, she combats this feminine inferiority in a way that anticipates certain forms chosen a century later by a number of women fighting for the emancipation of their sisters: by assuming attitudes and dress traditionally considered masculine. A tragic feminist—because her battle is an individual one, more intuitive than logical, a contradictory one since it in fact seeks what it rejects, and one doomed to failure— deep in her heart of hearts Emma would like to be a man. It is thus more than by chance that in her visits to the château de La Huchette, her lover's home, she plays at being a man—"she combed her hair with his comb and looked at herself in his shaving mirror"—and (in a gesture of frustration that a psychoanalyst would label a characteristic sign of penis envy) even falls into the habit of clenching between her teeth "the stem of a large pipe" of Rodolphe's. Nor are these the only occasions on which Emma acts in ways that transparently reveal the unconscious wish to be a man. Her biography abounds in details that make this attitude a constant from her adolescence to her death. One of them is her manner of dress. Emma often adds a masculine touch to her attire, and takes to wearing men's clothes; what is more, the men in her life find this attractive. When Charles meets her for the first time, at Les Bertaux, he observes that "a pince-nez framed in tortoise shell, like a man's, was tucked between two buttons of her bodice." On her first horseback ride with Rodolphe, that is to say, on the day that her liberation from the bonds of matrimony begins, Emma is symbolically wearing "a man's hat." As her affair with Rodolphe goes on and she becomes more daring and imprudent, these outward signs of her identification with the virile begin to be more and more noticeable: as though to "shock everyone," the narrator says, Emma goes about with a cigar in her mouth, and one day we see her step out of the Hirondelle "wearing a tight-fitting vest, like a man's": this masculine attire strikes the villagers as being so outlandish that those who had given her the benefit of the doubt as to her infidelity "doubted no more."

This propensity of Emma's for going beyond the limits of the second sex and invading the territory of the first betrays itself, naturally, in ways less evident than her style of dress. It is implicit in her dominating nature, in the swiftness with which, the moment she notices any sign of weakness on the part of the male, she immediately takes over from him and forces him to assume female attitudes. In her relations with Léon, for example, their respective roles change very soon, and it is always she who takes the initiative: it is she who goes to Rouen to see him, rather than vice versa; it is she who asks him to dress in a certain way so as to please her, she who advises him to buy new curtains for his rooms, she who more or less orders him to write poems to her. Because Léon is tightfisted and has inhibitions about indulging himself, Emma ends up sharing the expenses of the hotel where they make love. Léon is the passive element, she the active one, as the narrator points out: "he never disputed any of her ideas; he went along with all her tastes; *he was becoming her mistress, more than she was his.*" But precisely because Léon plays the feminine role that his energetic mistress forces upon him, Emma feels frustrated and is contemptuous of him, *because in her eyes he behaves like a woman*; her identification with the male mentality is thus total. The day comes when Léon stands her up because he can't manage to shake Homais; the thought then crosses her mind that the notary's clerk is "incapable of heroism, weak, common, *more spineless than a woman*, and a penny-pincher and a coward besides."*
Emma is forever doomed to frustration: as a woman, because the woman in the fictional reality is a subjugated being to whom

---

* All italics in these quotations mine. (M.V.L.)

the world of dreams and passion is forbidden; as a man, because she can reach that world only by turning her lover into a nonentity, incapable of arousing in her an admiration and a respect for the so-called *virile* virtues, which she has failed to find in her husband and seeks in vain in her lovers. This is one of the insoluble contradictions that make Emma a pathetic character. Heroism, daring, prodigality, freedom are, apparently, masculine prerogatives; yet Emma discovers that the males in her life—Charles, Léon, Rodolphe—become weaklings, cowards, mediocrities, and slaves the moment she assumes a "masculine" attitude (the only one that allows her to break the bonds of slavery to which those of her sex are condemned in the fictional reality). Thus there is no solution. Her horror at having borne a daughter, so bitterly criticized by the self-righteous, is the horror of having brought a feminine being into a world in which life for a woman (one like herself at least) is simply impossible.

In her marital relations too, the male-female roles are very soon reversed; Emma becomes the dominant personality and Charles the dominated. She sets the tone, everything is always done her way, at first only about the house, but later in other domains as well: Emma takes over the task of making out the patients' bills, obtains a power of attorney that will enable her to make all the decisions, and gradually becomes the lord and master in the family. She obtains this status with little difficulty, for all it takes to turn her weak-willed husband into a tool is a little guile or a bit of wheedling; but if necessary she does not hesitate to use forceful means, as when she backs her husband into a corner by demanding that he choose between her and her mother-in-law. Emma's hold over Charles does not end with her death, for it grows even stronger following her suicide. The first thing Charles does after she has breathed her last is to decide to have a splendid, romantic funeral, as would suit her tastes. Later on, he contracts her spendthrift habits, her fancy notions, thus bringing on his ruin, exactly as Emma has brought catastrophe upon herself. The narrator sums up this situation in a moving image: "She was corrupting him from beyond the grave."★

Moreover, in the fictitious reality Emma's case is not unique; there are two other women who assume masculine roles without feeling as frustrated as Madame Bovary by so doing. In both instances the women are matriarchs who take over the man's role in the marriage because of the husband's weakness. Charles Bovary's mother becomes the head of the household when the couple meets financial ruin, and in like manner Charles's first wife, the narrator tells us, "was the master" from the moment the couple married. There is a difference, naturally. These matriarchs are not feminists in the usual sense of the word; their reversal of the roles is in no way a sign of rebellion; on the contrary, it implies resignation. They take over the role of the man because there is nothing else they can do, given the fact that their husbands have rejected it and someone in the household must make decisions. In Emma's case, masculinity is not only a function she assumes in order to fill a place left empty but also a striving for freedom, a way of fighting against the miseries of the feminine condition.

A Binary World

The fictitious reality also has as a distinctive sign a mysterious ordering based on the number two. It is organized by pairs:

★ The only one who saw, with his usual critical acumen, that one of Emma's greatest charms was the mixture in her personality of masculine and feminine traits was Baudelaire. In his review of the novel he wrote that Flaubert "was unable to keep from infusing virile blood into the veins of his creature, and Madame Bovary, in the most energetic and ambitious elements of her character, as in her strong capacity for dreaming, remained a man. Like Pallas, sprung forth fully armed from the brain of Zeus, this strange androgyne harbored all the seductive charms of a man's soul in a most attractive woman's body." The review appeared in the October 18, 1857, issue of *L'Artiste* and was later reprinted in Baudelaire's *L'Art romantique*.

everything that exists gives the impression of being one and its double, and life and things a disturbing repetition of each other. In this binary world, one is two, that is to say, everything is itself and its replica, at times identical, at times deformed; almost nothing exists for itself alone, since almost everything is duplicated in something that confirms and denies it. This symmetry may be traced in characters and in actions, in places and in objects. The fictitious reality, unlike the real one, does not give the impression of increasing and multiplying freely, chaotically, but, rather, of doing so within the framework of an inflexible overall plan, obeying an immanent law or universal virtuality which no one and nothing can escape, which has replaced individuality by duality as the basic unit of life. The animate and the inanimate are subject to the fateful dynamics of the formation of pairs, thereby constituting a system of relations that has no rational explanation: in this sense the fictitious reality is not historical but magical.

The clash of objective and subjective reality is a dramatic constant in Emma's story. Emma does not differentiate between them; she can live reality only in an illusory way or, rather, she *lives* the illusion, tries to give it concrete form. In the novel, illusion and reality are opposite versions of one and the same thing, two inseparable sisters, the one beautiful, the other ugly. Reality reveals its sordid aspect by contrast with the embellished image of it traced—with the aid of romantic novels—by Emma's imagination, and in strict parallel, this subjective reality reveals its color, loftiness, and richness (its illusory nature: its impossibility) when it is set against its gray and wretched objective version. Each, thus, is essential to the other and both are indispensable for the constitution of the fictional reality, which results from this dialectic between the "real" and "ideal" faces of life. On March 21, 1852, Flaubert writes to Louise Colet: "The entire value of my book, if it has any, will lie in my having been able to walk straight across a hair suspended above the double abyss of the lyrical and the vulgar (which I want to fuse in a narrative analysis)." To have succeeded in doing so is not everything, but it is nonetheless one of the merits of the novel that it is in fact built on pairs of opposites, each member of which is the intimate and necessary complement of the other of the pair and yet retains its own specificity, thus giving the fictitious world a nature all its own. It is also in this conjunction of contraries—illusion and reality or, as Flaubert puts it, the "lyrical" and the "vulgar"—that *Madame Bovary* fulfills, in its own way, the aim of the novel to embrace totality: in the fictitious reality it is not only that which exists that shapes life; the nonexistent also contributes its share. One of the most oft-repeated commonplaces concerning *Madame Bovary* is the statement that this novel did away with romanticism with one stroke and inaugurated the realist movement. It would be closer to the truth to speak of a romanticism brought to completion rather than of a romanticism denied. The romantics described the subjective version of the real, by exclusive choice (Lamartine, Chateaubriand) or as a matter of preference (Hugo), substituting illusion for reality. In *Madame Bovary*, Flaubert extended this truncated reality, adding to it the half that had been abolished by the romantic imagination (without, however, suppressing romantic illusion, as Zola, Huysmans, Daudet were later to do). In the novel the components of romantic love all make their appearance: sentimental outpourings, tragic fate, the rhetoric of inflamed passion. If separated from its context, the amorous duo between Emma and Léon that goes to make up almost the whole of the first chapter of Part Three seems to be prototypical of a romantic novel. The context, however, reveals what a great proportion of unreality the two lovers' fine phrases contain: the conscious or unconscious lies they tell each other, the traps and self-deceptions of which they are the victims, the distance separating their words and the facts. The space that the narrator sets between reality and illusion is not meant to be taken as an absolute condemnation of the one by the other: the scene is not a farce. These delicate mistruths that the two lovers put forward are always moving, because they reveal their thirst for some absolute, for sensual fulfillment, for beauty—the necessity of illusion, and their effort to bridge, with words, the abyss between their ideals and their true condition.

The system of dualities around which the fictitious reality is organized is not built upon what dialectics calls the identity of contraries, but, rather, on their reciprocity: they are not eventually united in a superior synthesis but instead coexist as different elements, which nonetheless attain full reality only as a function of each other. While Flaubert was writing *Madame Bovary*, he gave Louise Colet his *Notes de voyage* describing his travels in the Orient, and Louise was shocked by his description of Kuchuk Hanem, the celebrated Egyptian prostitute with whom Gustave had spent a single, albeit intense, night of love. Louise was of the opinion that the courtesan was demeaned by the portrait, which included a description not only of her cosmetic refinements but also of her bedbugs. Flaubert's reply reads as follows: "You tell me that Kuchuk Hanem's bedbugs degrade her in your eyes; for me, they are what lent her incomparable charm. Their nauseating odor mingled with the scent of her skin, dripping with sandalwood oil. I want there to be a bitter bite to everything, an eternal jeer in the midst of our triumphs, and desolation at the heart of our enthusiasm. That reminds me of Jaffa, where, as I entered the city, I breathed in at one and the same time the fragrance of the lemon trees and the stink of corpses; the cemetery, fallen into ruin, revealed to the eye half-rotted skeletons, while the green trees dangled their golden fruits. Don't you appreciate how complete this poetry is, how it represents the great synthesis? All the appetites of the imagination and of the mind are satisfied at once; it leaves no trace behind" (letter of March 27, 1853). The formula that Flaubert employs ("the great synthesis") suggests an intimate commingling. The nauseating odor excites him because it is mingled with the fragrance of sandalwood, and this perfume in turn because it contrasts with the other, while neither of the two loses its identity in an intermediate, hybrid blend; it is by grating against each other as they cohabit on the prostitute's body that these two dissonant presences define each other, and it is this relationship of antagonistic fraternity, of jarring proximity (like that of the scents of lemons and of decaying human flesh in Jaffa) that fascinates Flaubert. As his memories of the courtesan of the Nile and of the cemetery in Palestine prove, such dualities are possible in real reality. In the fictitious reality they will be *necessary*. In real life they may manifest themselves; in the fiction, things, persons, and events will give the impression of manifesting themselves *only* through dualities, in the form of contrast, as in these cases, or in the form of resemblances. The quotation is of further interest, because in it we see Flaubert catching a glimpse of how the association of opposites can lead him to realize his aim of embracing everything: it will enable him to satisfy *all* the appetites both of the imagination and of thought, to reject *nothing*. In the fictitious reality, in like manner, this ambition finds expression in the binary system: each object, event, or person, being at once itself and its contrary, a totalization equivalent to what the whole aspires to represent manifests itself, synthetically, in each and every part of the narrative. Flaubert's drive to embrace the whole of reality did not originate with *Madame Bovary*. Five years before beginning the novel, he wrote Louise: "Beneath beautiful appearances I for my part search out ugly depths; and beneath ignoble surfaces I try to discover mines of devotion and virtue. It's a relatively harmless mania, which makes you see something new in a place where no one would ever suspect it exists" (letter of September 5, 1846). Besides enhancing the possibility of discovering something new, this approach to what is human prevents the overly schematic distribution of virtues and vices, furthers the realization that one and the same person may at one and the same time be, in different respects, both good and wicked, and leads to a view of life that takes into account its contradictory complexity, its polyvalence.

One of the domains in which the reality/illusion binomial systematically manifests itself in the fictitious world is language. Depending on whether they are actual occurrences or written accounts, the nature of the very same sequence of events changes; the two versions clash. On being committed to writing, reality becomes a lie. In *Madame Bovary* letter writing, journalism, books are agents that make reality less real. If we were to believe only what the novels, the newspapers, or the letters in the book tell us, we would have a false version of the fictitious reality; we would know certain facts, not as they really came about, but as the characters believe—or would like it to be believed— that they came about. In the fictitious reality, to write is always to deceive; writing is the realm of fantasy. Emma's inability to adapt to life can be traced in large part to the books she reads, to the romantic fictions that have shaped in her mind an ideal reality that does not coincide with the real one (this means that these novels falsify life). Hence, sensible people like Charles's mother fear Emma's fondness for novels. They are not wrong. That Emma's dissatisfaction has its roots in books can be clearly seen from the episode that immediately follows the one in which she gives herself to Rodolphe. Madame Bovary thinks she is entering the world of the heroines of fiction; she is certain that illusion is at last on the point of becoming reality: "She remembered then the heroines of the books she had read, and the lyrical legion of those adulteresses began to sing in her memory with sisterly voices that entranced her . . . She herself was becoming, in real life, one of that imaginary company . . ." If Emma had not read all those novels, it is possible that her fate might have been different (as might Don Quixote's had he not read romances of chivalry); perhaps she might have borne her lot with the same oblivious calm and complacency as the other bourgeois matrons of Yonville. The lies of fiction filled her head with appetites, restless yearnings, dreams. Like books, the journalism of the fictitious reality is another great creator of illusions: the difference lies in the fact that the illusions of the novels are beautiful and noble, while those of the journalism in *Madame Bovary* are sordid and base. The press appears as something pretentious and contemptible; Homais's pedantry comes pouring out in the form of an article, full of hyperbole and quotations from the classics, that gives an entirely false impression of the agricultural fair at Yonville. The novel shows the two planes on which this event takes its place in human memory: the historical and the rhetorical; what actually happened and its verbal deformation as perpetrated by the pharmacist. What in fact was a popular fair full of absurdities and tragicomic elements becomes, in words, a supremely refined ceremony, a festival honoring patriotism, progress, and science. Worse still are the lies that *Le Fanal de Rouen* perpetuates when Homais, leaping into action with what the narrator rightly calls "the wicked cunning of his vanity," pens venomous little fillers against the Blind Man of Yonville, whom he detests because he has not been able to cure him. The newspaper is an effective provider of an essential prop for the moral ambiance in which the characters live and move: lies. Thus it is educated people—the people who are best-read—who are the worst liars. Those who tell the truth are generally stupid fools, such as poor Charles Bovary, or simple folk, such as Emma's father. Léon, Rodolphe, Emma, Homais, on the other hand, continually deceive other people and themselves. And when they have recourse to the written word, they surpass themselves in their ability to invent untruths, to turn reality into unreality. A prime example of this is the letter that Rodolphe writes to Emma to break off their affair, on the eve of the day that they have set for running off together. Using the technique of intercutting with the same mastery as in the episode of the agricultural fair, the narrator shows us, in two admirable pages, one of those contradictory dualities typical of the fictitious reality, the falsehood and the truth of a situation. The letter to Emma that Rodolphe is shown writing systematically belies what he is thinking and feeling, and vice versa. His hand pens melancholy, long-suffering, generous phrases describing the sacrifice he is prepared to make in order to keep Emma from making the reckless error of eloping with him. His mind, on the other hand, is occupied by a single thought, freeing himself from a mistress who has become a nuisance. From the clash between his words and his feelings the true personality of Rodolphe suddenly comes to light. In the fictitious reality there is always a divorce between what is experienced and what is written; they form a dichotomy embodying those elements whose conflict is the source of the novel's dramatic power: reality and illusion.

If we analyze the setting in which the story of Emma Bovary takes place, we discover that the locales are arranged symmetrically, by like pairs or diametrical opposites. The life of the Bovarys unfolds in twin towns. What distinguishes Tostes from Yonville? Both tiny Norman villages, each with its one long street lined with houses, its typical local characters, its monotonous life, both surrounded by exactly the same sort of countryside with scattered farmhouses and a network of roads up and down which the *officier de santé* travels endlessly visiting his patients, the one town seems to be the exact replica of the other. When, after Emma's crisis, the Bovarys move from Tostes to Yonville, the name of the setting changes but not its nature: topographically and sociologically it is still precisely the same. But Tostes is only one of the points of reference for Yonville: the other is Rouen. If Tostes is its double, Rouen is its antithesis, the city where life is different and endlessly varied, where Emma finds consolation for having to live in a stifling country town: it is from there that the periodicals and novels that set her to dreaming come; from there that Lheureux brings the luxury items and the clothes with which she tries to fill the emptiness of her life and cloak her anguish; there that balls and theatrical performances are held; there that there is enough space and sufficient numbers of people for her to pass unnoticed and have an illicit love affair. Yonville/Rouen are the two poles between which—beginning with her affair with Léon—Emma's life rebounds, the two focal points of her duplicity. Each of these settings, by virtue of its size and nature, reflects one side of the double life of the heroine. Yonville, the village, is the dullness of marriage, boredom, right thinking, and prejudices, the routine of household tasks and responsibilities, circumspection and the reining in of instinct, the meanspirited totting up of bills and debts. Rouen, the city, with its cathedral and its hotels, its restaurants, public squares, islands, is the heady excitement of adulterous passion, extravagance, untrammeled instinct, revelry, unconventionality, folly. The relationship between Yonville and Rouen is that of communicating vessels: each one reveals its physiognomy by contast with the other. Just as Emma's double life finds its geographical materialization, in a manner of speaking, in the Yonville/Rouen duality, so her two amorous escapades are each connected with a fixed setting. Rodolphe is the château de La Huchette and Léon the Hôtel de Boulogne. The contrasts between the two locales suggest those of the lovers: the château with its cold stones, its lonely corridors, and its elegant alcoves mirrors Rodolphe's refinement, wealth, aristocratic tastes, and calculating spirit; the hotel, a mere stopping-off place and a temporary refuge, Léon's instability, his bourgeois manners and mentality. In the fictitious reality, moreover, there are two châteaux: La Huchette is a modest version of La Vaubyessard. Despite its small size, Yonville, on the other hand, affords itself the luxury of having two identical inns, each with its own billiard room, situated directly across the street from each other, irreconcilable enemies competing for the custom of the limited local clientele: the Lion d'Or, run by the widow Lefrançois, is a replica of the Café Français, run by Tellier. This duplication of physical settings ensures that there will also be two farms: Les Bertaux, where Emma was born and spent her childhood, and the Maison Rolet, on the outskirts of Yonville, where Berthe Bovary is brought up.

The system of paired opposites can also be seen in the city/country opposition that pulses throughout the book; through the workings of the symmetry that rules the novel, descriptions of the rural and the urban are kept in precise balance. Thus the celebrated description of Rouen, as seen through Emma's eyes as the Hirondelle reaches the top of the hill overlooking the city, has its exact counterpart in the description of the countryside at the confines of Normandy, Picardy, and the Ile-de-France, where Yonville is situated, that opens Part Two of the novel. As follows naturally from this evenhanded distribution of description between countryside and city, Emma gives herself for the first time to one of her lovers in each of the two décors: to Rodolphe amid nature, in a scene in which the narrator intertwines the description of the dialogue of the couple with that of the plants, the trees, the flowers, the sky around about them; and to Léon in the streets of a city, following an itinerary that comes close to being a detailed map of the whole of Rouen. The settings of the scenes in which Emma's adulteries take place correspond to the two lovers' social and professional status: Rodolphe, the aristocratic landowner, with tastes that have a hint of the feudal about them, makes love on the grass, alongside a pair of saddle horses, in the open air; Léon, the notary, a product born of the city, of bureaucracy, makes love in the heart of a city.

The pairs Tostes/Yonville, Yonville/Rouen, country/city are the settings in which the action of the novel takes place objectively. But there is another scenic pair, an antithetical one also, which, though it appears only intermittently, is highly significant, for like the dichotomy between what is experienced and what is written, it embodies the basic opposition between reality and illusion that underlies the entire fictitious world. The binomial opposition in question is that between province and capital. Paris does not make its appearance in the novel on an objective plane but on a subjective one: by way of the myths, the fabrications, the exaggerations that echo in the very name of this distant place, inaccessible to provincials. The province is the reality; Paris, the illusion to which, at the beginning of her marriage, Emma transports herself in her imagination with the aid of a map: closing her eyes, she makes her way along ideal boulevards, makes purchases in chimerical shops, hears around about her the rumble of dream carriages rolling over the paving stones, and sees phantasmagorical gas lamps gleaming in the shadows. And Paris is that city which Homais's cliché-ridden imagination turns into an orgy of masked balls, where actresses drink champagne and make love with students, and the latter, the darlings of high society, seduce wealthy ladies of Saint-Germain who sometimes marry them; but for Homais it is also the dangerous territory in which one can be led into evil ways and gulled by clever rascals. For Dr. Canivet, who, unlike Homais, detests progress, Paris is the place the "inventions of the devil" come from. In the fictional reality Paris is not a physical place but a mental one, a creation of provincials into which they project their terrors and their lusts; it is the opposite of the reality within which they live out their lives.

If the pairs of places are primarily antithetical, the pairs of objects of the fictitous reality are most often identical. It is this aspect of the novel that has led to the most detailed commentaries on the workings of the binary system in *Madame Bovary*.*

* See, for instance, Claudine Gothot-Mersch, *La Genèse de "Madame Bovary"* (Paris: José Corti, 1966), p. 266; Durry, p. 180; and in particular Claude Duchet, "*Roman et objets: l'exemple de* Madame Bovary," in *Europe*, September–October–November 1969, pp. 172–201.

But in general Flaubert's critics, unconsciously influenced by their obsessive bias in favor of "verisimilitude," have reproached him for his "mania" for duplication (Duchet's term). The implication is that, since in real reality this systematic duality does not occur, it should not occur in the fictitious reality either. But if the latter were a mere photograph of the former, it would be a work not of creation but of information. It is the *added element*, the reordering of the real, that makes a novelistic world autonomous and allows it to compete with the real world from a critical point of view. The duplication of objects—like that of settings, events, or characters—is a tactic aimed at endowing the fictitious reality with its own qualities so as to free it from its model.

Outside different houses of Yonville, pairs of identical objects appear as emblems or ornaments: "two red and green apothecary jars" in the shop window of Homais the pharmacist, "two cast-iron urns" in the doorway of Guillaumin the notary, "two calico streamers" outside Monsieur Lheureux's dry-goods store, and "two poles" outside the barbershop. The two pairs of erotic slippers that steal into the story are more subtle: the first are a present from Léon to Emma, and the second, also a "love gift," are worn by Guillaumin the notary. A single object may appear twice, in sharply contrasting circumstances: Emma's wedding dress, for instance, a joyous, radiant white touch amid the fields on the day of the marriage procession, symbolizing the illusions of a young girl, serves years later as her shroud at her wake. One object can become two through the effect of covetousness, the "two traveling trunks," for instance, that Lheureux delivers to Emma though she has ordered only one; and one object that is the exact duplicate of another opens and closes an era: on arriving in Tostes as a newlywed, Emma spies the bridal bouquet of Charles's first wife; her last act before leaving Yonville is to burn her own bridal bouquet, yellow with dust, which she has come across in a drawer. Claude Duchet has discovered that in the chapter on the agricultural fair the number two appears eighteen times, as an accompaniment to the love dialogue of the "two lost souls," and that the duplication can be seen even in the decorations of the speaker's stand, "two long lengths of ivy," and in Homais's toast to "industry and the fine arts, those two sisters." The list is endless: on the mantel of the fireplace in the Hôtel de Boulogne are "two of those great pink shells in which the roar of the ocean can be heard"; standing on the dining-room table at Guillaumin the notary's are "two silver dishwarmers," and in his cravat "two diamond stickpins" gleam; Charles Bovary's boots have "two deep creases across the instep" and those of Binet the tax collector, because of his bunions, have "two parallel bulges"; two objects serve to frame Emma as "she remained standing there, her elbows leaning on the windowsill, between two pots of geraniums" or with "her elbow alongside her dinner plate, between the two candles burning down." This constant recurrence of double objects might appear to be a mere happenstance if this duplication were not also a marked characteristic of other domains of the fictitious reality. It is not an accident but a law of fate. In this world everything tends to exist in twos, to come in pairs whose members are either affirmations or negations of each other.

If we proceed from places and things to the narrative itself, we see that here too the magic law of duplication operates: events tend to repeat themselves. Emma has two lovers, Charles two wives, who leave him a widower twice over. Hippolyte is subjected to two operations: the one Bovary performs on him to straighten his clubfoot and the one when gangrene sets in and Canivet is obliged to amputate. There are two scenes depicting Emma being seduced, both identical in structure: in the one, Rodolphe's honeyed words, during the official ceremonies at the agricultural fair, mingle with the rhetorical clichés of the speeches; in the other, in the cathedral of Rouen, Léon's words to Emma are intermingled with the guide's encomium of the beauties and the curiosities of the church. The wedding procession that marks the beginning of the Bovarys' married life has its counterpart in the funeral procession in Yonville that marks the close of the story of the couple. There are two balls: the one at the château of La Vaubyessard, and the masked ball that Emma and Léon attend in Rouen, a sort of plebeian version of the earlier aristocratic evening party. There are two country fêtes, animated, noisy affairs bordering on the grotesque and ending in gargantuan feeds: Emma's wedding and the agricultural fair. Madame Bovary's suicide has a precedent: she feels for the first time like killing herself and is on the point of doing so the day she receives Rodolphe's letter making excuses for not running away with her. And she dies two deaths: the one illusory and the other real. In the first, Emma imagines that she is dying, surrounded by flowers, candelabra, prayers, in a neatly made bed, like the heroine of a romantic novel. The second death, the real one, forms a cruel contrast with this first one: the poison brings on terrible physical suffering and grotesquely distorts her features, as Charles, plunged into the depths of despair, and two other poor devils present at the scene look on. On yet another hand, Emma's poisoning is foreshadowed by an imaginary one, on the day that she comes upon Homais reading the riot act to Justin for having taken a receptacle from the *capharnaüm* for Madame Homais to boil currant jam in; the pharmacist, beside himself with rage, recalls that the receptacle had been sitting next to the arsenic on the shelf, and Madame Homais, horrified, imagines the tragedy that could have ensued: the whole family might have met their death. The Homais children thereupon begin "to scream in anguish, as though they could already feel terrible pains in their bellies": it is Emma who will emit these screams of pain when she actually poisons herself.

The parallel dreams of Emma and Charles constitute a fa-

mous dichotomy of the novel. In them the free-floating imagination of each of the two builds images that reflect the abysmal
differences between their respective ambitions and characters.
As Charles imagines a serene, sedentary, domestic future, in
which happiness is the fruit of the repetition of the same acts,
and of gradual material progress—Berthe will grow up, come
to resemble her mother more and more, become an incomparable housekeeper, wear the same straw hats as Emma, so that
from a distance people will take them for sisters, and eventually
find a good husband who will make her happy—Emma dreams
of a future that means a violent break with her present life,
leaving no place whatsoever for Yonville, for Charles, or for
their daughter. Her fantasy takes her, with her lover, to distant
lands full of picturesque local color, where splendid cities with
white marble cathedrals and soaring bell towers are succeeded
by groves of lemon trees, enchanting fishermen's villages, and
a tropical hut within a grove of palm trees: the landscape and
the climate of this vision are as torrid as passion itself. Each
dream takes on its precise meaning by virtue of the other: the
splendor of Emma's brings out the dullness of Charles's, the
selfishness of hers becomes all the more evident by contrast to
the all-important role that the family plays in his, and so on.
In no other dichotomy of the novel is the symmetrical disposition that characterizes the fictional reality as rigid as here,
where the narrator has devoted a very nearly identical number
of words to each of the two dreams.*

Situations, facts, images, and forms repeat themselves (although the contents differ). The arrival of Dr. Canivet in Yonville to amputate Hippolyte's leg prefigures that of Dr. Larivière
when Emma is dying: in both cases the physician's visit is an
event that arouses the excitement, the admiring curiosity of the
townspeople, and in both instances the doctors give an impres-

---

* Or, at any rate, an identical number of lines: thirty for each in the Garnier edition.

sion of impetuosity, aggressiveness, overweening authority, as though they had come to take possession of the place, rather than to cure a patient. Gestures are repeated: at their last assignation, Emma and Rodolphe remain for a moment with their fingers intertwined; no doubt they have done so many times during their affair, but the narrator specifically states that this gesture is the exact repetition of another, *the one on the first day*: "Like the first day, at the agricultural fair!" Thus their relationship begins and ends with the very same image: two clasped hands. Père Rouault loses Emma twice, and on both occasions he is moved to do the very same thing. When Emma marries, the old man accompanies the newlyweds a short way down the road. He says goodbye and starts back home, but on arriving at the top of a hill—on the road to Saint-Victor—he turns around to watch them disappear in the distance and weeps. He does exactly the same thing as he leaves Yonville after having come to Emma's funeral. The narrator emphasizes the repetitive nature of the episode: "But when he reached the top of the hill, he turned, as once before he had turned around on the road to Saint-Victor, on parting from her." Emma's wedding and her death culminate in two identical poses: an old man surveying a landscape from the top of a hill, his eyes full of tears and his heart filled with sadness. Here one person does the same thing two times; in other cases the same event is enacted twice, each time by a different person. After Emma's death, Charles finds Rodolphe's letter, the one breaking with her, in the attic, the very place where she had taken refuge on the day she received it, and he is as pale and shaken as she had been long before: "And Charles stood there, motionless and open-mouthed, in the very spot where once, even more pale than he, overcome with despair, Emma had longed to die."

One form of the binary system of the fictitious reality is duplicity, that is to say, the ability of the characters to be two different beings at the same time without others noticing. This is not a characteristic of certain of them but of all of them alike: men and women, in certain circumstances, subjected to certain predisposing factors, become two people. They do not always do so deliberately, to hide their feelings from others; sometimes this invisible parthenogenesis takes place spontaneously, as happens to Charles the first time he visits Les Bertaux. It is dawn, the medical officer is jogging along on horseback half asleep, and suddenly he has a sort of dream that he is two Charleses at once, that he is experiencing two situations and two times at once. He has a sudden "double vision" of himself: "He saw himself double, at once a student and a married man, lying in his bed as he had been just a while before, walking through a surgical ward as in bygone days. In his mind the smell of poultices mingled with the fresh smell of dew; he heard both the sound of iron curtain rings running along the rods around the hospital beds and his wife as she lay asleep." The "doubling" here is illusory; it is the product of a drowsing mind. Some time later, Charles's person will undergo a transformation whereby his outward behavior and his heart are set totally at odds with each other. Sniffing danger, Héloïse Bovary forbids him to return to the Rouault farm and the *officier de santé* obeys. But at the same time that he stops seeing Emma, he begins to love her, to see her in his mind's eye: ". . . the boldness of his desire protested against the servility of his conduct, and with a sort of naïve hypocrisy he told himself that this very prohibition against seeing her somehow gave him the right to love her." This incongruity, whereby a person when he acts is the opposite of what he is when he feels and thinks (we have already seen an example of this in the episode where Rodolphe writes the letter breaking with Emma)—in other words is two persons, one to himself and another to others—is a recurrent theme in the novel. When Emma discovers in her early days at Yonville that she is in love with Léon, her immediate reaction is to turn into a model wife in everyone's eyes, even Léon's (and it is on seeing this hardworking, unaffected, kindly, satisfied woman that Homais utters his memorable phrase: "She's a woman of extraordinary presence who wouldn't be at all out of place in a subprefect's residence"); nobody—except herself and the reader—knows that beneath this outward appearance of perfection and domestic felicity there lies hidden a woman "full of covetousness, rage, hatred." From this time on, all Emma's life unfolds beneath the sign of duplicity; till the day she dies there will always be two Emmas: the one that Charles and the townspeople of Yonville know and the one known only to herself and, at intervals, to Léon, Rodolphe, Lheureux.

The duplicity may be shared, an operation whereby two persons become "double" in order, on the one hand, to save appearances and, on the other, to realize their desires. This is what happens the first time that Léon and Emma are alone; their words amount to a banal exchange, while their eyes, their minds, their hearts carry on the real dialogue: "Had they nothing else to say to each other? Their eyes, however, held more meaningful converse; and as they forced themselves to utter trivialities, they sensed the same languor invading them both; it was like a murmur of the soul, deep, continuous, more clearly audible than the sound of their voices." This dividing of self of the human being, in order to satisfy his or her desires without violating the social conventions, is something that the characters do instinctively; only Rodolphe has a theory to justify duplicity. There are, according to him, two moralities. One, that of mediocre, mean, petty souls, and another, for certain elect, that allows every freedom and excess: "The petty one, the conventional one, the one invented by men, the one that keeps changing and shouting at the top of its lungs, is earthbound, boisterous, and vulgar, like that crowd of imbeciles you see down there. But the other one, the eternal one, is all around us and above us, like the landscape that surrounds us and the blue sky that sheds its light upon us." In reality, Rodolphe is a cynic and is here giving his method of seduction a trial; he doubtless has no particularly strong belief in this superior morality; Emma, however, does.

The theme of doubleness in general and of duplicity in particular is not a gratuitous one. In all probability its source is the constant dividing of the self implicit in the vocation of the writer of fiction. Anyone who follows this calling lives his* experiences in the same way that everyone else does; but on yet another hand, he observes them and uses them. As a consequence, he is and is not identified with these experiences; as he lives his life, he is someone who takes his distance from what he lives, and as he writes, someone who tries desperately to relive what he has lived, the better *to live it as a lie*. This duality doubtless explains why the themes of the double and duplicity are permanent ones in the novel. Something similar happens with regard to the theme of the outsider, in which the novelist projects the social status that his vocation forces upon him. Flaubert often said that he was two persons. He was speaking not only of the two different sides of his literary vocation—his lyrical-romantic bent, which whetted his appetite for history and exoticism, and his realist-contemporary one—but of what different people the man who lived and the man who created were. That was his answer to Louise Colet when she once reproached him for having written to Eulalie Foucault: "You say that I seriously loved that woman. That's not true. It's just that when I wrote to her, with the faculty I have for arousing myself with my pen, I took my subject seriously; *but only while I was writing*. Many of the things that leave me cold when I see them or when others talk about them excite me, irritate me, hurt me if I speak of them, and especially if I write."† Six years

* To avoid awkward constructions, I shall use masculine pronouns throughout this passage. Thanks to the resources of Spanish syntax, the writer in that language (as Vargas Llosa here) can choose *not* to specify gender. (H.L.)
† Letter of October 8, 1846. Flaubert's italics.

later, he repeats the same thought: "Yes, it's a strange thing, the pen on one side and the individual on the other" (letter to Louise, July 27, 1852).

We also note the predisposition of the fictional reality toward dualism with regard to the characters. They ordinarily make their appearance in pairs, suggesting the crystallization of a single essence in two different persons. This is true of the two fathers-in-law in the story: they are the most likable men in the novel, the most straightforward, the most consistent in their behavior. The outgoing, spendthrift Monsieur Bovary is a spontaneous, lighthearted sort, uncalculating and free of duplicity, on a moral plane very much like the simple, goodhearted Père Rouault. The two fathers-in-law escape, each of them in his own way, the two curses visited upon almost all the other members of the fictional society: mendacity and stupidity. The two physicians in the story (Charles is only an *officier de santé*), Dr. Cavinet and Dr. Larivière, have a great many things in common, although the latter has more prestige than his colleague: the superior, arrogant air with which they arrive in Yonville and deal with the townspeople, their monumental self-certainty, their professional coldness, which borders on the inhuman, their excellent appetite. Emma has two real lovers, but if the reader examines her love life attentively, it will be noted that the different stages that constitute it are each occupied by binomials or pairs, in which the real lover has a double or an illusory complement, an ideal figure with which Emma associates him: in the first stage, in Yonville, Léon is coupled in Emma's mind with the now-distant and almost mythical figure of the viscount of the château of La Vaubyessard, a personage who again haunts her mind when she begins her romance with Rodolphe; in the third stage, when she again meets the notary's clerk at the opera in Rouen, Emma weaves romantic fantasies around the figure of the tenor Lagardy and relates him to Léon, as she has previously linked Léon and the viscount. It is as if in order to be able to love a flesh-and-blood man, Emma needs the initial stimulus of an illusory one (although the viscount and the tenor actually exist, Emma endows them with a purely imaginary life), of whom they will be and must be a materialization (the fact that they are not constitutes her eternal defeat).

But the best example of this binary nature of the fictitious is, quite evidently, the Homais-Bournisien tandem. They are inseparable, symmetrical expressions and equivalents of ideological sectarianism and spiritual conformism. The pharmacist tirelessly parrots positivist dogmas, using the most rudimentary formulas and the most hackneyed arguments, bringing to this philosophy not the slightest personal contribution, exactly as the *abbé* mouths Catholic dogma in the form of clichés and crude examples. Adherents of apparently opposed ideologies, they have embraced them in identical ways: having made a handy act of faith that spares them from having to think for themselves and provides them with simple answers for every circumstance, they have submerged themselves in a sea of self-complacency. In the last analysis, the two of them—Bournisien and his deism, Homais and his materialism—represent one and the same form of human abdication. Together they embody the worst possible variety of Flaubertian *bêtise*: the intellectual sort. It has been said, not without reason, that in Homais and Bournisien Flaubert parodies the two ideologies that coexisted in the bosom of his family: his father's Voltairean, atheist scientism and his mother's Catholicism, and that he did so from the point of view, equally critical of both, that was his own: skepticism. What is certain is that Homais and Bournisien are the two sides of a single coin, as is masterfully dramatized in the chapter on Emma's death, when, like two marionettes whose strings are being pulled by the same puppeteer, they snore in perfect unison alongside her corpse laid out for the wake, or when, each according to his ideology, the one sprinkles holy water all about the room to chase away demons while the other pours chlorine water on the floor to kill germs.

What a ponderous machine a book is to put together, and
more important, what a complicated one!

—Letter to Louise Colet, September 13, 1852

But the *added element* is not exclusively a product of the subject and the characters; it also depends on the way in which the story is told. The distances from the real reality that we have noted—things becoming human and humans becoming things, men women and women men, the magic law of duality—help to give the fictional reality its autonomy. Its form is an even more important contribution to this end. Any novel that does not aim at doing away with the story element must resolve two problems: ordering in time and point of view. The entirety of events, persons, places, emotions must have an order of presentation, must constitute a chronology. The temporal structure of a novel is always a prime constituent of the *added element*, since the time of the fiction is never identical with real time (if only because the time of the chronology as *read* varies, depending on the skill and the choice of each reader). Moreover, the facts that go to make up the fictitious reality do not proliferate spontaneously: they are recounted by someone. This inevitable presence in any and every fiction, the narrator, is responsible not only for the time of the fiction—the way in which the facts are ordered—but also for the words that describe things and places and the words the characters say. It is the narrator who establishes the way in which the facts of the story are set forth—by presenting them, by hiding them, by relating them to one another—and the nature of these facts. Visible or invisible, one or multiple, trustworthy or suspect, the narrator, together with his attitudes—the points of view of a novel— imposes particular characteristics on the fictitious reality.

Chronological order and words, time and the narrator are, naturally, an indestructible unity; separating them is an artificial procedure, but there is no other way of showing the workings of the *ponderous and complicated machinery* that enables a fiction to create the illusion that it is true, to pretend to be alive.

The Four Times of Madame Bovary

In *Madame Bovary* time is not a homogeneous flow in which events succeed each other, steadily and irreversibly, like the waters of a river that the reader watches flowing past at a velocity that never changes. It is, rather, a heterogeneous current which, though it constitutes a series—a before, a now, and an after—consists of moments of movement and moments of motionlessness, of eddies, of changes of nature, with the result that the events and persons of the fictitious reality take on different degrees of certainty, depending on which of the four planes that constitute the temporal system of the novel they appear on. Sartre distinguishes two types of duration in *Madame Bovary*: "One of the singular and inimitable charms of *Madame Bovary* will be that the two durations are put before us simultaneously, the one lived in its slow repetitiveness, its tedious languor; the other oracular but hidden, a theatrical temporalization subtending the novelistic temporalization and manifesting itself on oc-

(168

casion by intersigns, revealing to us in these lightning moments that Emma is hastening to her ruin and is bent on fulfilling her destiny as a woman damned."* That is correct: in the novel, periods of unhurried development, of a slow succession of minor happenings, alternate with brusque accelerations in which, in a few lines, the action is condensed, gathers speed, multiplies into a monstrous occurrence, only to turn back once more into the same tranquil, methodical periodicity as before. But even though these two sorts of events have a different duration—Emma's numerous trips to Rouen and the instant when she swallows the arsenic, for example—they nonetheless belong to a single temporal plane, constitute one same time, even though they are of different importance. The four temporal planes I am speaking of establish a division between the events of the story that differentiates not duration but substance, and the fictitious world owes its complexity in good part to the changes wrought by the narrator by translating the story from one plane to another. That there are four temporal planes does not mean, of course, that the boundaries between them are sharply defined. The narrator conceals these transitions, and the reader is scarcely aware of the continuous shift of the narrative material. He notes only the consequences of these changes: the destiny and the ambiguity that permeate the actions, the very personal movement that they impart to the story. It is important that the narrator has been clever enough to create four different times, but what is more important still is the way in which he has distributed the narrative material between them in order to build the fictional reality.

* *Op. cit.*, Vol. I, p. 781.

A Singular or Specific Time

Let us look at the events that open and close the story. Here is the first thing that the narrator recounts:

We were in the study hall when the Headmaster entered, followed by a new boy still dressed in his clothes from home and a custodian carrying a big desk. Those who had been dozing suddenly awoke, and each one stood up as though interrupted at his work.

And here is the last thing (the reference is to Homais):

He has just received the cross of honor.

Above all else, there is not the slightest doubt as to the reality of these events. The narrator does not hesitate in the slightest; his revelations are categorical. In the initial one, we see the door of a classroom open, the headmaster enter, followed by a new pupil and a custodian carrying a desk, the schoolboys rising to their feet, pretending they have been surprised while hard at work. And in the final one the same tone of certainty: the Yonville pharmacist has received—in a past very close to the present in which the narrator situates himself—the decoration that he has coveted, and the "cross of honor" now gleams on a chest puffed up with pride. These events are not only certain, and not only did they happen at two different past moments—the first in a distant past and the second in an immediate past in relationship to the narrator; in both cases it is a question of facts whose singularity and authority are indisputable. These events have taken place, they occupied a concrete and transitory instant in the course of time, they were made up of a definite conjunction of unrepeatable gestures, attitudes, and movements, they ceased and now they are there, fixed and unmistakable in the development of the story, with their particular coloration, volume, solidity, anecdotal value, moral significance, and their varied range of significance, along with the other events of the novel. No one can question their truth, their originality, their uniqueness, or their situation in the fictitious chronology. They exist on an objective level of reality, independent of the subjectivity of the characters; both signify action and presuppose a flow, an orderly and progressive chain of events in which they were initially nothing, a possible future, and then a present that materialized in them, and subsequently a memory that endures, a past that recedes.

An important number of events in *Madame Bovary* appear, as in these two examples, with the characteristics of objectivity, specificity, mobility, and transitoriness. They constitute the *singular or specific time* of the fictitious reality, and we recognize that the story is situated on this plane when the narrator uses the preterit tense to report it (or the equivalent periphrastic forms: *"Il vient de recevoir la croix d'honneur"* is the same as *"Il reçut la croix d'honneur il y a peu de temps"*). When the narrator employs this tense of the verb, the novel attains its maximum dynamism and agility, for this is the privileged tense of action and movement; it is, above all, the events that make the story progress, transitions, episodic changes that are narrated on this plane of time. It is comprised primarily of human occupations, and also of perceptions and sensations whose exceptional and instantaneous nature the narrator wishes to stress. We find on this temporal plane the surprises of the novel, concrete events such as weddings, deaths, operations, adulteries, spectacles, small details such as the precise movements of characters from one place to another, and their sudden reactions to certain stimuli; the dialogues as well, which bare new elements, and a few rare references to natural surroundings and to objects that do not constitute a permanent setting but accidental, furtive, ephemeral presences. When the narrative material is located on this temporal plane, the fictitious reality is seen to be in a state of maximum animation and anecdotal effervescence; it is activity, exteriority in general, human action, and "history" in the sense that what the narrator is recounting has happened in this way, one single time, and will not happen again.

Circular Time or Repetition

Intercalated with the singular events are others related by the narrator which differ from the former because of their repetitive character and what we might term their abstract nature. They take the form of scenes which do not show a specific action but, rather, a serial activity that repeats itself, a habit, a custom. Here, for example, is how Charles's workday ordinarily ends, during the Bovarys' stay in Tostes:

He would come home from his rounds late at night, at ten, sometimes midnight. He wanted his dinner then, and since the maid had gone to bed, it was Emma who served him. He would take off his frock coat so as to be more comfortable as he ate. He would tell about every person he'd met, every village he'd been to, every prescription he'd made out, and complacently finish what was left of the beef hash, pare his cheese, munch an apple, pour himself the last drop of wine in the pitcher, then go up to bed, stretch out on his back, and the next minute be snoring away.

In the previous case, the narrative time was a straight-line progression; in this one, a rotation. The story moves but does not advance, circles round and round in the same place, is repetitive. The difference between this paragraph and the ones I cited as examples of *singular or specific time* is that, in the case of Charles Bovary's arrival at school and Homais's receiving of a decoration, what happened and what was related were identical, the event as it occurred was the event as it was narrated, and vice versa. Here, on the other hand, a gap has opened up between the two: there are links between what happens and what is narrated, but the two are different things. What happens is made up of the many nights, over a space of weeks and months, in which Charles, after visiting his patients, returned home, ate his dinner, and went to bed. Each one of these nights was a particular, unique occurrence, with certain untransferable characteristic details—the different menu, the particular garments he removed before sitting down at the table, the various words he used to tell his wife about his day, the different gestures, the varying number of yawns on each occasion—but these particularities and differences have disappeared in the recital. Instead of describing them one by one, the narrator has summed them up in an archetypical scene, which is none of those that took place but, rather, condenses and symbolizes all of them. In order to compose this résumé scene, he has left the particular out of account and recounted the general, the common and permanent traits of this sum of nights. Between what is lived by the characters and what is recounted by the narrator the coincidence is no longer absolute but relative: the text is now a less certain reflection of the facts; it is not their faithful portrait but a painting that takes its inspiration from them in order to create its own images.

The typical verb tense of this plane is the imperfect indicative. Many critics, beginning with Albert Thibaudet, are persuaded that this is the Flaubertian tense par excellence, the one in which he found it easiest to narrate and the one which he turned to the best account. He endowed it with an extraordinary flexibility, a diversity of function that it had never before had in the novel. Entire episodes of *Madame Bovary* are related in accordance with this system of abstractions that allows a maximum of facts to be reduced to a minimum of words, a long series of actions to be synthesized in just one, while giving at the same time the idea of duration, of recurrence, of the story moving forward. The three days of romance spent by Emma and Léon together in Rouen (Part Three, Chapter III) are almost exclusively narrated in this *circular time*:

They sat in the low-ceilinged room of a small restaurant, with black fishnets hanging at the door. They ate fried smelts, custard, and cherries. They stretched out on the grass and lay in each other's arms in an out-of-the-way spot beneath the poplars; and they wished that, like two Robinson Crusoes, they might live forever in this little corner, which seemed to them, in their bliss, the most magnificent place on earth. It was not the first time that they had ever seen trees, blue sky, a stretch of grass, that they had heard water flowing and the breeze sighing in the leafy branches; but they had doubtless never contemplated all that with wonder: it was as though nature had not existed before, or had begun to be beautiful only after their desires had been appeased.

What the narrator is describing is something generic and not specific, plural and not singular: images which sum up actions repeated several times by the lovers until finally they become a sort of routine, and which later on, in their memory, will doubtless be the ideal graphic balance of these three full days. Hence what the narrator recounts has both happened and not happened: these are synopses, ciphers, essences of acts. The material narrated on this temporal plane is not objective, as is that on the specific temporal plane. It is, rather, at once objective and subjective: it has its feet resting on the objective world, in the last analysis it is "history," since its point of departure is always events that have happened, but the upper half of its body is purely subjective, an interpretation that the narrator himself makes by abstracting in an image the family features of a series of events and excluding from each unit the differential elements. What is recounted undoubtedly occurred: but it is not certain that it always happened in exactly that way; the one thing that is evident is that it happened a number of times, that it consisted in a sum of similar acts of which what is narrated is a sort of emblem. When I say that what is recounted is events, I am using too restrictive a term; on this plane the narrator also describes feelings, thoughts, and in the example cited—the three days that Emma and Léon spend in Rouen—we can see the freedom with which he clears the limits between the outer world and the inner, the ease with which he narrates, within the same circular movement, what the couple did and what they felt. This circular or repeated time is that of reflection, of states of mind, of moods, the time that shapes the psychology of the various characters, the motivations that will later precipitate sudden events, the time of the minute details of ongoing daily life, social or family routine, by contrast to which the exceptional, unique, and transitory events of the singular plane will have an even more striking character. This circular plane is that of boredom and monotony, of the predictable, of the social (whereas the preceding plane was first and foremost that of the individual), and it is thanks to this plane that the fictitious reality has its particular duration—serene, rhythmic, majestic—and takes on its impressive breadth, for the images of this time permit the narrator to expand the material—each occurrence that is narrated represents many that have taken place—without multiplying the words. It is the time of places and of permanent objects, of a rural, urban, and domestic setting that has stability, for it frames many actions or prolonged actions.

Where the fictitious reality is most admirably described in this circular time—the whole of it gives the impression of a slow and powerful whirlpool, of a never-ending flow round and round and round—is in the account of the months of Emma and Léon's romance (Part Three, Chapter V). Emma is in the habit of going to visit Léon on Thursdays, using as a pretext her piano lessons in the city; she spends the day with him in Rouen and returns to Yonville the same night. The narrator reduces these dozens of trips made by Emma to spend the day with her lover to one ideal Thursday—a "master pattern" or "matrix" Thursday, and incorporates within this abstract day, a mere "figurehead" of the others, any number of tiny details, such as the mechanical gestures that Emma customarily makes as Hivert's coach arrives at the city gate: "Emma would unbutton her overshoes, put on a different pair of gloves, straighten her shawl, and, twenty paces farther on, step out of the Hirondelle." Nor have the couple's conversations been omitted; the narrator symbolizes in a fervent exchange the thousands of things that the lovers must have said to each other in these weekly assignations:

She would bend down toward him and murmur, as though breathless with rapture:
"Oh, don't move! Don't say a word! Look at me! There's something so gentle in your eyes, that does my heart so much good!"
And she called him "child."
"Do you love me, child?"

The reader has no certainty that precisely this scene with these very same words and gestures has ever taken place, but he understands that very often in the little room in the Hôtel de Boulogne there have been scenes very much like it, in which things of this sort have been said and equivalent gestures made. The narrator has thus accomplished several things at once: he has contrived to relativize the story, to stamp it with a special air of uncertainty, a rather mysterious nature (for the images take their distance from what they represent; they no longer serve things but instead are served by them), and to suggest an idea of permanence in motion, of static movement. All this reinforces the originality of the fictitious world.

When the narrator places himself on this plane, a relationship is established between what is narrated and what has occurred that is similar to the one that exists between real reality and fictitious reality. Just as this latter is not a servile reflection but an image which, despite its being forged from materials taken from the former, nonetheless constitutes an autonomous entity, so the narrator's voice in the moments of repeated time is a verbal entity which, even though it is sustained by the fictitious material, does something more to it than relate it: it also exists as a separate reality.

Immobile Time or Plastic Eternity

There are other moments in the fictitious reality in which time is neither linear and rapid nor slow and circular, but instead seems to have been volatilized. The action disappears, people, things, places remain motionless and, as though transported out of the nightmare of chronology, live an eternal moment. The fictitious reality shown on this plane is exteriority, form, perspective, texture, color; a plastic presence, a body that exists solely in order to be contemplated. Its grammatical tense is the present indicative and the best example of it is the opening pages of Part II describing Yonville:

> At the foot of the hill, after the bridge, a broad stretch of road begins, lined on both sides with young aspens, which leads you in a straight line to the first houses of the region. They are surrounded by hedges, and their yards are full of scattered outbuildings, cider presses, cart barns, and distilling sheds, standing here and there beneath leafy trees with ladders and poles leaning against them or scythes hooked over their branches. The thatched roofs, like fur caps pulled down over eyes, come a third or so of the way down the low windows, and each thick, convex windowpane has a bull's-eye in its center, like the bottom of a bottle . . .

No one moves, time does not flow, everything is matter and space as in a painting. When human beings are described on this temporal plane, they become no more than a pose, a facial expression, a gesture surprised by a camera lens, and the fictitious reality turns into a décor for the rigid figures in a wax museum. In the château of La Vaubyessard, as Emma passes by one of the rooms, she spies the following image: "Emma saw solemn-faced men grouped around the billiard table, their chins resting on their cravats, all of them with decorations on their chests, smiling silently as they made their shot. On the dark wood of the wall paneling hung great gilded frames, with names in black letters at the base." One and the same substance appears to provide the material for the gilded frames, the black letters, and the stone-like gentlemen with their decorations who, with their jowls buried in their cravats and a frozen smile on their lips, have been arrested by the description in this disturbing, grotesque, theatrical pose, just as they were about to tap the balls with their cues. In this case the "freezing" of the scene is done by a character: Emma's eyes capture the scene and make it eternal, snatching these billiard players from the flux of time, making a sculpture group of them. On many other occasions it is the narrator himself who interrupts the action, poses the characters in a certain attitude, and like the painter with his model has them remain motionless, holding the pose as he paints them. "She [Emma] was ripping out the lining of a dress, and scraps of it lay all about her; never raising her eyes, the elder Madame Bovary was cutting away with her squeaking scissors, and Charles, with his cloth slippers and the old brown frock coat that did him for a dressing gown, was standing looking on with his hands in his pockets, as silent as the others; nearby, Berthe, in a little white pinafore, was scraping the gravel of the garden path with her shovel." In this example, the imperfect is equivalent to a present: for the duration of the description, these figures *are* these frozen poses, this harmonious relation, the careful arrangement and the distance that separates them, the silence that envelops them. Like the figures in a family portrait set in a Flemish interior, the characters are not *doing* this or that; they are *being* it: their presence is their essence.

This temporal plane is that of description, that of things, that of the outside world, the one that gives the novel its physical depth, that materiality with which we invariably associate the name of Flaubert. When the fictitious reality is motionless time, the human voice disappears, as do intimacy, thought, feelings: life becomes mute and statuesque, inaction and plasticity. The language tends to be purely informative, to disappear into the object, and along with a stubborn concern for precision and exactitude, a decided propensity for the visual and the tactile suddenly makes its appearance in it. This time is, par excellence, that of the narrator: he acts as the principal intermediary between the fictitious reality and the reader; it is he, transformed into a pair of avid, petrifying eyes and wielding words as though they were paintbrushes, who assumes almost the entire responsibility for tracing the forms and revealing the contents. On the specific and the circular planes, the fictitious reality is almost always described by way of the conduct of certain characters; on this plane the narrator undertakes this mission directly.

This immobile time is also that of the "philosophy" of the fictitious reality—which I shall describe briefly in the following chapter: that is to say, those principles of an ethical, historical, or metaphysical order, which, being stipulated directly by the narrator, exist in a timeless mode, as fateful presuppositions not subject to the contingencies of evolution and change that are part of the fictitious reality.

Imaginary Time

On the three previous temporal planes a gradual progression from movement to repose, from the dynamic to the static can be noted. On passing through each one of them, the narrative material has been, successively, a precipitous and evident action, a serene and relative occupation, and finally, a theatrical and plastic immobility. It is now about to become an unreality. The three planes had something in common: the events, objects, and places described enjoyed a totally or partially objective existence, had an autonomous being, occurred, occupied a space in the fictitious reality. But there is another plane in the novel made up of persons, places, and things whose existence is uniquely subjective. They are not submerged in the fictitious chronology, they are not subject like the others to the terrible law of duration, they do not occupy concrete space: their realm is not that of history but that of the imagination. They exist in the characters' fantasies; they are beings that are dreamed or invented, the offspring of ambition, curiosity, frustration, and sometimes terror, as when Homais "had a sudden vision of underground dungeons, his family in tears, the pharmacy sold, all the apothecary jars scattered among strangers . . ." Only he (and the reader) envisions these catastrophes which have not happened and will not happen except in the fear-ridden consciousness of the pharmacist, the day he is summoned to appear before the bar of justice for practicing medicine without a degree. Those underground cells, those inconsolable tears, that pharmacy gone bankrupt are of a different nature from the events and persons of the preceding examples, because their being is parasitic upon Homais, and because they are not an expression of what they themselves are but of what he is: his bad conscience, his imagination have clichés as their one and only vehicle.

This is the time of the characters, their exclusive patrimony and responsibility. When the material is described on this plane, the narrator attains his greatest distancing from it, his greatest invisibility. It is the time of dreams and of nightmares, of intimacy, of unsatisfied desire (as when Rodolphe, who has just met Emma, pictures what her life must be like and mulls over what possibility he has of seducing her: "While he trots off to see his patients, she stays behind at home darning his socks.

How bored she must be! If she had things her way, she'd live in town, dance the polka every night! Poor little thing! Gasping for love like a carp on a kitchen table gasping for water. Three months of courting and that little piece of goods would adore you, I'm certain of it. It'd be ever so sweet, so charming!"). It is the time of fantasies, the time that gives the reader an intimate knowledge, through the images they create, of the culture, the intelligence, and, most important, the inventiveness of the characters, the way in which they build the unreal out of the real. The events and things that constitute this plane are not gratuitous; they do not serve as mere picturesque embroidery. In this story whose spinal column is the battle between illusion and reality, they represent one of the contending forces, the one that in the end is defeated. We must not be misled into thinking that because it is Emma who lives the fictitious unreality the most intensely it is her fantasy alone that peoples this temporal plane with resplendent things that do not exist. She is the principal creator of the imaginary in *Madame Bovary*, to be sure, but Homais too is an active fabricator of myths, as is Léon in his early years, when he dreams in Yonville of a legendary Paris and "the fanfare of its masked balls and the laughter of its grisettes" echoing from afar: "He furnished a dream apartment. He would lead an artist's life in it. He would take guitar lessons! Wear a dressing gown, a beret, blue velvet slippers! And already in his mind's eye he admired over his mantelpiece the two crossed fencing foils, with a skull and the guitar above."

The beings who belong to this *imaginary time* are self-consistent: they are "romantic" stylizations of objective reality, owed to reading, as in the case of Emma, or to naïveté and prejudice, as with Léon, Homais, Rodolphe. We have already seen how, with the aid of a map, Emma transported herself to Paris without ever leaving her house in Tostes: "She would close her eyes and see gas lamps flickering in the wind, and footboards of barouches unfolding with a great clatter as they drew up in front of theaters." These are images her imagination forges from materials drawn from the novels of her adolescence, from the stories told at school by the ruined aristocratic lady who used to come to work with the nuns, from the magazines and books she borrows from the *"cabinets de lecture"* in Rouen. This relation between the real and the imaginary can be seen very clearly when, after she has given herself to Rodolphe, Emma is certain that she is about to form "a real part of these fictions" and be a sister of "the heroines of the books she had read." And it can be seen, dramatically—since in this case the abyss that lies between the real model (Léon) and the fantasy (the man to whom Emma thinks she is sending her letters) can be measured—when Emma continues to write to him even though their affair has ended: "But as she wrote she felt the presence of another man, a phantom embodying her most ardent memories, the most beautiful things she had read in books, her most avid desires; and in the end he became so real and accessible that she palpitated with excitement, even though she was unable to picture him clearly, hidden as he was, like a god, beneath his multiple attributes. He dwelt in that azure realm where silken ladders sway beneath flower-scented, moonlit balconies. She sensed him drawing nearer, he was about to ravish her entirely in a kiss. And the next moment she would fall to earth once more, shattered; for these vague love raptures exhausted her more than the wildest orgies." We see in this paragraph the importance that the imaginary has for Emma; she feels such a powerful attraction to it that not even the evidence of the real can hold her back. Emma need only pick up her pen, think, or dream for the altogether ordinary notary to leave behind his fleshly envelope, his terrestrial gravity, and be transformed into an extraordinary being, to whose existence her "most ardent memories," the "most beautiful things she had read in books," her "most avid desires" have equally contrib-

uted. This substitute reality makes a rebel of Emma and gives
her the strength both to live and, in the end, to kill herself.

Though each of the other temporal planes has a corre-
sponding grammatical tense (either explicit or implicit), any
tense will do for this one: the tense of the verb becomes a mere
function of the plane on which the character who produces it
is narrated. In most instances, unreality is a future illusion, as
in the parallel dreams of Emma and Charles, when each of them
imagines a future that suits each perfectly, but there are other
cases in which it is a present illusion, as when, for example,
Léon little by little turns into a phantom as Emma writes to
him, and there are times when it may even affect the past, as
when Emma's imagination denies the lived reality of her life by
embroidering upon her memories of her early years.

I have said earlier that the temporal structure constitutes
an indestructible unity. By that I mean that what is most important is not the fact that there are four planes which give the
narrative material varying velocities, degrees of certainty, natures; it is, rather, their interdependence, the shifts from one to
the other, the way in which they modify and complement one
another. It is this system of harmonies and disharmonies, the
complexity of the whole, that enables the temporal structure to
produce the proper effect. A great orchestra made up of musicians provided with the very best instruments would get nowhere without a conductor capable of putting all the parts of
the score together and directing the performance of it. A beautiful concert, in the final analysis, is something more, something
other than the mere sum of the elements that have made it
possible. And now that we have had a look at the instruments
and the musicians, let us watch the orchestra conductor in action.

The Transformations of the Narrator

Who tells the story of *Madame Bovary*? Several narrators whose voices take over from one another so unobtrusively that the reader scarcely notices the shifts of perspective and has the impression that there is only one narrator. As with the temporal planes, the fact that there are several narrators—each of them assigned a different function—and the way in which the changes from one to another are brought about are of equal importance. The moment at which these transformations occur and their subtlety are likewise key factors in giving the narrative material its particular powers of persuasion. Here are the narrators of *Madame Bovary* or, better put, the different masks of the protoplasmic narrator:

A Plural Narrator-Character: The Mysterious "We"

Who is the narrator who, hiding behind the first person plural, begins the story? It is someone who is on the scene, a part of the world we are being told about. He is present in the classroom which Charles enters, preceded by the headmaster of the school; he hears and is doubtless a party to the scornful hazing to which the students subject the new boy from the country; later on, he and Charles live their school years together: "It would be impossible now for any of *us* to remember anything about him. He was an unremarkable boy, who played at recess, worked in the study hall, paid attention in class, slept soundly in the dormitory, ate with a will in the dining room."* There is no doubt about it: the person speaking has been something more than an observer: an active participant, an accessory, a character in the story. This spatial point of view—the narrator placed inside the narrated world—a device as old as the novelistic genre itself, would seem to have been chosen for reasons of verisimilitude, to make the story more believable. This is the case with the picaresque novel, where the hero tells the story of his life: the account takes on a greater degree of credibility in that it is a privileged witness who is offering it, someone who has firsthand knowledge: I was there, I can tell you the real story, I lived what happened. The narration takes on the appearance of historical witness.

But here things do not happen in precisely this way. This inhabitant of the narrated world does not speak of himself but of another, of others, of all the others except himself. He is present, yet we do not see him; he is simply a point of reference, a vision and a memory transmitting what he saw and learned at a certain moment, without showing himself. His identity is mysterious not only because of his reserve concerning his own person but because he speaks in the first person plural, which may indicate that he is not one but several characters. He might be a collective narrator: the *we* of the first chapter perhaps refers to the entire student body of the school or to a group of students. But he could also be just one of these schoolboys, who uses the plural out of modesty and a wish to remain anonymous. This uncertainty is essential to the character-narrator who opens the

* My italics. (M.V.L.)

story; he refers to himself only seven times, all in the first chapter, and then disappears, never to return. This spatial point of view, in which there is no distance whatsoever between the narrator and what is narrated, inaugurates the novel by establishing a great closeness between the reader and the story; throughout the whole of the first *tableau*—Charles's arrival in class, the teasing, the episode of the *casquette*, the penalty set by the teacher—in which the character-narrator's viewpoint is dominant, it seems as though we are about to read a personal confession, an autobiography. At the same time, the vagueness of the narrator—who is present but does not show himself, who limits himself to letting us know that he is a citizen of the fictitious world—arouses a curiosity paralleling that provoked by the story he is telling. In addition to giving the impression that the story he is telling is true, thereby fulfilling the traditional function of the character-narrator, the initial narrator of *Madame Bovary*, through the grammatical form behind which he conceals himself, lends a certain unsettling air of mystery to the narrative material.

The haziness surrounding the plural character-narrator facilitates his replacement by another: he vanishes, and his disappearance is not even noticed, because he was already very nearly invisible. After Charles has joined the class, another narrator now sketches in background material that the enigmatic *we* cannot know of: Charles's earlier life, his parents' marriage, the first lessons he received from the parish priest of his town, up to the time of his arrival in Rouen. The plural character-narrator then appears once more to sum up, in the sentence that I have cited, what sort of life at school this docile, diligent, but mediocre pupil had, whereupon he disappears once again, this time for good. A different narrator goes on to tell what happened to Charles when he left school, became a medical student, received his diploma as an *officier de santé*, married Héloïse Dubuc, a widow, and settled in Tostes. This narrator with whom, thanks to these four changes, the character-narrator takes turns telling the story in the course of the first chapter, is

The Omniscient Narrator

In quantitative terms, he has the principal responsibility for the story; it is he who recounts almost everything that happens and who describes almost everything that exists in the fictitious reality. He does not form part of the narrated world; he is outside of it and speaks in the third person singular. His attributes are omnipresence, omniscience, and omnipotence. But even though he is everywhere, knows everything, and is all-powerful, he invariably uses these divine faculties in a rigorously planned way, in accordance with a coherent rational system whose rules he violates only on extremely rare occasions (these transgressions are always venial and so infrequent that they never endanger the system). He witnesses and recounts with equal ease what takes place in the outside world and in the heart of hearts of the characters; he moves about freely in time, as in the first chapter, taking a leap backward to tell the story of Charles Bovary's parents and then a leap forward to return to the school in Rouen, and equally freely in space, as in this same chapter, in which he goes from Rouen to the nameless hamlet "on the border of the *pays de Caux* and Picardy" to which Charles's father retreats after failing as a textile manufacturer and a farmer, whereupon he, the narrator, returns just as swiftly to Rouen. The great tactical decisions that determine the narrative strategy of *Madame Bovary* fall on his shoulders: it is he who decides which facts are communicated to the reader and which are hidden from him and for how long, the temporal planes on which each episode, description, or theme is situated, and at what moment the narrative is transferred to the voice of one or another of the characters, or to their thoughts, feelings, movements, or to the natural setting and the things round about them. His extraordinary freedom—so vastly superior to that of a character-narrator—is nonetheless his greatest peril: any abuse, incongruity, or caprice in the use of his unlimited powers diminishes or destroys the power of persuasion of what is being narrated. In *Madame Bovary* he uses this freedom by limiting it to himself, in accordance with precise rules aimed at concealing his existence or revealing it in predetermined and inevitable circumstances. Hence this omniscient narrator is not one but two, depending on his degree of visibility and intrusion in the narrated world.

THE INVISIBLE NARRATOR

The majority of the material narrated in the third person singular is recounted by an absence that speaks, a glacial, meticulous observer who does not allow himself to be seen, who becomes indistinguishable from the object or the subject of which an account is being given. The rule that permits him to be invisible is that of objectivity: he tells what happens but does not qualify it in any way, limits himself to communicating what the characters do, cease to do, say to themselves or to one another, without ever revealing his own thoughts, his reactions to the world being recounted. He lacks subjectivity, is as indifferent as a movie camera that could also film the invisible; he has no desire to prove, only to present. Since he scrupulously obeys this inflexible law of objectivity, he achieves his purpose. The reader believes he doesn't exist; he has the feeling that the narrative material is engendering itself before his eyes, that it is its own beginning and end:

His father, Monsieur Charles-Denis-Bartholomé Bovary, once an army surgeon's aide, involved around 1812 in a conscription scandal and forced around this time to leave the service, had then turned his personal charms to advantage to come by a dowry of sixty thousand francs and a bride, the daughter of a dealer in knitwear who had fallen in love with the figure he cut. A handsome man, a braggart, given to clanking his spurs, his side whiskers meeting his mustache, his fingers always loaded with rings, and dressed in flashy colors, he had the air of a swashbuckler and the glib tongue of a traveling salesman.

The invisible narrator is the main axis of the Flaubertian theory of impersonality, the instrument that allowed this idea to be put into practice. It was while he was writing *Madame Bovary* that Flaubert became convinced that the work of art must give the impression of being self-sufficient, and that in order to achieve this effect it was absolutely necessary that the narrator disappear altogether. "The artist must arrange things in such a way as to make posterity believe that he never lived" (letter to Louise Colet, March 27, 1852). This invisibility requires that the narrator assume an impassive attitude toward what he is recounting, forbids him to interject himself into the narrative to draw conclusions or pass judgment. His function is to describe, not to absolve or condemn. In this same letter to Louise, he insists that all literature with a moral is intrinsically false: "There would be a fine book to write about literature that attempts to prove something; from the moment you prove, you lie. God knows the beginning and the end; man, the middle. Art, like Him in space, must remain suspended in the infinite, complete in itself, independent of its producer." Beginning in this period, his correspondence is full of similar passages; what he told Louise he will later tell his friends Louis Bouilhet, Mademoiselle Leroyer de Chantepie, George Sand, the Goncourts. His belief that the narrator (Flaubert said "the author," "the producer," "the artist," and this is the origin of a grave misunderstanding) must be completely impartial is not limited to the ethical or social aspect of the story; it also means that he is not permitted to rejoice at the happiness of his characters or pity their misfortunes: his one and only obligation is to communicate them. It is not surprising that readers conditioned by the romantic novel to see not only the misfortunes of the characters described but, along with them, the feelings of commiseration or wrath that such misfortunes provoke in the narrator (and should provoke in them, the readers) accused Flaubert of being "cold," "dehumanized," and of performing "autopsies," when they read, for instance, of Emma's death agony in *Madame Bovary*, recounted with the most uncompromising objectivity by the invisible narrator:

Her breast immediately began to heave rapidly. Her whole tongue lolled out of her mouth; her rolling eyes dimmed like two lamp globes going out, so that one might have thought her dead already but for the terrifying acceleration of the movements of her ribcage, shaken by furious gasps, as though her soul were battering against its prison walls to free itself.

The one who makes himself invisible, by narrating in the third person, by maintaining an impenetrable neutrality toward what happens in the fictitious reality, not venturing an opinion, not drawing moral or social lessons from the story, not allowing himself to be moved by the experience of the characters *is the narrator of the novel, not the author.* The narrator is always someone distinct from the author, another of the latter's creations, like the characters, and undoubtedly the most important of them, even in the cases in which he is an invisible narrator, for all the other characters depend on this secret personage. The author of a novel becomes a divided self, invents a narrator (or several of them), and it is he who adopts the attitudes of impassibility and objectivity, or any other, as for example in a romantic novel, in which the omniscient narrator is usually a visible presence, a subjectivity which tells of itself as it tells the story. Flaubert's critics do not make this distinction and therefore propose a debatable version of his theories. The fact that Flaubert did not clearly distinguish between author and narrator in his letters does not excuse them: one need only read his novels to know that he made such a distinction in practice. His theories have meaning and force if a differentiation is made between the two; if they are confused with each other, they are gone with the wind, they make no sense. For, as it is fanciful to think that an author can create without making any use whatsoever of his experience, it is no less so to imagine that a man of flesh and blood, with a definite intellectual and emotional life, can do away with his ideas, passions, instincts, obsessions at the moment of creation in order to turn himself into a narrating impersonality, into a data-communicating machine. Impassibility and objectivity are simply clever, surreptitious ways of turning this subjectivity into narrative, a strategy in which conclusions, demonstrations, and sentimental reactions in the face of what happens in the fictitious reality appear to transpire naturally, to be breathed forth in the reader's direction by what is recounted, rather than being forced upon him by a dictatorial narrator. Instead of passing judgment directly, the author does so from his invisible standpoint, deviously: by organizing the material in a given way, by linking the episodes in a certain manner, by illuminating or casting a shadow over the conduct of the characters at opportune moments, by choosing certain revealing incidents, provoking certain dialogues, providing certain descriptions. Many years after having published *Madame Bovary*, this was Flaubert's view of the matter, which he communicated to George Sand in an incomparable formula: "I don't even believe that the novelist should express *his* opinion concerning the things of the world. He may communicate it, but I am not in favor of his stating it.* In fact, thanks to the invisible narrator, he does not state it: he communicates it by osmosis, suffusing the narrative material with it, turning his subjective world into the objective world of fiction.

* Letter of August 10, 1868. Flaubert's italics.

The invisible narrator existed in the novel before *Madame Bovary*, but ordinarily he took over the narration only for brief periods, almost through inadvertence on the part of the author, who (particularly if he was a classical novelist) entrusted most of the telling of the story to an omniscient and intrusive narrator who constantly takes turns with the characters as teller of the story and sometimes is a veritable pest in the fictitious reality. The invisible narrator had never before had the primordial function that he has in this novel, and no author before Flaubert had ever worked out such effective techniques for concealing the narrator's existence.

Though the invisible narrator is the principal omniscient narrator in *Madame Bovary*, he is not the only one. Despite his having such unshakable ideas on the subject of impassibility and objectivity, Flaubert happily did not apply them as though they were dogma. He was a creator who sometimes theorized, not a theoretician who wrote novels, and in the domain of creation, as in that of history, praxis always goes beyond theory. There are moments when the omniscient narrator ceases to be invisible; absence becomes presence. The groundwork for these sudden appearances is always carefully laid, and they play an important function in the narrative strategy. They are the moments in which the invisible narrator is replaced by

THE PHILOSOPHER-NARRATOR

The omniscient narrator manifests himself at certain times—it must be emphasized that they are rare—in the form of intrusions which betray, for the brief space of a word or a phrase, the existence of a being who is a stranger to the fictitious reality. A number of these intrusions are, quite evidently, involuntary ones, lapses on the narrator's part, as when, in the middle of an impersonal description of the region where Normandy, Picardy, and the Ile-de-France come together, he sticks his nose in to opine: "This is where they make the worst Neufchâtel cheese in the entire district," or a little later on when he rounds off with a touch of irony the description of the brief period of affection and attentions that Emma showers on her daughter in her first days in Yonville: Madame Bovary's lyrical maternal effusions, he says, would have reminded "anyone not from Yonville" of "La Sachette in *Notre-Dame de Paris*."★

But there are occasions when the omniscient narrator deliberately brushes characters and objects aside to occupy the foreground of the story and voice, professorially, a philosophic maxim, a moral judgment, an adage or an aphorism, a rule of life that is concretely illustrated by the event that he has just recounted or is about to recount: ". . . for there is not a bourgeois alive who in the heat of his youth, if only for a day, a minute, hasn't thought himself capable of boundless passions, the loftiest of undertakings. The sorriest little womanizer has dreamed of sultanesses; in the heart of every notary lie the remains of a poet." No character is speaking; the narrator himself formulates this general and unappealable law of bourgeois conduct to explain Léon Dupuis's conformism, his transition from the young romantic he was in Yonville to the calculating, prudent man he now is in Rouen.

The momentary interruptions in the action or the description so that the magisterial voice of God the Father may sum up what has been narrated in an ethical, sociological, psychological, or historical rule is a classic device in the novel, and here Flaubert is following a tradition. He is not doing so in a mechanical way, however, for he gives the device a personal stamp. The philosopher-narrator makes his appearance only at certain important moments, and his passage is always a swift one; his presence raises the fictitious reality to a solemn, abstract plane only for a few seconds, so that the march of the narrative

★ A character in Victor Hugo's *Notre-Dame de Paris* whose child was stolen by the gypsies. She became a recluse, spending her days in a little cell on her knees worshipping a pink satin slipper that had belonged to her child.

will not be obstructed, broken up, diverted by the intrusion. Besides its abruptness, the voice of the philosopher-narrator possesses another invariable characteristic: a tone of authority. It never falters, it speaks categorically, as when, after the invisible narrator has reported that Léon on his return from Paris is no longer the timid young man that Emma has known but a man of experience, bold and sure of his way with women, the story comes to a halt so that a divine voice may deliver the following words: "One's aplomb depends upon the surroundings: one does not speak in the drawing room in the same way as on the third floor back, and the rich woman seems to have all her banknotes on her person, in the lining of her corset, protecting her virtue like a cuirass."

Flaubert gives a particular coloration to the hallowed device of the interruption of the magister-narrator: he reduces his interventions to certain opportune circumstances (I have found no more than half a hundred appearances of the philosopher-narrator), endows them with certain permanent qualities—brevity, generality, peremptoriness—and disposes these summary verdicts, general conclusions drawn from the particular or partial morals of the story, in such a way that they rhythmically punctuate the narrative. In the final analysis, it is evident that the collection of statements by the philosopher-narrator forms one plane of the fictitious reality: the ideological plane. Not the ideology of this or that character, but the immanent one in that society, shared by everyone, the basic system of ideas in which the characters are born, live, and die, and which is sufficiently lax to leave room within it for contradictory ideologies of classes, of social groups, and even of individuals. Hence these tendencies constitute a valuable part of the fictitious reality, an indispensable complement of the material conveyed by the *words in italics*. The two together form the moral, political, religious, and metaphysical parameters within which the men and women of the novel move, the roots of their behavior patterns and their sentiments. Although both merge to form the rhetorical or philosophical level of the fictitious reality, the words in italics and the magisterial pronouncements are not the same thing. The italicized words have a limited radius; they express *relative and concrete truths*, the beliefs, myths, or prejudices of a specific group—a family, a school, a profession, a sex, a social class, a region—from whom the omniscient narrator sometimes takes a critical and ironic distance (in which case the italics underline what a vicious and perverse deformation of reality the particular cliché, proverb, or turn of phrase is), whereas the philosopher-narrator always expresses unilateral *abstract and absolute truths*; his sentences lay claim to being human reality captured in a verbal formula, as when he begins the chapter following Emma's death agony by defining people's reaction to death in the following terms: "The death of someone always releases a sort of aura of stupefaction, so difficult is it to grasp this unexpected advent of nothingness and resign oneself to believing that such a thing has actually taken place."

The philosopher-narrator expresses something more permanent and universal than the sayings and adages in which the ideology of a community is reflected: certain innate qualities, a general human essence which precedes persons and within which concrete existences take form, representing a variant or mode. When Emma, for instance, brought to ruin by her debts, runs to Rodolphe to ask him for three thousand francs and he answers that he does not have that sum, the philosopher-narrator materializes to inform us that mixing money and love endangers the latter, because money matters quickly cool it and kill it: "He was not lying. Had he had it doubtless he would have given it to her, unpleasant as it usually is to act so generously; of all the cold blasts that blow on love, a request for money is the iciest and the most devastating." While the italicized passages constitute the rhetorical level on a subjective plane—beliefs and ideas of the characters—the thoughts put forward by the philosopher-narrator do so on an objective plane: what he says aspires to be scientific knowledge, a mathematical formulation of human nature. The two planes combined structure the world of ideas and beliefs on which the beings of the fictitious reality base their judgments, do good and wreak evil, arrive at the right or the wrong conclusions, are base souls or noble ones, ordinary human beings or unusual ones, conformists or rebels.

Singular Character-Narrators

By this is meant the voices of the characters themselves in the brief periods in which, without the mediation of the omniscient narrator, dialogue or monologue takes the place of description. This occurs when the dialogue is not "described" but is set directly before the reader, thanks to a short but total disappearance of the invisible teller from the scene. In most instances the shift is detectable if one pays close attention to the graphic signs: lines of dialogue are preceded by a dash, set in quotes, or separated by a series of ellipsis dots, without indication of the speaker. In the agricultural fair episode, three character-narrators take over from the omniscient narrator, each of them telling in turn his or her own story, in a few brief words, recounted in the first person singular. The three alternating voices are those of Emma and Rodolphe (standing on a balcony) and of the official down below who is giving out prizes:

"Just this morning, for example, when I came to your house . . ."
—To Monsieur Bizet, of Quincampoix.
"Could I have had any idea that I'd be coming here with you?"
—Seventy francs!
"I was about to leave a hundred times, and yet I followed you, I stayed with you."
—Best manure.

"As I would stay this evening, tomorrow, every day, all my life!"

—To Monsieur Caron, of Argueil, a gold medal!

"For I've never been in such completely charming company as yours."

—To Monsieur Bain, of Givry-Saint-Martin!

"So I'll carry the memory of you away with me."

The omniscient narrator has entirely disappeared, his distant voice and invisible gaze displaced by the immediate, personal voices of the characters, telling their story themselves. In addition to the main shift—character-narrators rather than the omniscient narrator—there are secondary ones, as the three characters succeed each other as narrative voices (Rodolphe, the chairman, Emma). In other cases, though the character's speech is accompanied by a brief tag of the invisible teller's ("he said," "he stated," "he continued"), it is so long that the reader loses sight of this reference; the voice of the character submerges that of the omniscient narrator, and the reader gradually notices that a transformation has taken place. Though the beginning of it bears the mark of the invisible teller ("he said"), this speech by Rouault, for instance, offering Charles consolation following the death of his first wife, goes on for so long that it turns into a monologue, a first-person narration:

"I know what it's like!" he said, clapping him on the shoulder. "I've been through the same thing! When I lost my poor departed wife, I went out into the fields so as to be by myself; I fell to the ground at the foot of a tree, I cried, I called out to the good Lord, I told him all sorts of nonsense; I would have liked to be like the moles I saw hanging in the branches, with worms crawling in and out of their bellies; to be dead, in a word. And when I thought of how other men were holding their good little wives in their arms at that very moment, I'd begin pounding my stick on the ground; I was out of my mind, you might say; I couldn't eat; the very thought of going to a café made me sick to my stomach—you'd never believe it. But you know, little by little, what with one day chasing away the one before, a spring on top of a winter and a fall after a summer, it all went away, bit by bit, drop by drop; it passed, it left, it went down inside, I mean to say, because there's always a little part of it that never goes away, down deep, you might say . . . a weight, right here, on your heart! But being as how it happens to all of us, a person shouldn't let himself go either, and want to die because other people are dead . . . You must get hold of yourself, Monsieur Bovary; it won't last forever! Come and see us; my daughter thinks of you every so often, I'd like you to know, and she says it seems like you've forgotten her. It'll be spring soon; we'll take you out rabbit hunting so as to take your mind off things a little."

Certain critics maintain that the dialogue in *Madame Bovary* counts for very little, but this is not so. In the opening chapters the predominant form taken by the story is description, naturally, and except in the very first scene, the voice we hear almost without a break is that of the omniscient narrator. But things change following the Bovarys' arrival in Yonville, a sequence that opens, in fact, with a great collective conversation in the Lion d'Or. From that moment on, the voices of the characters are heard more and more often, until in Part Three of the novel— from the beginning of Léon and Emma's affair to the end— dialogue becomes unquestionably the principal form of narration. Thus the function of these character-narrators assumes greater and greater importance as the story proceeds.

These are not the only instances in which there are changes from the omniscient narrator to character-narrators. Sometimes this happens, in a less evident but more original fashion, within a single paragraph when, without the forewarning of a paragraph indentation, a dash, or quotation marks, a voice involved in the action, that is to say, that of a character, ends a sentence that the invisible narrator has begun. This, too, is indicated, however, by a graphic sign: the character-narrator's sentence or word is in italics.

The Words in Italics:
The Rhetorical Level

In *Madame Bovary* there are a little over a hundred words or phrases which the author marked to be printed in italics so as to differentiate them from the remainder of the text. In some cases this typographical distinction follows the customary practice. Like other authors of his day and earlier, Flaubert uses italics for the title of a book, a periodical, or the name of an opera, for an Anglicism, an Italianism, or a Latinism of Homais's, or for a regional expression, such as *cheminots*, the little rolls in the shape of a turban that are eaten in Rouen during Lent; for nicknames, for the cant word of a group (the boys in the school in Rouen call the entering pupil a *nouveau*); or to make it clear that a word is a phonetic rendering: *Charbovari*.

But these cases account for only a minimal number of the words in italics. All the rest constitute a bold and unprecedented use of this device, an innovation as regards narrative point of view. Critics do not appear to have noticed this. The only one to have paused to ponder this curious italicization of certain words and phrases was Thibaudet, who pointed out that this indicates that they are not part of the author's language but examples of the clichés used by the townspeople of Yonville. He remarks elsewhere that through this use of clichés Flaubert is citing bourgeois speech as other authors cite Latin and that these hackneyed words and phrases foreshadow the *Dictionnaire des idées reçues.*★ Both observations are correct but do not go far

★ *Op. cit.*, pp. 204 and 275.

enough. The function of these italics is much more varied, affecting the axis of the novelistic structure constituted by the changes of narrator.

Here is an example. Charles's mother has taught him, as a child, to play the piano, to sing a few romances:

But of all that Monsieur Bovary, who cared little for culture, said that *it was useless.* Would they ever have the money to send him to state schools, buy him a practice, or set him up in a business? Besides, *with a little brass, a man always gets ahead in the world.* Madame Bovary bit her lips in silence, and the boy roamed the village.

The *style indirect libre*—the so-called free indirect style that is the one *technical* contribution of Flaubert's that critics point to—very clearly consists of an ambiguous form of narration, in which the narrator tells what he is recounting from a viewpoint so close to the character's that the reader at times has the impression that it is the character himself who is speaking (in this paragraph, for instance, the phrase: "Would they ever have the money to send him to state schools, buy him a practice, or set him up in a business?"). The root of the *style indirect libre* is ambiguity, a doubt or a confusion as to the point of view, which is no longer that of the narrator but still is not that of the character. A brief glance at the example I cite suffices to show that the phrases in italics are a different case. Here ambiguity has given way to certainty: within the paragraph, for a very brief moment but beyond question, there is a substitution of one narrator for another, a double shift of voices. At the beginning of the paragraph, the one who is carrying the story forward is the omniscient narrator, but in the middle of this first sentence an intrusive voice chimes in and is superposed upon the narrator's. Monsieur Bovary has said that it is "useless" for his wife to teach all these things to the boy, and the narrator picks up this voice and repeats with the father what he has said, while at the same time still manifesting his own existence: it is for this reason that he uses the imperfect tense. Thus in the first phrase in italics two narrators coexist:

1. A singular character-narrator, Monsieur Bovary, whose presence is betrayed by the italics, a typographical sign that enables the invisible narrator to take his distance, to step aside from the narrative without disappearing altogether; and

2. The omniscient narrator, a voice recounting the story to another voice, a furtive shadow but nonetheless still detectable, thanks to the tense (the imperfect) that is characteristic of him and distinguishes him from the intrusive voice.

The invisible narrator then goes on with the story till the next phrase in italics. Here there is no longer a coexistence, the double voice turns into a single one: the omniscient narrator is relieved by the character-narrator. It is unquestionably Monsieur Bovary who says that *with a little brass, a man always gets ahead in the world*. In addition to the italic type, the tense of the verb has changed, and this present consummates the exile, for the brief lapse of the phrase, of the invisible narrator. But the latter returns immediately to recount that Madame Bovary bit her lips and said nothing and the boy roamed the village. Hence in a few lines of text we have witnessed a number of changes of narrator. Two voices have been conjoined to narrate the episode, without the need of ellipsis dots and paragraph breaks— the usual forewarning of a change of speaker in the traditional novel. The point of view has shifted five times; we have been brought closer to the fictitious reality and been taken farther away from it: we began by seeing it from the outside, with the invisible narrator; then we were taken inside it to listen to what took place through the voice of a character; then we found ourselves outside once more, after which we came back to the voice of the same character as before and returned outside again.

This is what is important about the italics. In many cases, as in this one, they signify a change of narrator, a very rapid shift of the point of view. The italics, naturally, are superfluous; Flaubert might have dispensed with them, as does a modern novelist, who does not hesitate to intermingle the voices of an omniscient narrator and character-narrators in a single sentence if he believes it necessary to do so. This flexibility of point of view is possible today thanks to the fact that one day there was someone who did exactly that for the first time. And the one who began to bring about the changes that permit such flexibility—emphasizing them with a graphic sign to avoid confusion, perhaps frightened by his own audacity, perhaps without really realizing what a revolution he was starting by breaking down the rigid separation between omniscient narrator and character-narrator, who had never before shared the same sentence—was Flaubert, in *Madame Bovary*. I needn't stress the advantages that these changes bring to narrative: they make it more supple, condense it, and at the same time—and this is something essential to the totalizing nature of the novel—they allow the part (the sentence, the paragraph) to reproduce that totality that the novel as a whole aspires to embrace. A small bit of text narrates a fact from two perspectives simultaneously: that of an impartial observer and that of the actors in it. Here, for instance, is how the invisible narrator and Charles's mother take turns recounting the bad impression Emma makes on her mother-in-law: "She thought her *too hoity-toity for their position in the world*; they ran through wood, sugar, candles *at the same rate as some great mansion*, and the amount of charcoal burning in the kitchen would have been enough to cook a meal for twenty-five!"

But the italics have other uses besides indicating changes of narrator; in many cases, the voices of characters who are introduced into the voice of the invisible teller and silence it for a moment utter nothing but commonplaces. These phrases, that is to say, constitute the rhetorical level of the fictitious world: they are expressions coined by a community, not by isolated individuals, bearing the impress of prejudices, beliefs, a way of seeing and living reality. *With a little brass, a man always gets ahead in the world:* this maxim of the elder Monsieur Bovary is indicative of a pragmatic, optimistic philosophy, of a fierce individualism, of the mentality of the winner, who believes it a rule of life that where there's a will there's a way. The formula that Charles's father unthinkingly takes as gospel truth exemplifies what Marx called a "fetish," an element of the ideological superstructure of the fictitious reality which, in point of fact, Emma's life—the historical level of that reality—belies. Madame Bovary's story proves that will is not the key to success, that it is not enough to be bold and imaginative to make one's way in this world. When we read the opinion of Emma expressed by Charles's mother: "She found her *too hoity-toity for their position in the world*," this voice is not only uttering a picturesque phrase, characteristic of a certain moment and a certain place in the history of the French language. Above all else, it bespeaks a prejudice-ridden narrow-mindedness. An entire conformist class, with an acute class consciousness, prudent, convinced that everyone must be content with what he has and not try to escape from the economico-social pigeonhole that he or she occupies, that preaches resignation as a prime virtue, expresses itself by way of the words from her mouth. When they utter phrases such as this, the characters lose their identity as individuals and embody an entire community. Thus, curiously, these voices— the character addressing the reader without intermediaries—that are what is most dynamic, most vividly alive in the narrative are at the same time what is deadest. What we are listening to are robots, through which a protean, abstract ventriloquist speaks: a family, a trade guild, a religion, a moral code. In this sense the italics stand not only for a change in narrator but, simultaneously, for another change as well: that of the level of reality. When these voices appear, the narration rises (or descends) from a psychological or historical plane to the rhetorical level on which, through crystallized forms of language, the intellectual and moral patterns of a collectivity are expressed.

The particular movement that the changes of narrator and of level of reality give to the narrative, the swift, subtle substitutions little by little create that special substance, the fictitious reality. This process of building, developing, organizing, completing, in accordance with rigorous and coherent changes of time, space, and level of reality, transforms its conjoined elements, all of which proceed from real reality, into something different. The countless changes become *natural* thanks to Flaubert's style, to a versatility whereby each of them achieves its effect within a continuous whole, and whereby the permanent and the provisional, the stable base and the sudden break, are made compatible.

Obstructive Images

Style was Flaubert's great obsession, the root of the enormous suffering each book represented to him. His correspondence abounds in passages bearing witness to his struggles in *"les affres du style"*—"the throes of style"—and if one consults the manuscripts it is stupefying to see how meticulously each sentence has been composed, ripped apart, and recomposed, the scrupulous attention that has been paid to the exigencies of sonority, harmony, precision, and visual effect. When he prophesies in his letters, however, that his great merit in *Madame Bovary* will have been to raise prose to an artistic level that up until then only verse had attained, he is not thinking of what is, to me, the greatest conquest of his style—what I would call its functionality—but, rather, of formal virtues, not directly dependent upon or irremediably linked to what seems to me to be the first obligation of novelistic prose: telling a story. He is undoubtedly thinking, rather, of the ability of such prose to move the reader by virtue of its music and its plastic values, and omitting its narrative task from consideration. This is the explanation of the images—or at any rate of a good number of them—that loom up proudly here and there in the fictional space, as solid and conspicuous as sculpture groups. They are carefully constructed, and usually they round off a description or an episode. At times, above and beyond the artistic effect they create, they are useful because the aptness of the comparison gives visible form to the psychological, moral, or symbolic connotations of an episode, sets them in relief—as, for example, the metaphors that appear in the description of the fiacre in which Emma and Léon take their erotic journey, that hired cab "sealed tighter than a tomb and tossing like a ship." But there are admittedly too many tropes of this sort; too often they are forced, so strained that they are not at all in keeping with the perfectly feigned naturalness of the overall style. Instead of enhancing the power of persuasion of the narrative, they weaken it. At one point, Flaubert realized the danger and wrote to Louise that his novel was beginning to teem with metaphors, as with lice: "I think my Bovary is going to move along, though I'm bothered by my penchant for metaphor, which has decidedly gotten the better of me. I am devoured by comparisons, as one is by lice, and all my time is spent crushing them to death; my sentences swarm with them" (letter of December 27, 1852). He didn't kill enough of them. Instead of raising the "artistic" level of the novel, these images at times give a mannerist turn to his style that badly dates it, and a number of them are facile and of questionable taste: the one, for instance, that compares Charles's happiness after his second marriage to digestion: "His heart full of the night's bliss, his spirit at peace, his flesh content, he would go off ruminating his happiness, like those who keep savoring, after dinner, the taste of the truffles that they are digesting."

On the other hand, Flaubert does not appear to have been aware of the importance of his major discovery: the *style indirect libre*. I have not found in his correspondence a single "theoretical" statement regarding this narrative method, which is, in fact, the key to the suppleness of his style, the technique that permits him to effect the constant changes, the harmonious conjunction of different perspectives that enable him to structure the fictitious reality on several planes at once. I do not mean to say that he did not know what he was doing when he employed this stylistic procedure in *Madame Bovary*, but rather that, in all likelihood, he regarded it largely as a device, something that preoccupied him because of the effects that could be obtained through its use—and not, like the metaphors, a matter to be pondered in and of itself—and that he may not have suspected how subversive this technique would turn out to be in the history of the novel.

The "Style Indirect Libre"

Flaubert's great technical contribution lies in his bringing the omniscient narrator so close to the character that the boundary lines between the two vanish, in his creating of an ambivalence in which the reader does not know whether what the narrator says comes from the invisible teller or from the character who is soliloquizing *mentally*: "Where, then, had she learned this corruption, so profound, so dissimulated that it was almost immaterial?" Who is the subject who thinks this? Is it the invisible teller or Léon Dupuis who is the author of this disturbing question concerning Emma's innermost nature? The cleverness of the device lies in Flaubert's having undermined the narrator's omniscience; he no longer knows everything, he has doubts, his power has diminished tremendously, and is now precisely that of a character. And since there is a character—Léon Dupuis—who, according to the context, perceives and suffers from Emma's "corruption" more and more intensely as time goes by, the reader has the impression that a transubstantiation has

taken place, that it is perhaps Léon and not the invisible teller
who asks himself this question.

It is the style always employed to give an account of intimate facts (memories, feelings, sensations, ideas) *from the inside*, that is to say, to bring the reader and the character as close
to each other as possible. There were, naturally, monologues
in novels before *Madame Bovary*. At certain moments the characters talked to themselves and told themselves what they felt,
thought, or remembered. But this is precisely where the difference lies: they *talked* to themselves, rather than *thinking* to
themselves. Even when the narrator notes: "So-and-so thought,"
and then exits from the narrative, what remains behind in the
story is a voice, a character theatrically reciting the story of his
inner life, describing his subjective life from outside, by way
of logical discourse—which rarely differs, grammatically or
conceptually, from that of the dialogue between characters. By
relativizing the point of view, the *style indirect libre* finds a way
into the character's innermost depths, little by little approaching
his consciousness, drawing closer and closer as the intermediary—the omniscient narrator—appears to vanish in thin air. The
reader has the impression of having been introduced into the
deepest recesses of the characters, to be listening, seeing consciousness in movement before it turns into oral expression or
before it even feels the need to do so; in a word, he feels that
he is sharing a subjectivity. The method that Flaubert uses to
achieve this effect is a clever use of verb tenses, and of interrogation in particular. Here is an example in which the happiness
that marriage to Emma brings Charles is described; thanks to
the *style indirect libre*, the entire description appears to be (is?) a
silent monologue by Charles himself:

Up to now, had any part of his life been enjoyable? Was it his
years at school, where he had lived shut up behind those high walls,
alone amid schoolmates brighter than he or more clever in class, who

laughed at his accent, who made fun of his clothes, and whose mothers came to the visitors' parlor with pastries tucked in their muffs? Was it later, when he was studying medicine and never had enough in his purse to go dancing with some little working girl who might have become his mistress?

Critics have pointed out that the *style indirect libre* consists of a particular use of the imperfect, that it is the Machiavellian use of this tense of the verb that imperceptibly shifts the narration from the outer world to the inner one, and vice versa. The interrogative form is almost always a complementary device to facilitate this subtle transition from one plane to another, so that the change from omniscient narrator to character-narrator will not cause breaks in the story and will pass unnoticed. The imperfect, moreover, is not absolutely indispensable; in certain cases, the suppression of the verb is sufficient to represent the mental life of the person, for the space of an instant, like a flash of lightning: "Père Rouault would not have been displeased to have someone take his daughter off his hands, for she was of little use to him around the place. In his heart, he didn't hold it against her, being of the opinion that she was too clever to spend her life farming, *an occupation accursed by heaven*, since it had never yet made anybody a millionaire." There is no doubt that it is the omniscient narrator who is speaking at the beginning and end of the passage, that it is the invisible teller of the story who is describing what Père Rouault thought of his daughter. There is a gradual approach in the paragraph to the consciousness of the character. The first sentence is distant; the narrator is describing something he knows and what he knows is far removed from him. In the second sentence, on the other hand, the character is closer to the invisible teller and to the reader (the key word is the adverbial phrase *in his heart: intérieurement*), and doesn't the sentence that I have underlined appear to be an exclamation that crosses the mind of Père Rouault himself? But certainly not its conclusion ("since it had never yet made anybody a millionaire"), where it is clear that the omniscient narrator is speaking again. The prose of *Madame Bovary* owes to the *style indirect libre* its flexible quality, its ability to expand and contract, which enables it to effect all these changes in space and in time without the rhythm and the unity of the narrative being altered.

The *style indirect libre* is logical. Later Joyce will violate these logical norms in order to provide an even closer approximation of mental life, creating what has become known as stream-of-consciousness narrative. This would doubtless not have been possible without Flaubert's invention. The *style indirect libre* represented the first great step by a novelist to narrate a character's mental processes directly, to describe his or her inner life, not through its outward manifestations (acts or words), by way of the interpretation of a narrator or an oral monologue, but by *representing it* through writing that appeared to situate the reader in the very heart of the character's subjectivity.

THREE

THE FIRST
MODERN NOVEL

If the book I'm having such difficulty writing turns out
well, I'll have established, by the very fact of having
written it, these two truths, which to me are axiomatic,
namely: first, that poetry is purely subjective, that in lit-
erature there are no beautiful subjects, and that therefore
Yvetot is as good a one as Constantinople; and that con-
sequently one can write about one thing as well as about
any other. The artist must raise everything to a higher
level: *he is like a pump; inside him is a great pipe reaching*
down into the bowels of things, the deepest layers. He
sucks up what was pooled beneath the surface and brings
it forth into the sunlight in giant sprays.

—Letter to Louise Colet, June 25–26, 1853

The Birth of the Antihero

On May 26, 1845, Flaubert writes to Le Poittevin: "You know
that beautiful things do not admit description." That is an egre-
gious lie; the romantics of the day were doing nothing but
describing beauty to the point of tedium. For them the beautiful,
to be sure, centered around two poles of reality: Quasimodo
and the pretty little gypsy girl. In romantic novels, people,

things, and events are either beautiful or horrible, attractive or repellent. The sublime, the monstrous, the exalted, the horrible in life and their novelistic transformation into something that has dignity and casts an artistic spell are the great romantic conquest. What is excluded from the romantic novel is that area of the human whose faces, objects, and actions are not as repugnant as Quasimodo or as charming as Esmeralda: the overwhelming percentage that constitutes normality, the humdrum everyday background against which the exemplary figures of heroes and monsters stand out. This intermediate limbo will be metamorphosed into "beauty" in *Madame Bovary*, where everything is equidistant from these extremes and corresponds to the dull, flat, dreary existence of ordinary people. I do not mean to say that Flaubert was the first to represent the petty bourgeoisie in the novel, whereas the romantic novel had described a feudal and aristocratic world. Balzac's novels are full of characters representing all strata of the bourgeoisie—including the rural provincial bourgeoisie—and yet this does not prevent his heroes (many of them, at any rate) from having the polar character (they are either admirable or execrable) typical of the romantic novel. It is not the world of the bourgeoisie, but something vaster, covering all social classes transversally, that Flaubert transforms into the central material of *Madame Bovary*: the realm of mediocrity, the gray universe of the man without qualities. For this reason alone it would deserve to be considered the prototype of the modern novel, very nearly the whole of which is built around the scrawny figure of the antihero.

Flaubert arrived at the conclusion that mediocrity was profoundly representative of the human several years before writing *Madame Bovary*. It is a subject that keeps cropping up in his letters from 1846 on: "To deny the existence of lukewarm sentiments because they are lukewarm is to deny the sun if it isn't high noon. There is as much truth in half-tones as in violent colors" (letter to Louise, December 11, 1846). "It is not great misfortunes that make for unhappiness, not strokes of great good fortune that make for happiness, but the fine and impalpable fabric of a thousand banal happenstances, a thousand dull details that go to make up a life of radiant calm or of infernal agitation" (letter to Louise, March 20, 1847). Five months later he returns to the same subject, expressing himself in similar terms: "It is not in fact great misfortunes that are to be feared in life, but minor ones. I am more afraid of pinpricks than of saber blows. In like fashion, we have no need of continual acts of devotion and sacrifices, yet constantly need from others at least the outward signs of friendship and affection, in a word, kind attentions and politenesses" (letter to Louise, August 29, 1847). This conviction that life is not made up solely of polar extremes, that in the majority of cases happiness and misery are simply the gradual and imperceptible accumulation of ordinary, trivial occurrences, that what is petty and opaque is more characteristic of man's nature than the great and the luminous, means that when Bouilhet and Du Camp, after their reading of the *Tentation*, suggested to Flaubert that he choose an "ordinary" subject for his novel, they were putting into words something that already existed as a possibility in their friend's mind. For from the very beginning, these ideas had been intimately bound up—as everything in Flaubert's life was—with literature. In 1847 he had told Louise Colet: "Beautiful subjects make mediocre works."* He was exaggerating, to be sure, since a "beautiful subject," well executed, can produce an extraordinary work, but it is interesting to note that four years before *Madame Bovary* he was already defending plebeian subjects. There is no question but that he was doing so in the name of a veristic conception of the novel: the mean and the vulgar impress him as being legitimate subjects because they are true, because they represent human experience. When he is writing *Madame Bovary* he says

* Undated letter, 1847, *Correspondance*, Vol. II, p. 49.

as much in no uncertain terms, in an image that foreshadows Faulkner's famous figure in which he compares men on earth to a handful of insects on a bitch that she could shake off at any moment. "But isn't Society the infinite tissue of all these pettinesses, these underhanded tricks, these hypocrisies, these miseries? Humanity swarms on the globe, like a filthy handful of crab lice on a vast pubis" (letter to Louise, June 25–26, 1853). *Madame Bovary* is, in fact, a world of beings whose existences are made up of pettinesses, hypocrisies, miseries, and banal dreams. Besides signifying a rupture with the eponymous worlds of the romantic novel, this begins the era of the contemporary novel, in which heroes shorn of all moral, historical, psychological grandeur will drown in mediocrity as a matter of course, until finally, in our day, as a culmination of this process of deterioration, in the work of writers such as Samuel Beckett or Nathalie Sarraute they come to be mere residues, entities living in a larval state, an agitation of vegetable tropisms, or going further still, in the novels of a Philippe Sollers scarcely more than a murmur of words. This progressive diminution of the character—which will not end in the death of the novel, as certain pessimists fear, but rather, in all probability, in an opposite process of rehabilitation of the novelistic hero, though on different bases—no doubt began with the first published novel of this man who in the final years of his life prided himself on having constructed a narrative based on "normality": "I have always endeavored to go to the heart of things and to dwell on the most all-embracing truths; and I have deliberately avoided the accidental and the dramatic. No monsters, and no heroes!"*

But this rule is not perfectly observed in *Madame Bovary*, despite what Flaubert says, for he has not sacrificed the exceptional creature: Quasimodo appears fleetingly in the streets of Yonville, transformed into a blind man covered with pustules,

---

* Undated letter to George Sand, December 1875, *Correspondance*, Vol. VII, p. 281.

(216

and Emma owes several of her traits to the adorable gypsy girl in Hugo's *Notre-Dame de Paris*. That is why I have said that Flaubert's "realism" is not so much a romanticism rejected as a romanticism carried to completion. *Madame Bovary* enlarged the idea of realism that ruled in his day and gave new impetus to the novel as the genre whose aim is to represent the whole of reality. At exactly the midpoint of his writing of the novel, Flaubert wrote to Louise that *everything* in life ought to be raw material for creation: "It was once thought that only sugar cane gave sugar. Today it is extracted from almost anything; it is the same with poetry. Let us extract it from anything, it doesn't matter what, for it lies in everything everywhere: there's not an atom of matter that does not contain thought; and let us get used to the idea of regarding the world as a work of art whose procedures we must reproduce in our works" (letter of March 27, 1853).

The Novel Is Form

In order to make what up until then had appeared, by anton-omasia, to be an anti-artistic subject into a beautiful one, Flau-bert naturally used form. This led him to the certainty that there are neither good nor bad subjects, that any subject may be either, depending exclusively on how it is dealt with. This seems self-evident to us today; but in Flaubert's day the following formalist profession of faith to Louise was subversive: "That is why there are neither noble nor ignoble subjects and why, from the stand-point of pure Art, one might almost establish it as an axiom that there is no such thing as a subject, style being in and of itself an absolute manner of seeing things" (letter of January 16, 1852). The romantic novelists, like their predecessors, had always put this theory into practice, but they had not posed the problem intellectually; on the contrary, they had always said that the beauty of a work depended on such factors as sincerity, originality, the sentiments implicit in the subject. Moreover, in the nineteenth century, as in those before, a number of poets had reflected on the absolute importance of form, but this had not been the case with novelists, not even the greatest of them. We must not forget that up until that time the novel had always been considered to be the most plebeian, the least artistic literary genre, the sustenance of pedestrian minds, whereas poetry and the theater were the noble, elevated forms of creation. There had been novelists of genius, of course, but they had been intuitive geniuses, who willingly acknowledged their role as second-class creators (sometimes after failing as creators of the first rank, that is to say, as composers of poems and tragedies), whose mission, in view of the popular tastes of their public, was to "entertain." With Flaubert we encounter a curious paradox; the same writer who turns the world of mediocre men and earthbound spirits into the subject of a novel notes that, as in poetry, in fiction as well everything depends essentially on form, the deciding factor in determining whether a subject is beautiful or ugly, true or false, and proclaims that the novelist must be above all else an artist, a tireless and incorruptible craftsman of style. His task, in short, is to bring about a symbiosis: by means of an exquisitely pure art (an aristocratic art, as he puts it), he must breathe life into the vulgarity, the most universal experiences, of humanity. This is what he enthusiastically praises in Louise Colet's story *"La paysanne."* "You have condensed and set down, in an *aristocratic* form, a very ordinary story that falls within everyone's range of experience. And to me that is the true mark of strength in literature. Commonplaces are put to use only by imbeciles or by geniuses. Mediocre natures avoid them; they seek out the exceptional, the highs and lows."* I do not know if the Muse really managed to bring off this alliance in her story, but there is no doubt that Flaubert did so in *Madame Bovary* and

---

* Letter of July 12, 1853. Flaubert's italics.

that this is one of the great feats brought off in the book, as Baudelaire saw; in his words, the novel demonstrates that "all subjects can be either good or bad, depending on the way in which they are dealt with, and that the most vulgar ones can become the best."★

Laying claim to everyday subjects for the novel went hand in hand for Flaubert with the most stubborn exactingness in the realm of language; as he never tires of repeating in the letters of these years, and sums up in the following formula, his aim is to raise narrative prose to the lofty artistic status thus far attained only by poetry. He knows that if he succeeds in doing so, he will have elevated the "ordinary lives" that he tells of in his novel to the level of the epic: "To want to give prose the rhythm of verse (while at the same time keeping it very definitely prose) and to write of ordinary life as one writes history or epic (without at the same time falsifying the very nature of the subject) is perhaps an absurd undertaking. That is something I sometimes ask myself. But it is perhaps also a great experiment, and most original!" (letter to Louise, March 27, 1853). Just as he wishes his prose to vie with poetry for the virtues of sonority, precision, harmony, and rhythm, on other occasions he says that it will have to have, like drama, swiftness, clarity, and passion: "What a beastly thing prose is! It's never finished; there is always something to do over. A good prose sentence must be like a good line of verse, *unchangeable*, as rhythmic, as sonorous. That at least is my ambition (there is one thing I'm certain of: there's no one who has ever had in mind a more perfect type of prose than I have; but as for the execution, what weaknesses, good Lord, what weaknesses!). Nor does it strike me as impossible to give psychological analysis the swiftness, the clarity, the passion of purely dramatic narration."†

★ *Op. cit.*
† Undated letter to Louise Colet, July 1852, *Correspondance*, Vol. II, pp. 468–69.

As the author of *Madame Bovary* saw it, these two preoccupations—how to use a banal subject to maximum effect and
an obsessive concern for form—were indissociable. Curiously
enough, his disciples—both close and distant—were to separate
the two and *take sides for the one against the other*. Even in our
own day we can distinguish two lines of descent among novelists, irreconcilable enemies, yet both recognizing Flaubert as
their master. The battle between "realists" and "formalists,"
who have in common only their regard for *Madame Bovary* as
a precursor of their own works, is one that began during Flaubert's own lifetime. The most immediate influence exercised by
the novel was on the generation of Zola, Daudet, Maupassant,
Huysmans, writers who considered it a model of the type of
realism that they officially enthroned in French literature. In the
prologue of his *Pierre et Jean*, Maupassant states that the following naturalist axiom has been passed on to him by Flaubert
himself: that everything has the possibility of being a good
literary subject, no matter how insignificant and trivial, since
"the least thing has within it a touch of the unknown," and
Emile Zola devotes the most enthusiastic study of his *Les Ro-
manciers naturalistes* to Flaubert. For this movement which made
everyday subjects the major theme of narrative art and which
had as one of its primary aims the replacing of exceptional
characters by ordinary people who are the faithful reflection of
a social milieu, the great literary fresco in which Charles Bovary,
Homais, Bournisien, Rodolphe, Léon, and above all Emma had
been portrayed was an object of worship and a model to em-
ulate. The same is true of other literatures that embraced the
theses of the naturalists: in Spain, for instance, where the best
nineteenth-century novel, *La Regenta*, by Leopoldo Alas, owes
a great deal to *Madame Bovary*. The naturalists, however, did
not prove to be orthodox practitioners of the concept of realism
embodied in Flaubert's novel. *Madame Bovary* won for fiction
certain new areas of human experience, without thereby ex-

cluding those which for centuries had constituted the principal domain of the art of narrative. This totalizing process was arrested, and novelistic art impoverished, because the naturalists concentrated exclusively on the description of everyday life and the social, and because they adopted formal devices which they repeated mechanically in novel after novel. A few of Zola's books are still readable and there is no question that the artistic quality of Maupassant's stories is remarkable, but taken all in all, naturalism represented a loss rather than a gain, for its practitioners often neglected form. "For a thing to be interesting, one need only observe it for a long time," Flaubert had said.* Quite true, but in his case what proved to be interesting as literary material was then subjected to scrupulous formal treatment, capable of giving it the status of art. The ordinary—the normal—takes on a literary life only if the creator succeeds in imbuing it with a certain exceptional character (just as the exceptional lives in literature only if it takes on the outward appearance of a certain normality), that is to say, if it seems to be a unique, privileged experience. What is remarkable in *Madame Bovary* is that its mediocre beings, with their earthbound ambitions and pedestrian problems, impress us, by virtue of the structure and the writing that create them, *as beings who are out of the ordinary within their ordinary manner of being.* Many movements that proclaimed themselves realist failed because for them realism consisted of taking bits and pieces of ordinary everyday reality and describing them with the greatest fidelity but a minimum of art. The one thing does not exclude the other: the choice of a "realistic" subject does not free a writer of narrative of formal responsibility, because, whatever his subject matter may be, everything in his book will ultimately depend on form. Flaubert noted a disdain for the purely aesthetic element in those writers who called themselves his disciples and was horrified.

* Undated letter to Le Poittevin, September 1845, *Correspondance*, Vol. I, p. 192.

It was for this reason that he refused to acknowledge the role of founder of a school that they conferred upon him, and many times expressed his violent aversion to realism ("I am thought to be enamored of the real, whereas I loathe it; for it is out of hatred for realism that I have undertaken to write this novel," he wrote to Madame Roger des Genettes, the novel in question being *Madame Bovary*),* not because this word reminded him of subject matter that repelled him, but because it connoted a disinterest in "style" and "beauty," which for Flaubert were literature's *raison d'être*. He made his meaning clear to George Sand, who had remarked upon the enormous influence that he enjoyed among young writers: "Speaking of my friends, you add the words 'my school.' But I'm ruining my disposition trying not to have a school! I reject all schools, *a priori*. Those writers whom I often see and whom you mention are out to track down everything I despise and worry very little about matters that torment me. I regard technical detail, documented local facts, in a word, the precise historical side of things as quite secondary. I aim at *beauty* above all else, while my fellows scarcely give it a thought. Where I am beside myself with admiration or horror, I find them unmoved."†

This absorbing aesthetic passion is as essential to *Madame Bovary* as is the appropriation of ordinary life as an acceptable subject for the novel. An entire series of writers, among them some of the greatest modern prose stylists, admire this formal aspect while rejecting or neglecting the other, and thus declare themselves Flaubertians for reasons that are the opposite of those of a Zola or a Maupassant. Foremost among them is the artist-novelist par excellence, the most intelligent and refined of writers of fiction of his era, the master juggler of point of view, the magus of ambiguity: Henry James. He came to know Flau-

---

* Undated letter, October or November 1856, *Correspondance*, Vol. IV, p. 134.
† Undated letter, end December 1875, *Correspondance*, Vol. VII, p. 281.

bert personally in the last years of his life, and has left a moving image of what Sunday afternoons were like in the little apartment in the Faubourg Saint-Honoré, when writer friends gathered there to chat with Flaubert. In a study published in 1902, James crowned Flaubert "the novelist's novelist," stressing almost exclusively the artistic splendor that the novelistic genre had acquired thanks to the author of *Madame Bovary*.★ A subtle and penetrating essay, and as partial and arbitrary a one as Zola's (through for opposite reasons), it sums up with great exactitude what form meant for Flaubert and his method of work, which, he says, consisted of finding a style that would enable him to "feel" a subject, unlike romantic novelists, who believed that it was necessary to "feel" the subject in order to be able to express it adequately. James's view that the form of *Madame Bovary* is rich and the material poor is less persuasive, though symptomatic, and his criticism that Flaubert was incapable of creating "rich and interesting" characters in the novel (in reality Flaubert was *trying* to do precisely the contrary) is frankly absurd. Despite James's reservations concerning several of Flaubert's books (in 1883, in his *French Poets and Novelists* he committed a gross error of judgment, deeming *L'Education sentimentale* a novel of no interest), he was the first to recognize, in *The Art of Fiction*, that it was thanks to Flaubert that the novel had come to be one of the great artistic forms in Europe. A direct line of those who have claimed descent from Flaubert on aesthetic grounds can be traced to our own day, when, as I have noted before, the French authors of the New Novel, formalists if ever there were such, called him their precursor for having looked upon literature, a century before them, as a problem of language. In the two collateral branches of the Flaubert lineage, one of the most important of the "artistic descendants" (to distinguish them, in a handy formula, from the "realists") was

★ "Gustave Flaubert," included in *Notes on Novelists* (New York: Scribner's), 1914.

Proust, for whom this predecessor is above all the master of style, a narrator able to identify himself totally with what he describes, to disappear in the object of his description, which, Proust says, is the only way of giving life and truth to what is being described. The author of *A la Recherche* praises primarily the silences or blanks of his style, that is to say, his talent for narration by omission, his use of the hidden fact.* Proust was not as great an admirer of Flaubert as he was of Balzac, but it is probable that his debt to the former was in fact greater. Flaubert's descriptive method, the *style indirect libre*, as we have already seen, opened a door to the subjectivity of the novelistic character and for the first time enabled the life of the mind to be represented directly. In *Madame Bovary* this system is almost always employed to show how the human mind, on receiving any sort of stimulus from reality, brings dead experiences back to life through memory, how every profoundly lived sensation, emotion, or event is not something isolated but the beginning of a process to which, over time, memory will contribute other senses and meanings as new experiences supervene. Memory as something ineradicable, a stubborn battering ram against time, recovering with each new incident what has already been lived, is a constant in *Madame Bovary*, and from this point of view the book can be seen to be an antecedent of Proust's prodigious adventure: re-creating a reality as a function of that preponderant level of experience, memory, which organizes and reorganizes the real, which perpetually re-creates what its great enemy and purveyor, time, continually destroys.

---

* *"A propos du style de Flaubert,"* in *Chroniques* (Paris: Editions de la Nouvelle Revue Française, 1927).

Interior Monologue

With regard to narrative technique, critics have unanimously stressed the importance for the modern novel of the *style indirect libre*, invented by Flaubert. Thibaudet was the first to point this out: "The *style indirect libre* circulates everywhere today, something we owe beyond question to Flaubert, to the imitation of Flaubert."* It is not a question of imitation, however, at least in the case of authentic creators capable of using forms developed by others in an original way (whereupon these forms cease to be the forms of "others" and become their very own). Imitation in literature is not a moral problem but an artistic one: all writers use, to varying degrees, forms that have been used before, but only those incapable of transforming these plagiarisms into something personal deserve to be called imitators. Originality consists not only of inventing techniques but also of pointing the way to a new, enriching use of techniques already invented. The significance of the *style indirect libre* lies not so much in the fact that this device for showing interiority is used by countless contemporary novelists in the same characteristic way that Flaubert used it but in the fact that it was the point of departure for a series of techniques which, by revolutionizing traditional narrative forms, have enabled the novel to describe mental reality, to provide a vivid representation of a character's inner psychological life. The *style indirect libre* is, on the one hand, an antecedent of Proustian discourse and its slow, oleaginous reconstruction by memory of time past, and on the other hand, the most immediate precedent for the inner monologue, as first conceived by Joyce in the final episode of *Ulysses*, and later perfected and diversified (so as to represent not only the "normal" workings of consciousness but also different types of psychic "abnormality") by Faulkner. Thus the entire vast psy-

* *Op. cit.*, p. 246.

chologistic sector of the modern novel, in which, in one way or another, the dominant perspective in fictitious reality is the human mind, is a tributary of *Madame Bovary*, the first novel in which an attempt was made to represent the functioning of consciousness without having recourse to its external manifestations, as had been the practice up until then.

The Techniques of Objectivity: The Behaviorist Novel

Criticism, on the other hand, has been blind—perhaps because of the Manichaeanism omnipresent in contemporary thought that requires that everything be univocal, that nothing partake at one and the same time of two contrary principles—to the relation between Flaubert and the branch of contemporary narrative that is (superficially speaking) the adversary of the psychological tendency. I am speaking of the so-called behaviorist novel, in which acts predominate over motivations, in which the primary focus of the narrative is not on the inner world of ideas and feelings but on the outer world of conduct, objects, places. Is it not obvious that this kind of novel—which describes without interpreting, shows without judging, places the primary emphasis on the visual, and endeavors to be "objective"— shares certain undeniable "family traits" with the tireless preacher of impersonality and impassibility and hence with the first novel in which these theories were embodied? Impersonality, which Flaubert required of the novel, also tempted a number of poets of his time. The Parnassians, with Leconte de Lisle at their head, attempted to eliminate the subjectivity of the author and called for a serene art, a poetry that would have the solid and visible beauty of natural landscape or of group sculpture. But poetry soon took another direction, subjectivity regained its rights, and in modern poetry the objective tendency is no doubt the one least highly esteemed. In the novel, on the other hand, it has lasted on into our own day, and in certain countries and certain periods—the United States, the period between the two world wars—it dominated narrative writing and produced such highly talented novelists as Dos Passos and Hemingway. General features characterizing the objectivist tendency are a preference for the narrative point of view of the omniscient narrator whom I have called the invisible narrator and the key role that description plays in it. Certain critics attribute the invention of the invisible narrator to Hemingway, because of the brilliant use he made of this point of view, and others point out that its appearance in the novel was a consequence of the movies. In reality, as we have already seen, it is the ruling point of view in *Madame Bovary* and Flaubert was the first to experiment with certain forms of writing as a means to this end. As for description, I should like to quote a passage from Geneviève Bollème concerning the status this technique came to have in the novel thanks to Flaubert: "Whereas before him description entered into the novel only to support it, to make it more truthful, and its role was merely incidental, it becomes for him the one and only experience whereby it seems possible to express the movements of life. It is description that is the story because it is analysis and expression of the feelings that things symbolize or support, becoming one with these feelings as they become one with things."* Geneviève Bollème thus establishes a line of descent between Flaubert and those writers who, like Robbe-Grillet, an inveterate "voyeur," have practically reduced the novel to this one procedure. What is certain is that after *Madame Bovary* description came to fulfill a major function in novels narrated by an invisible teller, for the simple reason that one of the most effective tactics for concealing the existence of the omniscient narrator is to make of him an impartial and meticulous gaze, eyes that observe the fictitious reality from a distance

* *Op. cit.*, p. 268.

that never varies and a mouth that relates what those eyes see with scientific precision and total neutrality, never allowing so much as the hint of an interpretation to creep in. Flaubert used the invisible teller to give what is recounted an autonomy, to make the fictitious world appear to be sovereign. This aim explains why description in his hands became something more than a complement of the story (Geneviève Bollème calls it his "one and only" instrument; I would only go so far as to say the principal one, since dialogue and monologue also play a role in *Madame Bovary*). The same thing occurs in the modern behaviorist novel, and for the same reasons. The narrator of Sánchez Ferlosio's *El Jarama*, for instance, and of the majority of novels of the "critical realism" that was the height of fashion in Spain in the fifties and the beginning of the sixties, is a tireless describer of the objective world: the meticulously detailed, impersonal, apparently disinterested enumeration of behavior, objects, and places effaces the presence of the narrator. There are countless modern novelists who, like Flaubert in *Madame Bovary*, have used objective description to make the teller of the story invisible. In their novels the verisimilitude of what is recounted depends on this invisibility. This is precisely the reverse of what happens in a classic novel, in which the verisimilitude ordinarily depends on the power of persuasion—that is to say, on the direct and personal *presence*—of the omniscient narrator, an intruder often more visible and active than the characters themselves.

Bertolt Brecht and Flaubert or Paradox

But there is an important domain of contemporary literature—having more to do with the theater and poetry than with the novel—that does not accord at all with Flaubert's theories concerning the impassibility and the neutrality of the creator, his condemnation of literature that seeks to *prove*, and the autonomy of the work of art in relationship to life. I am referring to that pedagogical and ethical current according to which historical truth and artistic truth are inseparable, and which assigns literature the responsibility of educating people ideologically, by describing to them the problems they are experiencing, by furnishing them with the proper interpretation of the causes and effects of these problems and the weapons to remedy them. Within this tendency, the greatest figure—not only because of the high artistic level of his work, but also because his clear and cogent thought provided the principal theoretical basis for this aesthetic—was Bertolt Brecht. I have always been tempted to compare him to Flaubert, because curiously enough, despite the fact that each of them represents one of the two extreme views as to what the vocation of the writer and the nature of the work of literature should be, they have, it seems to me, something in common: in their respective oeuvre, each of them achieved, in yet another case of the contradiction between intention and realization in which literature abounds, results quite the opposite of the goals they had originally set themselves.

Both of them were at once great creators and great theoreticians of their art (though Flaubert's theories are set forth only in personal letters and in a prologue of a few brief pages); their works represent the apogee of the movement they founded or contributed decisively to founding. On the other hand, it is hard to imagine two artists more antipathetic to each other. The two of them took something similar, however, as a point of departure: hatred of the "bourgeois." It is true, nonetheless, that in Brecht the word "bourgeois" signifies an exploiting social class, the one which owns the means of production, whereas in Flaubert it is little short of a synonym for all of humanity, except for a mere handful of writers. ("I for my part include in the word 'bourgeois' the bourgeois in a work smock as well as the bourgeois in a frock coat. It is we, and we alone—the educated, that is to say—who are the People, or better put, the tradition of Humanity").* Brecht was a man with generous social ideas, sensitive to the injustice of which the majority of humanity is the victim, and an optimist as well: he believed that this situation could change through revolution and that literature would contribute to this change by opening people's eyes and awakening their consciousness to the "truth." For him, the principal mission of literature was to proclaim and spread the truth, and one of his most famous theoretical texts is, in fact, the analysis of the *Five Difficulties* that the writer must skirt if he is to fulfill this obligation successfully. These are the basic ideas inspiring his theories on epic theater, his condemnation of Aristotelian mimesis—art as the imitation of nature—and the techniques for distancing. Flaubert, by contrast, was a profoundly self-centered individual, unmoved by social injustice and concerned throughout his life only with problems that affected his own person and literature. On the pretext of hating the bourgeois, he hated and despised humanity; he loved literature because it seemed to him to be a way of escaping from life and having his revenge on it, and his view of history was pessimistic in the extreme: the future would always be worse than the present, which was worse than the past, and there was no solution for any of man's problems, nor did this state of affairs strike him as unjust, since it was precisely what humanity deserved. This black, haughty skepticism regarding human destiny is, perhaps, the hidden explanation for his theory of impassibility, for his defense of an indifferent, objective art, in which everything takes its course without emotion or outside intervention, of a literature without a moral: "*That is how humanity is*; the task at hand is not to change it, but to know it," he wrote to Mademoiselle Leroyer de Chantepie.†

* Undated letter to George Sand, May 1867, *Correspondance*, Vol. V, p. 300.
† Letter of May 18, 1857. Flaubert's italics.

What is paradoxical is that the artistic products of these two contrary attitudes are also contrary to the theories of their authors. Brecht the democrat writes a body of work which, in practice, seems to presuppose that his public is infantile or stupid: everything must be explained to it and emphasized repeatedly so as not to allow the least error, a single wrong interpretation to creep in. Literature assumes the guise of a class in which the author, a stern teacher, goes over a lesson with his pupils, one that includes a certain number of stories and their morals, a few fables and the exclusive truths that they illustrate. The reader or the spectator has the "message" forced upon him (with genius sometimes), along with a story and some characters, and is allowed no escape and no choice: literature thus becomes, like dictatorships, something that leaves no other alternative than total acceptance or total rejection. Proselytizing, paternalistic, doctrinaire, it is an art that is, in a profound sense of the word, religious, not only because it is addressed to men who are already believers or catechumens, but because it demands of them—despite its apparent dogged appeal to reason—from the outset, and before all else, an act of faith: the acceptance of a single truth that exists prior to the work of art.

The ever-contemptuous Flaubert, by contrast, brought into being a body of work which in practice presupposes (since it requires them) the maturity and the freedom of the reader: if there is *one* truth in the work of literature (because it is possible that there are several and that they are contradictory), it is hidden, woven into the very pattern of the elements constituting the fiction, and it is up to the reader to discover it, to draw, by and for himself and at his own risk and peril, the ethical, social, and philosophical conclusions of the story that the author has set before him. Flaubert's art respects, above all else, the reader's initiative. The technique of objectivity is aimed at reducing to an absolute minimum the "imposition" of a particular view that every work of art inevitably entails. I do not maintain, naturally, that Flaubert's novels are free of all ideology, that they do not set forth a particular vision of society and of humanity. I do maintain, however, that in his case these ideas are not the cause but the effect of the work of art, which for the creator is not merely the consequence of a prior truth which he possesses and transmutes into fiction but the precise opposite: the search through artistic creation for a possible, and previously unknown, truth. Where Brecht and Flaubert differ is that in the latter the ideology is implicit in the fiction; it is a conceptual structure that results from what is created and never precedes it, something that lies in the depths of the story, and on being confronted with this submerged truth the author and the reader have precisely the same right to dive down after it and bring it to light. A frequent result of Flaubert's artistic strategy is that the author's intentions go astray in the course of creation and come to be replaced by a moral, political, or philosophical intention generated by the fiction itself, which may well conflict with the conscious ideology of the creator. The Flaubertian strategy of artistic creation inevitably introduces a principle of relativity, an ambiguity of interpretation, by the very fact that it excludes any explicit message from the work of art. The possibility of a univocal reading is thus precluded: the interpretation will always be exterior to what is created, something added that may well vary as the work echoes and re-echoes in each period or each person. It is the reader who, depending on his intelligence, his convictions, and his experiences, must relate fiction and reality, connect (or disconnect) the imaginary and the lived. Paradoxically, the novelist who hated humanity conceived a literature that respected the reader, in which the latter is treated as an equal and shares with the author the task of finishing the work by deciphering its meaning, whereas the writer who loved humanity conceived a literature that implies a disdain, or at least a stubborn mistrust, of the reader, since all it demands of him is obedience and credulity.

Literature as
Negative Participation in Life

There is, finally, one other aspect of Flaubert that appears to me to be of particular pertinence today. It has to do not with what *Madame Bovary* contributed to the novel but, rather, with the way in which Flaubert assumed his vocation, thereby setting what may well be an apposite example for those novelists who, in our time, still have a lofty conception of their calling. As a result of the specialization that industrial development brought in its wake and of the advent of modern society, fiction today has a more and more disquieting tendency to branch off in two different directions: a literature for popular consumption, manufactured by professionals with varying degrees of technical skill whose one aim is to turn out, as mechanically as a production line, works which repeat the past (as regards both form and content), with a slight cosmetic touch of modernism, and which as a consequence preach the most abject conformism in the face of the established order (the best-sellers of the capitalist world and the flag-waving, self-congratulatory, officially approved literature of the socialist world fall alike within this category), on the one hand, and on the other a literature of the catacombs, experimental and esoteric, that has given up before the fact any attempt to win a hearing for itself from the public that consumes the other sort, and instead meets self-imposed demands of artistic excellence, bold experimentation, and formal creativity at the price of (and, it might said, a maniacal insistence on) isolation and solitude. Thus, on the one hand, whether through the workings of the crushing mechanisms of supply and demand of industrial society or through the flattery and blackmail of the patron state, literature is transformed into an inoffensive occupation, a means of harmless diversion, shorn of what was once its most important virtue, the critical questioning of reality thanks to representations which, by drawing from this reality even its smallest element, added up to works that were at once its revelation and its negation, and the writer is transformed into a domesticated, predictable producer who propagates and promotes the official myths, having unconditionally surrendered to the reigning interests: success, money, or the crumbs of power and comfort that the state hands out to docile intellectuals. On the other hand, literature becomes a matter of specialized knowledge, remote and sectarian, a super-exclusive mausoleum of saints and heroes of the written word, who have haughtily handed over to writer-eunuchs the task of confronting the public, yielded the mandate to communicate, and buried themselves alive to save literature from ruin: they write to one another or to themselves, they say they are engaged in the rigorous task of investigating language or inventing new forms, but in practice they are multiplying each day the locks and keys of this redoubt in which they have imprisoned literature, because at heart they harbor the terrible conviction that only in this way, far from the promiscuous confusion in which the media, advertising, and the pseudo-products of a publishing industry that caters to a mass readership reign supreme, can an authentic literature of creation flourish in our day, like a hothouse orchid, hidden away, exquisite, preserved by hermetic codes from being sullied and cheapened, accessible only to certain valiant confreres.

In the face of this problem, Flaubert's case is an edifying one. He wrote at a period when, because of industrial growth, an enormous expansion of the literary market was about to take place and the novel adopted as the most popular genre among those social sectors won over to reading. For the first time there was to arise, along with the new society, the danger that the writer's literary vocation would be emasculated because of his dependence on industry; the danger, in other words, of writing becoming less a vocation than a profession, which in practice would amount in numerous cases to the writer's being coopted

by a certain sector of society, to a much more effective control
of his work than that exercised by the old system of aristocratic
patronage. We see in Flaubert an anguished intuition of this
danger. It lies behind the phobia he always had about publishing
what he wrote, the repeated statements in his letters, throughout
his life, that he is writing but is determined that nothing from
his pen is ever to see print, for reasons that always seem confused; they doubtless were not clear to him either, but they can
probably be summed up as an obscure fear that his freedom
would be threatened if he allowed himself to be caught up in
the industrial mechanism. The Industrial Revolution, the rise
of new classes to key economic and political posts, the democ-
ratization of education and culture in France were not a cause
for rejoicing for Flaubert; they filled him with horror. His letters, for instance, to George Sand, who had more or less liberal
leanings, boil with sarcastic gibes and insulting remarks on the
subject of universal suffrage—the most extravagant absurdity
imaginable, according to him—political participation by the
majority, representative institutions, or the mere idea of the
universalization of culture. The fall of the Second Empire de-
moralized him, because he was persuaded that in a bourgeois
democracy there would no longer be a place for art, that "useless
pastime," as he called it, that is to say, for what to him was
life itself. This anarchist mandarin said again and again that
literature to him was not a public service but a therapy against
despair, a way of tolerating a life that seemed odious to him.
Dozens, even hundreds, of paragraphs from his letters could be
cited as proof that, for him, writing was a selfish compensation,
a cowardly, imaginary way of giving expression to deeply buried impulses: "I was born with a whole bunch of vices that
never poked their noses out the window. I love wine and don't
drink. I am a gambler and have never touched a playing card.
Debauchery delights me and I live like a monk. I am a mystic

at heart and I believe in nothing," he wrote to Louise Colet in the midst of recounting the story of a woman who is trying to rebel against similar repressions (letter of May 8–9, 1852). There is one letter in particular, tirelessly cited by his enemies, which contains this proud affirmation of an individualist, this expression of lofty contempt for the rest of humanity: "I am simply a bourgeois living in retirement in the country, occupying myself with literature, and asking nothing of others: neither consideration nor honor nor even esteem. So they will get along without the bright light of my understanding. All I ask in return is that they not poison me with their candles. That is why I keep my distance."* A few months later, to Mademoiselle Leroyer de Chantepie: "The one way of tolerating existence is to lose oneself in literature as in a perpetual orgy" (letter of September 4, 1858). Ten years later, to Princess Mathilde: "For want of the real, one tries to console oneself by way of fiction,"† a statement which, when accompanied by this one three years later, also to Princess Mathilde, explains what I call the "added element": "When we find the world too bad, it is necessary to take refuge in another" (letter of May 3, 1871). Two years later he is even more explicit when he writes to George Sand that literature is his passion because it conjures life away: "The minute I no longer have a book on hand or am not dreaming of writing one, I could *howl* with boredom. Life seems tolerable to me only if one can conjure it away."‡

I think these quotations suffice to show how sincerely and how stubbornly Flaubert clung to a view of himself as a marginal member of society and how he always believed that his literary vocation was a direct consequence and an expression of

---

* Undated letter to Maxime Du Camp, early July 1852, *Correspondance*, Vol. II, pp. 452–53.
† Undated letter, June 1868, *Correspondance*, Vol. V, p. 378.
‡ Letter of July 20, 1873. Flaubert's italics.

this marginality.* I think the upheaval that the birth of industrial society (and along with it the rapid development of the upper and middle bourgeoisie) represented for culture in general, and for literature in particular, should be given as great weight in explaining Flaubert's hermetism as his family situation. In any event, it is evident conditions were such that the result of this desperate, stubborn single-mindedness with regard to his vocation, lucidly chosen as a citadel against the world, might well have been an aesthetic of incommunicability or of the suicide of the novel, an art in which the artist's social and psychological marginalization would have a formal equivalent, that is to say, an art of the particular, of the fragmentary, of the inexpressible, of destruction. From a vocation whose roots lay in a furious rejection of all humanity there might have been born a literature in which language was not a meeting place but a shield, a boundary line, a tomb, a proof of the impossibility of reconciling art and dialogue in the tumultuous new society.

And yet this did not happen; Flaubert was not the genius-inspired gravedigger of the novel. His pessimism did not take the form of a literature of silence, a solipsistic virtuosity, an aristocratic linguistic game with rules that barred common folk from playing. From his world *apart*, Flaubert, through literature, engaged in an active polemic with this world he hated, made of the novel an instrument of negative participation in life. In his case pessimism, disillusionment, hatred did not stand in the way of the communication indispensable to literature, the only thing that can assure it a function in society more important than being an idle luxury or a superior sport. Instead, they made the dialogue between creator and society a tense, daring, intimate, and above all seditious enterprise. Flaubert was

* It is obvious that this marginality was a psychological and moral attitude and not an economic reality in someone who was in a position to devote all his time to writing because he had an independent income, but this distinction is of little importance as regards the point I am trying to make.

eighteen years old when he wrote: "If I ever take an active part in the world, it will be as a thinker and a demoralizer" (letter to Ernest Chevalier, February 24, 1839). He kept his word scrupulously and, in so doing, indicated the bold yet possible and fundamental mission that literature might fulfill in this new society to which, owing to the growing concentration of power and the development of technology, everything would tend to be planned, controlled, oriented, centralized: constituting the negative force ("evil," as Bataille would say), the forever uncontrollable redoubt of dissatisfaction and criticism, that corrosive *margin* from which everything is questioned, relativized, or contested, the last bastion of freedom. Literature for Flaubert was this possibility of forever going beyond what life permits: "That is why I love Art. It is because there, at least, in this world of fictions everything is freedom. All appetites are appeased there, everything is possible, one is at once its king and its people, active and passive, victim and priest. No limits; humanity for you is a puppet with little bells you set a-jingle at the end of a sentence the way a jester does at the tip of his shoe (I've often had my revenge on existence in this way, to my complete satisfaction; I've enjoyed any number of pleasures all over again with my pen; I've come by women, money, travels) . . ." (letter to Louise Colet, May 15–16, 1852). All this means that all this pessimist need do is pick up his pen for a certain feeling of confidence to come over him, for a sense of security, of heady pugnacity to take the place of disillusionment and paralysis. The wounds and disappointments he receives at the hands of others (or fancies he receives) are transformed, through the intermediary of literature, into acts of aggression against society: "Damn and blast it! We must brace ourselves and shit on the humanity that's shitting on us! Oh! I'll have my revenge! I'll have my revenge! Fifteen years from now, I'll take on the job of writing a big modern novel and parade the whole lot of the bastards past!" (letter to Louise, June 28–29, 1853).

This fury, bordering at times on the apoplectic, was in reality a healthy one, causing Flaubert to build a literary bridge (though admittedly one whose planks were insults) to the society from which he felt himself exiled. Thus his vocation produced a work that was what great literature has always been: at once a cause and an effect of human dissatisfaction, an occupation thanks to which a man in conflict with the world finds a way of living that suits him, a creation that examines, questions, profoundly undermines the certainties of an era (beginning with manners and morals, in *Madame Bovary*, and ending with culture and the very notion of knowledge, in *Bouvard et Pécuchet*, the novel he was writing when he died). Rage, in Flaubert's case, was constructive: "Against the stupidity of my era I feel waves of hatred that suffocate me. Shit keeps coming to my mouth, as in a strangulated hernia. But I want to keep it, fix it, harden it; I want to make a paste of it and smear the nineteenth century with it, the way they coat Indian pagodas with cow dung, and who knows? Does it perhaps have a chance of lasting?" (letter to Louis Bouilhet, September 30, 1855). Yes, it has lasted, and curiously enough, the product of such rancor is today an irreplaceable source for any complete understanding of the society that inspired this work and a contribution of the first order to the shaping of the modern spirit; that is to say, with time it has taken on a positive and beneficent sign. As Flaubert predicted, those who condemned his work in the name of the moral and aesthetic values of the era have come off rather badly ("From this mouth they tried to close, they'll be left with a gob of spit on their face," he told Dr. Jules Cloquet as the court suit was about to be brought against *Madame Bovary* [letter of January 23, 1856]). It may well be that rage saved Flaubert from a hermetic aestheticism, that it infected his books with that negative virus that is the secret of their accessibility: for a novel to be harmful, it is indispensable that it be read and understood. This is perhaps a useful lesson for a writer of today. The author of *Madame Bovary* understood full well that genuine literature would always be *dangerous* ("Moreover, style, art in itself, always appears insurrectional to governments and immoral to bourgeois," he wrote in the preface to Louis Bouilhet's *Dernières chansons*), and demanded that it be accepted as such, as a counterweight to normality: "Abnormality is as legitimate as the rule" (letter to Louise, October 26, 1852).

In all Flaubert's works, even those that may be regarded as an escape into history, the novel is always an appeal of one man to other men to meet in the realm of the verbal imaginary in order, from there, to see how insufficient the life is that these works so prodigiously redeem and reject, save and condemn. Without renouncing his pessimism and his despair, transforming them, rather, into material and impetus for his art, and carrying the cult of the aesthetic to an almost superhuman degree of rigor, Flaubert wrote a novel capable of conjoining originality and communication, social value and quality. For, in this intransigent formalist, form was never divorced from life: form was life's best defender.

When he saw *Madame Bovary* in print for the first time, in the *Revue de Paris*, Flaubert wrote in dejection to Louis Bouilhet: "This book is much more indicative of patience than of genius, of labor than of talent" (letter of October 5, 1856). One hundred eighteen years later, combining the master's words in a different way, we may compose a more apt sentence concerning this book that we love: His genius is wrought of patience; his talent is the work of labor alone.

Elviria, Málaga
April 1974